Suddenness:
On the Moment of Aesthetic Appearance

European Perspectives

European Perspectives

European Perspectives
A Series in Social Philosophy and Cultural Criticism

Lawrence D. Kritzman and
Richard Wolin, Editors

European Perspectives seeks to make available
works of interdisciplinary interest by leading
European thinkers. By presenting classic
texts and outstanding contemporary works, the
series hopes to shape the major intellectual
controversies of our day and thereby to
facilitate the tasks of historical understanding.

Suddenness:
On the Moment of Aesthetic Appearance

Karl Heinz Bohrer

Translated by Ruth Crowley

Columbia University Press
New York

Columbia University Press
New York   Chichester, West Sussex
Copyright © 1994 Columbia University Press

Plotzlichkeit: Zum Augenblick des asthetischen Scheines
Copyright © 1981 Suhrkamp Verlag, Frankfurt am Main

Library of Congress Cataloging-in-Publication Data
Bohrer, Karl Heinz, 1935-
    [Plötzlichkeit. English]
    Suddenness : on the moment of aesthetic appearance / Karl Heinz
Bohrer ; translated by Ruth Crowley.
        p. cm. -- (European perspectives)
    Translation of: Plötzlichkeit.
    Includes bibliographical references and index.
    ISBN 0-231-07524-3
    I. Title. II. Series.
    AC35.B6713 1994
    111'.85--dc20   93-29695
                                                                  CIP

∞

Casebound editions of Columbia University Press books are printed on perma-
nent and durable acid-free paper.

Printed in the United States of America
c 10 9 8 7 6 5 4 3 2 1

Contents

Preface

The essays in this volume share a common inquiry: To what extent can the boundary between the aesthetic and the nonaesthetic phenomenon be represented by means of the temporal modality of "suddenness"? Suddenness is understood here as an expression and a sign of discontinuity and nonidentity, as whatever resists aesthetic integration. It is significant enough that representative authors of the nineteenth and twentieth centuries, to the extent that they themselves reflected art and stood outside the sphere of influence of German Idealism, repeatedly hit upon the concept and image of suddenness. But that addresses only half the question. In the texts of the first half of this volume, which have something of an advocate's tone, the question is left open. The second half contains the actual problem: To what extent can an interest in aesthetic constructs lead not merely to historical but also to systematic insights into an incommensurability in the structure of fictional language by analyzing the temporal modality of the sudden? This modality of the moment that is no longer identical with history began in the early romantic period (Friedrich Schlegel, Friedrich Schleiermacher, Heinrich von Kleist), found its previously undiscovered theorist in Friedrich Nietzsche, and was put through conceptual and aesthetic variations by modern authors like Marcel Proust, James Joyce, Robert Musil, and Walter Benjamin. This will be discussed in the second part of this book.

From its beginning, the concept "suddenly" has been implicated in an aesthetics of a "New Mythology" that was discovered by the early romantic school, was conceptually formulated and grounded by Nietzsche, and was passed on in a divinatory way by the French surrealists (Aragon) and Walter Benjamin. That concept also provides an instrument for investigation that seems heuristically more fruitful than models (such as Critical Theory or the history of philosophy) that look for continuity between fiction and reality, individual insight and universal rules, but usually only lead to tautologies. Its advantage over related methodologies, such as the concept of the incommensurable that was used by Adorno and transcendental hermeneutics (Heidegger, Gadamer), lies in the fact that the aesthetic boundary is retained as a pure event of perception. This does not mean that teleological, ontological, or normative "transcendence" comes in by the back door. Suddenness characterizes not simply the certainty of aesthetic perception but also a contingency in the structure of the elements of fictional language.

In his *Aesthetische Theorie* of 1970, Theodor Adorno emphasized the sudden mode of appearance of works of art in connection with his criticism of Hegel's ban on the "beauty of nature." Adorno even saw in suddenness "reproductions of the primordial shudder." On the other hand, he designated as "transcendence" the "moment of appearance" of what the aesthetic adds, the aesthetic "more." It is the transcendence of a "truth content." In this manner, the practitioner of historical dialectics reintroduced the aesthetic norm he had rejected in the case of Idealism. For all his criticism of Hegel, Adorno remains indebted to the dialectical method. That method granted the work of art a space to exist only beneath the Idea, which Adorno is finally unable to deny. As much as Adorno condemned the latter's depredations in the aesthetic realm, he does not deny its constitutive character. Just as Hegel, while perceiving it perfectly well, subsumed "appearing" itself under the "appearing of the Idea," in Adorno the suddenness of aesthetic epiphany ultimately vanishes in the truth content of the work of art, which achieves closure in a utopian fashion. The dilemma of Adorno as dialectician is that he was unable to admit the aesthetic of the sudden that was preparing itself in his work. Although he admired the beginnings of this idea in the Romantic period, he shied away from its consequences. The coordination of his concepts "writing," "meaning," and "transcendence" is also reminiscent of Jacques Derrida's paired categories, "power" and "meaning," "writing" and "difference" (*L'Écriture et la différence*, 1967). But then again, all this is cloaked by the dialectical reconciliation of oppositions.

Adorno, with all due respect, considered Nietzsche an "aesthetic reactionary," although he failed to mention Nietzsche's concept of "appearance," probably because he does not consider it capable of being incorporated into a theory, in contrast to Hegel's aesthetics. Nietzsche rehabilitated the "beauty of nature" that Hegel had banned, with serious aesthetic consequences. Nietzsche was the first to take into account in a theory the dual aspect of the aesthetic subject and the aesthetic construct, in his concepts of "the appearing of appearance" and of the "moment" that foreshortens the "horizon"—both concepts that are problematic.

Although our inquiry into the structure of suddenness overlaps with the French poststructuralists, particularly with several cultural-anthropological and phenomenological categories in Foucault (zero point, suddenness) and Derrida (difference, metaphor), it is formulated independently of and without systematic reference to these theories. It was inductively developed from observing the subjective linguistic behavior of the romantic authors I have named. Still, the points of congruence are not accidental. Central motifs of Foucault and Derrida recur to the aesthetic schemata of early German romanticism (Schelling), Nietzsche, and phenomenology (Husserl). Thus the detour via the French is not necessary, because the sources lie closer to home. The authors of these "origins" share an orientation toward anthropological materials and the symbols of those materials, bypassing the regulative idea of teleological history that had been elevated to a system by the Enlightenment and classicism. The concept of the "beauty of nature," suppressed by Hegel and reintroduced by Nietzsche, is a prime symbol for this orientation. Once the "beauty of nature" was again permitted, the characteristics of preclassical sensualism and of the rhetoric of the sudden again became visible, which did not subject the beautiful to the terror of having to legitimate itself.

The extent to which the beautiful itself then became a terror belongs to the posthistory of suddenness. For reasons of manageability and methodical abstinence with respect to teleological historical ideas, we do not mix that posthistory with the subject matter of the present essays.

Baroque allegory (Benjamin), the millennium (Musil), Attic tragedy (Nietzsche), New Mythology (Friedrich Schlegel)—these are central conceptual images or mythologems that, mindful of nature and death, produce no continuity between Being and the world of purposes. By withholding themselves from mediations of meaning, they offer themselves for a concept of the artifact and of the human soul that could maintain itself alongside current attempts to establish a context encompassing aesthetics and history, all the more so because these attempts always founder on their ethical and philosophical-historical premises. The anthropological-aesthetic symbol, on the other hand, opens up the possibility of regression and progression that secures the freedom of the future as long as no concept contains it. The sudden is thus not simply a category for the phenomenality of the work of art in consideration of its aesthetic effect; it also marks the barrier against a concept of time distorted by the history of philosophy or a theoretical system. We do not mean to deny that within the concept of suddenness we can recognize historically distinct positions of language and reflection. The following essays provide no justification for these different positions, but the problem is the central theme in the discussions of Nietzsche and of the utopia of the literary "moment" in the second part. To put it simply, at the end of the nineteenth century the sign "suddenly" experiences a dramatization of its reflection of time that corresponds to the modern period's love of speed, as Reinhard Koselleck has shown. This difference, however, is not compatible with the model of progressive history. Instead, it attests to the nonidentity of aesthetic experience and historical meaning. A theory of temporalization of the distinguishable positions on suddenness is reserved for a historical aesthetics of the sudden.

Because the lectures and talks in his volume were delivered over great intervals and were not presented to the same audiences, it was impossible to avoid repetitions and variations of the problem. In the versions in this volume, which have been reworked, those repetitions are not eliminated. Each of the nine essays can for that reason be read on its own even though the second part tries to answer or systematically resolve the questions and theses of the first part.

I thank Guido Kohlbecher of Koblenz for his proofreading.

K. H. B.

Suddenness:
On the Moment of Aesthetic Appearance

Part One

1 | Raids on the Cultural Norm: Literary Knowledge and Subjectivity

I

To put a problem in a context—of the history of ideas, the history of a discipline, or any other history—is not to solve it. Cultural presumptions only obscure the problems associated with art. We must approach art in a more spontaneous, original, and individual way. Academic scholars have nearly succeeded in robbing even the question of the relationship between art and knowledge of its urgency. But that relationship has always troubled thinkers; witness Plato's charge that art is a lie, Bacon's intellectual hierarchy (*scala intellectus*), the progressive disturbance postulated by the romantics. Does art become less significant as knowledge increases? The Schlegels categorically denied that proposition; Hegel laconically elevated it to a certainty.

After the romantics, interest in this problem dwindled markedly. Only the Marxist heirs of classical aesthetics continued to ponder the problem of the relative value of literature and "truth"; they resolved the conflict one-sidedly in favor of truth. The late romantic thinker Theodor Adorno was one of the few who continued to remind us, in an appropriately paradoxical way, that we have not solved the problem:

What is deadly about the interpretation of art, moreover, even philosophically responsible interpretation, is that in the process of conceptualization it is forced to express what is strange and surprising in terms of what is already familiar and thereby to explain away the only thing that would need explanation.[1]

Is art then always beyond our conceptual reach, as the one incommensurable human activity? Can art thus forever escape distortion by critics on the basis of its epistemological or ideological content? Paradoxical though this is, it is correct—and troubling.

But who writes strange or troubling works today? In most cases, literature has already conceptualized itself before criticism and science have had a chance to try their hands at it. Adorno's fine pieties took for granted a concept of literature shaped by Proust, Kafka, Beckett, and Joyce. Those authors never tried to compete with philosophers or journalists, because they were secure in their position.

It is a different story with today's best-known West German authors, for all their stylistic awareness and artistic conscience. In their most recent books Grass, Böll, Frisch, Lenz, Zwerenz, and Kempowski, with their zeitgeist-driven eloquence, constantly invite criticism of the theoretical reflection, the data, and the cognitive content of their works and as constantly come to grief. Why, for instance, is Grass' utopian novel so boring? The simple answer is that Wolf Lepenies' study, *Melancholie und Gesellschaft* (Melancholy and society), on which Grass draws, had already said everything important on the topic. It did not become more interesting when Grass regurgitated it in metaphors.

Only naive readers or those who obey cultural dictates unthinkingly still automatically expect to find something "higher" in a novel than in a theoretical work. Instead, we occasionally discover passages or footnotes in works of theory that are more daring and bolder than anything in literature. At least they put to shame the kind of literature that institutional critics pompously guard to keep it from revealing an open secret. That secret is that regardless of which prose style is currently in fashion, authenticity yesterday or realism today, other intellectual means of communication will always surpass literature in the field of knowledge unless it relies on what makes it unique: imagination.

No one reads Robbe-Grillet's novels any more, but his uncom-

promising decision against realism, against "content," still has
intellectual dignity. He knew, more than two decades ago, what
many West German authors have yet to grasp: that journalism,
contemporary history, psychobiography, and biography have
sucked Balzac's material dry. In the meantime, realistic, psychological, political documentary and confessional literature have come
to dominate the field. Even such theoretically attuned authors as
Heissenbüttel and Wellershoff praised Heinrich Böll's novel *Group
Portrait with Lady* for its research and its documentary style. It
would never occur to people who are susceptible to current fashions
in ideology to respond as Joseph Breitbach did: that he did not
need autobiographical motivation to write, because he had imagination.[2] Followers of the current fashion would try, in their dull,
reasoned way, to temper his response by pointing out that everyone
has private psychological motivations and is determined by class
experience, and no one would notice his pointed irony.

Even if we believed that realistic narration can imitate and
mirror back its age, that belief would not survive exposure to the
many novels of contemporary history. In their infatuation with
techniques and formalistic matters, critics and literary scholars
have forgotten the most important quality of a book: its historical
intelligence. Few have noticed that despite all innovations—documentary style, script form, montages of authenticity—these novels
pander to a naive realism.

A sense of history is the single source of anticipatory acts of
imagination. We can chart its atrophy by examining what has
happened to the classic texts of the modern period (Joyce, Proust,
Woolf). Scholars have dissected their inimitable, unique constellation of emphasis and historical era into a set of analytical characteristics and then denatured them to technical stylistic prescrip-
tions such as "interior monologue" and "stream of consciousness."
A concomitant of this interest in formal features is the assumption
that labeling something as "authentic" or "documentary" is giving
it a stamp of approval.

On the other hand, the historical imperative that Lukács announced in *The Theory of the Novel* has become virtually meaningless.[3] It serves as a mere injunction to authors to resolve the
problems of alienation in an optimistic way. Those who like to
quote maxims from the philosophy of history usually deploy them

in support of a worldview, whether utopian, existential, or Marxist. Such a use does not give evidence of historical intelligence.

We might find historical intelligence in a work of speculative
literature that has not yet conformed to any of the dominant motifs
of society because it sees through the latter's blandishments. To be
sure, ideological uncertainty, that deplorable lability of the aesthetic, is a necessary precondition for this speculative literature.
Take, for instance, the allusions to literature in the appendix to
Oswald Wiener's *Die Verbesserung von Mitteleuropa, Roman* (The
improvement of Central Europe: A novel). Many consider Wiener
a fascist because he voices spontaneous objections to the manipula-
tive and manipulated idea of progress. Those objections are an
aspect of his intellectual and spiritual predilection for a speculative,
rather than an ideological, utopia, which erupts where it will.

Wiener's novel could teach us to distinguish between metaphorical performances and cognitive acts. But such extensive allusions
made Wiener's rousing attack on our social dignity just another
exhibit in the museum of culture. It becomes just one more example of what gives the discipline of literary studies its rancid pun-
gency—where the discipline has not stoically rolled in carrion
itself. The work makes us participate in the offensive process by
which entrenched culture coopts imaginative invention.

What is important about such invention, however, is what the
culture cannot integrate: the way it takes us by surprise and forces
us to think something we have never thought before. Then we
gaze off into the distance like Baudelaire's stranger, with a bovine
stare of extreme concentration: "I love the clouds . . . the clouds
drifting by up there . . . there . . . the wonderful clouds."

But this vagueness—does it not serve to unmask the ideology of
the speaker? Is that not the formula of the bourgeois, socially
alienated artist? Yes, it is. Alienation creates the distance necessary
for perception. It is the feeling of being on the heights that comes
about in reading whenever the words attain the speed of thought.
Words about our age, perhaps. But when Böll and Grass write
about our age, their language lacks this speed. Their words and
associations for the last decade have been like those thick-bellied,
slow ships of the Spanish Armada, which the darting British ships
shot into flames before they could attack.

The pretentious prose of Grass, Böll, and Frisch teaches us
something about the cognitive deficit of literature, if we compare

it to the poems of Hans Magnus Enzensberger or Nicolas Born. The first group of writers never lets us forget that we are reading literature and that their age is not our age (although they constantly claim that it is). In contrast, if we read a book by a sociologist about how the interest in evolution replaced an interest in natural history, we feel that we are in the laboratory of the spirit. The more objective the text, the more full of facts, the more it challenges my subjectivity and makes it possible to interrupt my fact-clogged stream of consciousness at any point.

Suddenly. Suddenly it becomes possible, without a clear change of mood, to put aside the scientific text and to read poems that have nothing to do with it except that they too allow me to take hold of my own sudden time and teach me that there is a special connection between my time, time past, and time future. The sociological text and the poetic text share a consciousness of the age in its political, psychological, and epistemological dimensions that relativizes my own present moment.

The melancholy of the age: the historical process has lost its emotional force and consists for us only of mechanical acceleration, stasis, or repetition. That is an insight into the present state of our perception of the age: the demolition of our expectations, our submersion in a postrevolutionary condition, the attrition of the repertoire of historical metaphors. The tension intellectual poetry can engender arises whenever a poet immediately couples an emotional gesture with an insight that can be expressed conceptually. This is how theoretical and literary works can coexist simultaneously in our consciousness: literature does not eventuate in scientific knowledge, but the two types of works touch upon each other within the scope of our deliberations about, for instance, the way in which we can always interpret our age anew.

The prime modern example of cognitive prose, Robert Musil's *The Man Without Qualities*, begins with a passage that reduces anthropologically or historically defined certainties about the age to purely atmospheric data and that opens a view to a utopian horizon:

> There was a depression over the Atlantic. It was traveling eastwards, toward an area of high pressure over Russia, and still showed no tendency to move northwards around it. The isotherms and isotheres were fulfilling their functions. The atmospheric temperature was in proper relation to the average annual temperature, the

temperature of the coldest as well as of the hottest month, and the aperiodic monthly variation in temperature.[4]

The subject of this laconic description is the end of an era: "It was a fine August day in the year 1913."[5] The subject was also Musil's consciousness on one day or many days at the end of the 1920s. It reflects his awareness of the era that just preceded the brave new world of 1933, when a single powerful wave swept before it all those competing ideologies that had been the object of Musil's scientific suspicion.

The accomplishments of contemporary intellectual poetry highlight the deficit of the contemporary novel. It should be possible to fill a novel with reflection and argument. Compared with Musil's tensed, historically attuned imagination, compared with what have been called "intellectual" or "narrator-free" novels,[6] however, very few postwar historical novels achieve their historical or political goal. Günter Grass' *The Tin Drum* is one that does. Grass' novel succeeds because its grotesque style, its baroque concentration on detail, its mythological tone, correspond perfectly to the age it reflects and to the age in which it was written. The novel's aesthetic means duplicated the era's consciousness..

The same means in later works, especially in *Local Anesthetic*, were tired repetitions that degenerated into mannerisms because they no longer had a function in the context of the work's political themes. The rage for detail evokes only a dull sentimentality. The art industry feeds on this style without any cognitive function. The bourgeois epic, the realistic novel, remains astonishingly successful. Any genuine theoretical or scientific content, however, falls far below the standard once set by the intellectual novel. So we begin to look for a less opulent form. Apart from a new intellectual poetry, the literary form that most closely approximates the intellectual novel is the essay. But what sort of essay?

II

A misunderstanding lies in wait here. For a long time everyone who thought about the matter—including Lukács, Bense, and Adorno—considered the essay to be by definition the prose form with a specific affinity for cognitive content. What arouses suspicion, however, is the criterion they gave for this affinity. In 1910 Lukács wrote that the essay always addresses "something that is already shaped, or at least something that already exists."[7] Because the essayist does not shape something "new" from formless matter but is limited to preformed material, Lukács asserts that he or she need only write the "truth" about this material. In 1958 Adorno referred to Lukács' piece on the essay and repeated that the essay deals with "specific, culturally preformed objects."[8]

Despite his passion for experiment, in 1952 Max Bense also appealed to authorities in the tradition of intellectual history, among them Pascal. Bense attributed to the essayist a concern with the "tendency" of that "existence" whose "essence" the poet elaborates and increases "in an ontological sense."[9] All three interpreters and advocates of the essay share the view that the essayist's primary task is to interpret art and literature. At this point we must begin to question the possibility of the essay as prose dedicated to knowledge. If it is so closely coupled to material already articulated in language, it must present a backward-looking, traditional form of intellectual perception. Historical coloration and ideological differences should not obscure the point that Lukács, Bense, and Adorno speak of the essay in its latest, culturally conservative form, and they speak of it in a culturally conservative way.[10]

For the last fifty years, the essay has been the form in which "intellectuals" (as Bense has it) have expressed themselves. That has been especially true since the end of World War II, when the reconstruction of bourgeois civilization helped to obscure the fact that the newly resurrected essay form was often really only a degenerated form appropriate to the educated bourgeoisie. As a neutral expression, the essay could continue to exist in the periodicals of "inner emigration." The essay in this sense was not a form in which one could continue to prescribe method and style, not even when it is as perfect as Adorno made it. In fact, Adorno's essays exhibit the very qualities that an essayist prose of the future should avoid. True, Adorno's text on essays brilliantly and acutely chastises the academic disciplines for their attempt to regulate the "intellect." What Adorno wrote twenty years ago could well serve as the basis for a new attack on the effrontery of contemporary academic inquiries in the field of aesthetics. His language, however, exhibits the vacuous generality that makes a blunt instrument of the culturally conservative essay. The all-knowing attitude, the wonderfully arrogant intimidation of the academic Philistine, is useful in the attack on such opponents, but there is no trace of spontaneity or discovery.

Adorno himself relies exclusively on the norms created by traditional culture. His urbanity is innocent of the pain and hatred that would be a psychological or even psychotic goad to creation of something new. He remains ironically a part of the essay tradition that flourished in the prose of Thomas Mann and Hofmannsthal. That is why Adorno is unable to articulate his reference to the "romantic conception of the fragment"[11] in an anti-idealistic manner. Even when he speaks of the "breaks" in the romantic style of thought, which does not "gloss them over" because "reality is fragmentary,"[12] Adorno smoothes things over very well. In contrast to Walter Benjamin, his point of reference, Adorno's essays and his idea of the essay form ignored the "fragmentary" composition of the romantic essay at the very point where the genre broke through the culturally preconstructed context not only in a premonitory sense but categorically, in Friedrich Schlegel's "Über die Unverständlichkeit" (On incomprehensibility, 1800) and Heinrich von Kleist's "Über die allmähliche Verfertigung der Gedanken beim Reden" (On the gradual completion of thoughts while speaking, 1805–1806).

These essays have in common their understanding of cognitive acts as an event—an event that suddenly becomes aware of itself, an event that cannot be measured, not even logically, by what is already in existence. What is modern about this idea of cognition is that in contrast to the comparable mystical linguistic theory, it no longer requires positing God as the Other but instead displaces the Other into the aesthetic act of exploratory language itself. Schlegel's proposition "that words understand themselves better"[13] and Kleist's idea "that the ideas that are most clearly thought receive the most confused expression"[14] are not merely commentaries on a psychological critique of knowledge, but they bear on the type of knowledge itself. They anticipate the avant-garde mode of modern perception within which a contemporary intellectual prose would be possible. This knowledge flares up "suddenly, with a flicker" in order to pull "language" to itself and to bring "something incomprehensible into the world."[15] Kleist's "incomprehensible" something and Schlegel's "incomprehensibility" are not meant as semantic or stylistic criteria for scientific or philosophical language. They are hallmarks of an exclusive intellectual movement. They indicate a kind of prose that stands midway between fixed concept and newly discovered sign, a prose that is still in the future and therefore utopian. Those are the elements of the romantic essay that had been forgotten a hundred years later by the proponents and practitioners of the culturally conservative essay.

The most significant element that was forgotten was suddenness as a mode of aesthetic perception. That mode guaranteed or at least anticipated something structurally new, and it also corresponded directly to Schlegel's and Kleist's reflections on the French Revolution. Suddenness, the category of radical temporalization so central to the modern literary awareness, is no esoteric cipher but has a concrete and elementary reference. The fragmentary nature of romantic literature—Adorno described it formalistically as a method and an intellectual style; it is commonly misunderstood as random association—this fragmentary nature is the appearance of the sudden in prose. It is only through suddenness that the constellation is created with which the aesthetic figures of romantic prose—paradox, cipher, irony in Schlegel, and emotional excitement and astonishment in Kleist—are always firmly bound to the perception or intelligibility of an event in the historical, revolutionary process. The despised romantic "occasionalism" is the morality of the split second, the annunciation of the potentially universal for the particular. At certain times, however, specific sentences are more dangerous than general principles. That is true of Kleist's sentence: "Perhaps, in this manner, it was finally the twitch of an upper lip or the ambiguous fingering of a cuff that actually toppled the order of things in France."[16]

As a prose sketch, the romantic essay cannot be reproduced. But we must recall it, because the actual source of its intellectual power has been repressed by the "literary" essays of this century. As a result, what gave the essay its sovereignty is no longer associated with it: the enunciation of new cultural norms. Where the new, culturally conservative essay refers to romantic texts, it has been either a fruitful misunderstanding (Thomas Mann) or a desire to sidestep conflict by smoothing it over (Adorno). Both Mann and Adorno have a weighty, enlightened argument for making the essay reflect, rather than create, cultural norms: their skepticism about whether "the primordial" is possible and desirable in the essay. Their concept of the essay reflects the "myth," the "blind context of nature" that perpetuates itself even in culture. According to Adorno, that is the "true theme" of the essay.[17] He does not distinguish between primary nature and secondary reflection. The origin matters no more to him than the superstructure, and he mounts a polemic against those who mistakenly wish to claim literature for the primordial when he sets the essay this task of ideological criticism:

> It [the essay] does not glorify concern with the original as more primordial than concern with what is mediated, because for it primordiality is itself an object of reflection, something negative. That corresponds to a situation in which primordiality, as a standpoint of the spirit in the midst of a societalized world, becomes a lie.[18]

There is no more pointed formulation opposing the illusionist theory of literature that held sway in the academy when Adorno wrote these words. On the other hand, the statements are perceptive and succinct only as long as the reactionaries to whom they are addressed remain in our sights. Without this adversary, the same sentences read like a decree rendering the essay conceivable only as cultural philosophy. Thomas Mann's creative naiveté functions as a comment on the intellectual frustrations that Adorno recommended. Mann related to what is "culturally preformed"–to apply Adorno's terminology to him—as though it were an "autonomous entity,"[19] as if the culture he described were its opposite, that is, nature. Adorno was able to penetrate this state of affairs all the more easily because he never suffered the embarrassment of writing anything primary. If he had, he would have spent less time considering the dialectical relationship between culture and nature, origin and reflection, and more time on the difference between what is "preformed" and what is "daring, anticipatory,"[20] a difference he himself acknowledged. Adorno learned how "daring" applied to a new kind of essay by reading the prose of Walter Benjamin. The quality of daring distinguishes primary expression as a reflex of the artistic impulse from secondary, trivial belles-lettres. In 1929 Benjamin was still able to identify himself with surrealism, which he considered the "latest snapshot of European intelligence,"[21] but in 1956 Adorno could only look back on surrealism.[22]

The historically based disenchantment with the contradictions and illusions of the avant-garde movement, however, becomes prettification and illusion itself when it undertakes to deny suddenness as a structural feature of imaginative acts of writing. Such an intention, with its critique of ideology, coincides willy-nilly with the "literary" claptrap of *tout comprendre, c'est tout pardonner*, with which the culturally conservative essayists urbanely dismissed the suddenness of the early romantics and the surrealists. Admitting as an object of reflection only the material of the critic of art and civilization, those essayists are able to reduce, ontologically or dialectically, everything that is seen, experienced, or read to preformed patterns of the existing intellectual culture and its concepts. That is completely different from bringing these unmediated forms into relation to mediated forms. Where the unmediated, sudden compulsions to expression fall away, what arises is the essay form as cultural obedience of higher minds, providing one more example of the cultural norm: the methodical disabling of literature. That has shaped our notion of the essay. That kind of essay will not serve as the prose form we need, in which sudden imagination and acts of cognition spur each other on. A present and future prose of cognition would have to coincide somewhere with the structural element of suddenness as it existed in the early romantic essay. The name "essay" already leads us astray, unless we think of it as the term Musil used to circumscribe a prose form that emerges from a utopian frame of mind and possesses romantic qualities. In chapter 62 of *The Man Without Qualities*, Ulrich adulates the "utopian idea of essayism."[23] Musil describes the method of the essay as one that "takes a thing from many sides without comprehending it wholly—for a thing wholly comprehended instantly loses its bulk and melts down into a concept."[24] This is consistent with Adorno's view that the essay "rebels against the doctrine, deeply rooted since Plato, that what is transient and ephemeral is unworthy of philosophy—that old injustice done to the transitory, whereby it is condemned again in the concept."[25]

But unlike Adorno, Musil was guided by a "fantastical precision." This enabled him to write in the utopian essay style himself, to write in a style "entirely and wholly exact" without saying more than that what he was describing did not exactly correspond to anything similar that had been described earlier. The utopian style "sticks to facts," does not look at "the whole," and does not draw knowledge "from great and eternal verities."[26] This ironic skepticism toward the universal, this epistemologically frivolous view that "the element of uncertainty had come back into repute,"[27] this adventurous tendency to think "hypothetically" and to feel "mistrust of the usual assurances and safeguards"[28]—such instabilities characterize Musil's essays. They are meant to fill out the empty spaces we sense between knowledge and literature: "A man who is after the truth sets out to be a man of learning; a man who wants to give free play to his subjectivity sets out, perhaps, to be a writer. But what is a man to do who is after something that lies between?"[29]

III

What should he do, indeed? And who has already done such a thing? Without overburdening Musil's utopia, we can recognize contemporary examples of an essayistic literature that has managed to square the circle, to find a language that is relevant to the increase of knowledge while still maintaining a distance from the cultural norm and its concepts, to combine unflagging awareness with erupting spontaneity. In theory, we cannot exclude even the naive storyteller from these contemporary examples. The raw immediacy of a subjective experience would not necessarily be excluded from this concept of the prose essay merely because it uses an aesthetic stratagem to satisfy the need for truth. This concept of the essay, however, excludes that successful kind of novel in which the dominant ideologies of an enlightened upper middle class are incessantly reproduced: as the leisure occupation of the cultured architect, of the more highly organized man in general, with his mistress and his refined joy as a vacation goal (example: the later Max Frisch). If this caricature of Musil's hypothesis can be avoided, to the extent that such a middle-value ideology exercises only the same educational functions as the moralistic periodicals of the eighteenth century, it fulfills its goal as moderated higher entertainment.

If, in our search for daring, intellectual literature, we are forced to exclude this refined type of novel, and experimental poetry that has knowledge as its theme has enclosed itself in a formal hermeticism, which prose writers represent our specific, elusive form? Arno Schmidt? Joseph Breitbach? Koeppen? Canetti? Canetti would be the most likely example among the older generation. Thomas Bernhard as well. And certainly Oswald Wiener, Lars Gustafsson, and Christian Enzensberger. And what about Hans Magnus Enzensberger and Wellershoff, both of them authentic theorists and essayists as well as poets and prose writers? In any case there is a boundary that separates Hans Magnus Enzensberger and Wellershoff. Enzensberger, although a rationalist, still builds into his prose the quality of the incommensurable. Wellershoff, however, places too much confidence in scientific content. There are certainly other writers; we must look for those whose language is characterized by the utopia of essayism, suddenness, and "fantastic exactitude." It is no accident that the authors I have mentioned, even though not all are essayists in the strict sense, have developed such a prose. Certain of the authors, of course, have an individual preference for the romantic period—Bernhard, Gustafsson. But apart from such special interests or elective affinities, which can explain analogies, it is surprising that the utopian essay prevails even though the times have changed so drastically.

But have they really? For the early romantics in one way, for Musil and Benjamin in another, a quasi-revolutionary inhibition of action became a style. They are revolutionaries without a revolution, intellectual revolutionaries in a sense. They wrote at historical moments when a collapse of the political system was imminent or had just occurred. They had a keen sense of historical tendencies, the tendencies of the new age, but did not really engage themselves in those tendencies. Indecisiveness, coupled with an anticipatory intellectual bent, produces the essay. To put it in an uncynical way: it is the indecisiveness of a person for whom something is always dubious, who is notoriously driven with a desperate exactitude to take refuge in the utopian. The contemporary prose writers I have named are such intellectual organizers and writers. The attitude of vague anticipation, the scruples about progress, the intellectual style combining regressive and progressive elements are their hypothetical attack on the world. No empty promise, but probably pure utopia. The whole attitude corresponds, as I have already said, to this mouse-gray unknown called the future, this intellectual *drôle de guerre* that has situated itself above the "heart of the people," in the middle, beyond the extreme positions. To mention these objective, material causes of the new old German essay is to deflect the false idea that such scientific prose is "objective" in comparison to a less aware prose. Its advantage over the conservative, belletristic essay is in its emphasis on the subjective surprise attack, which does not enjoy the higher favor with which the classical essayist constantly flirts. Its kind of subjectivity is only all the more aware of clichés and deploys defensive measures against them that resemble knowledge. One way to sort out moral and intellectual clichés is to recognize them as linguistic clichés and to take them into custody. This Wittgensteinian suspicion of simply naming, honed by writers like Heissenbüttel, Jandl, and even Handke, is one possibility. But it has little to do with the sudden or the emphatic that arises from the collision of surprise attack and historical-political development.

The other possibility is the kind of essay that Musil announced. Among the writers I have named, Christian Enzensberger and the Swede Lars Gustafsson approach it most closely. Gustafsson's *Utopias* (1969) and Christian Enzensberger's *Größerer Versuch über den Schmutz* (*Smut: An Anatomy of Dirt*, 1968) both produce that lye of subjective intellectual prose in which set, customary patterns of intellectual behavior, and abstract conceptualization in general, dissolve. Of course, neither Enzensberger nor Gustafsson refers to Musil. They have nothing to do with him and would fall into mere citation if they mentioned him, which would contradict the adventurous, even aggressive wit of their essay style. But the tension of both texts derives from the clash with or play against that abstractness of opinions that Musil, like no other writer, perceived and rejected. Even Enzensberger's and Gustafsson's subject matters demonstrate "the insufficiency of the usual guarantees": smut and the fantastic. Those are two elemental, affect-laden things or ideas of things. But there is more: these things or ideas of things share the property of evading exact conceptual definition. As things that are still unformed, they defy quick engagement and challenge everyone to get involved with them—to the chagrin of those who would define them.

Christian Enzensberger quotes Mary Douglas (*Purity and Danger*,

1966): "All margins are dangerous. Every conceptual structure is vulnerable at its margin."[30] Both essayists methodically get involved with dangerous margins: the fantastic is what critics of ideology agree we must reject as "reactionary," and smut is literally the incarnation of evil and has been since the beginning of time. Gustafsson stoically undermines a platitude of left-wing enlightenment; Enzensberger restores to smut its subversive power, which a conservative order had long since moralized away. To put it in terms of logic: in the language of these essayists, the aspects of fantasy and smut they deal with contradict the whole of the false idea of those subjects. These essayists understand something because, nonrhetorically and immediately, they take as not true what has been assumed to be true. This essayistic reflection does not have an epigonal, edifying relationship to the intellectual tradition. This is most clear in the way Enzensberger and Gustafsson use quotations. They quote abundantly, but their quotations neither establish an intellectual-historical relationship nor sanctify an argument, as they usually do in conventional essays, which substitute quotations for intellectual examination. Quotation in these two essayists does not serve as luxuriant, lovely, empty flirtation, nor is it a heraldic congress with great names. Here quotation is argument. But in contrast to scientific assertions, this argument does not present itself on the straight-of-way where all the world passes by. Instead, it lies in the gravel on the shoulder of the road, as if it were meant to be found by chance. We find it "suddenly." That does not mystify what we find but is only an indication that an individual temper has found something, that subjectivity has entered into the discovery. Although Enzensberger and Gustafsson necessarily rely on preconstructed material, although they can no longer literally journey into the unknown as Montaigne did—a clean sweep has long since taken place in that field—their curiosity, their vigilant suspicion, is as concrete as Montaigne's curiosity was. That was the main thing the belletristic essay lost; consequently, it became as sterile as a panel discussion hashing over only opinions. A concrete essayist, like Gustafsson and Enzensberger, does not record his opinions but instead conjectures about something. His subjectivity is not arbitrary but rigorous. It addresses the challenges of the world beyond the essay. The collision of this individual subjectivity and the external world allows the emergence of what gives Gustafsson's and Enzensberger's thoughtful pieces the dimension of incommensurability, what the sciences and academic disciplines cannot achieve, namely, scandal.

What does that mean? It is clearly no longer the sensation in the drawing room or the wild orgies in the halls of academe, which the surrealists were after. We can appreciate such pleasures today, but we do not get off so easily. Today's orgiasts must be more Spartan if they want to violate reason in such a way as to have something left afterward. Reason is the good conscience of the academic disciplines and the authorities, which have meanwhile become one and the same. Scandal arises only when the essay rapes reason with all the signs of official sanction: footnotes are properly placed and the rules of logic observed. But whereas academic disciplines pat themselves on the back and have lost their ability to think under the compulsion of theory, the essay continues to think, while avoiding pressing its results on anyone. Unintentionally, it becomes the perpetuation of romantic irony. That is the element of the fantastic in scandal: the contradiction of reason becomes fully apparent only when it seems to be most reasonable. Gustafsson closes his essay on the fantastic by almost elucidating its ambiguity, then backing off from explanations and restaging it.[31] The last sentence of Enzensberger's essay reads: "True and a lie."

NOTES

1. Theodor Adorno, "Looking Back on Surrealism," in Adorno, *Notes to Literature*, ed. Rolf Tiedemann, trans. Shierry Nicholsen (New York: Columbia University Press, 1991), 1: 86.

2. Joseph Breitbach, "Ich habe mich immer in die Welt projiziert: Gespräch mit Joseph Breitbach," in Manfred Durzak, ed., *Gespräche über den Roman: Formbestimmungen und Analysen* (Frankfurt/Main: Suhrkamp, 1976), p. 52.

3. Georg Lukács, *The Theory of the Novel*, trans. Anna Bostock (Cambridge, Mass.: MIT Press, 1971).

4. Robert Musil, *The Man Without Qualities*, trans. Eithne Wilkins and Ernst Kaiser (New York: Capricorn, 1965), 1: 3

5. Ibid.

6. Manfred Durzak, "Der moderne Roman: Möglichkeiten einer Theorie des Romans. Am Beispiel von Georg Lukács," in Durzak, ed., *Gespräche über den Roman*, p. 9.

7. Georg Lukács, "Über Wesen und Form des Essays: Ein Brief an Leo Popper," in Lukács, *Die Seele und die Formen: Essays* (Berlin: Fleischel, 1911), p. 23.

8. Theodor Adorno, "The Essay as Form," in Adorno, *Notes to Literature* (New York: Columbia University Press, 1991), 1: 3.

9. Max Bense, "Über den Essay und seine Prosa," in Bense, *Plakatwelt: Vier Essays* (Stuttgart: Deutsche Verlags-Anstalt, 1952), p. 24.

10. On the concept of cultural conservatism, see Hannelore Schlaffer, "Der kulturkonservative Essay im 20. Jahrhundert," in Hannelore Schlaffer and Heinz Schlaffer, *Studien zum ästhetischen Historismus* (Frankfurt/Main: Suhrkamp, 1975), pp. 140–69.

11. Adorno, "The Essay as Form," p. 16.

12. Ibid.

13. Friedrich Schlegel, "Über die Unverständlichkeit," in Ludwig Rohner, ed., *Deutsche Essays: Prosa aus zwei Jahrhunderten* (Neuwied: Luchterhand, 1968), 2: 12.

14. Heinrich von Kleist, "Über die allmähliche Verfertigung der Gedanken beim Reden," in Rohner, *Deutsche Essays*, 2: 39.

15. Ibid.

16. Ibid., p. 38.

17. Adorno, "The Essay as Form," p. 19.

18. Ibid.

19. Ibid.

20. Ibid.

21. Walter Benjamin, "Der Surrealismus: Die letzte Momentaufnahme der europäischen Intelligenz," in Benjamin, *Angelus Novus* (Frankfurt/Main: Suhrkamp, 1966), p. 200.

22. Adorno, "Looking Back on Surrealism," p. 86.

23. Musil, *The Man Without Qualities*, 1: 294.

24. Ibid., 1: 250.

25. Adorno, "The Essay as Form," p. 10.

26. Musil, *The Man Without Qualities*, 1: 294–95.

27. Ibid., 1: 295.

28. Ibid., 1: 298.

29. Ibid., 1: 302.

30. Christian Enzensberger, *Größerer Versuch über den Schmutz*, 2d ed. (München: Hanser, 1971), p. 29.

31. Lars Gustafsson, *Utopien: Essays* (München: Hanser, 1969), p. 24.

2 | "Anticipation" in Literary Value Judgments: On the Analytic Illusion

The question as to the relationship between literary criticism and the discipline of interpretation, more pointedly formulated of late, still suffers from a notorious uncertainty regarding the actual topic of discussion. One trend is to equate literary criticism and interpretation, in the wake of Anglo-American New Criticism—Wolfgang Kayser's early suggestions have taken root and continue to proliferate here.[1] Or—and this is the more advanced case—people confuse ethical, metaphysical values and metahistorical, ontological norms with the potential evaluative criteria of a scientifically based literary criticism. This is the trend of the more recent attempts at traditional doctrines of evaluation, from Wilhelm Emrich to Walter Müller-Seidel.[2] The more precise procedures of textual linguistics, which are more adequate to the text, are subject to the limitation that they intend to determine what makes a type of text aesthetically valuable but cannot do this for a particular, individual work.[3] Gadamer's hermeneutic approach,[4] meanwhile, which also includes Peter Szondi's reflections,[5] tends to disrupt the process of elucidation despite its emphatic and influential recuperation of subjectivity as a heuristic category, because it ultimately has recourse to the pieties of tradition as obligatory norms. Interestingly, even the most recent works to have exposed this problem—primarily works by Norbert Mecklenburg, Harro Müller, J. Schulte-Sasse, and Friedrich Nemec[6]—do not fill the gap. Their critiques of ideology or theoretical arguments also resort to categories of general philosophy that constitute only the framework within which they would like to see the relationship between interpretation and criticism determined, but that never fully explain this relationship.

The reason for this reluctance to say how literary criticism becomes literary evaluation lies in the old concern about the possibility of a theory of any model of aesthetic judgment, that is, in the aporia of presenting the intersubjectivity of a literary value judgment in a conceptually relevant way. In order to make methodological progress here, I suggest two operations:

1. Instead of ignoring or suppressing the part of the process of aesthetic perception that cannot be contained in a theory, we must express it so that its cognitive elements become cognizable.

2. Then we will have to search for a context in which theory is possible, a context that provides the act of aesthetic perception with data without the aftereffect of destroying its spontaneity.

I

On the first point, the existence of a phase of aesthetic reaction that is removed from general concepts corresponds only to the contradiction between scientific or theoretical thought and aesthetic, fictional acts. The conceptual, theoretical portion of modern art itself, a phenomenon that was already reflected in Friedrich Schlegel's idea of a progressive universal poetry and emphasized later by Imdahl and S. J. Schmidt,[7] does not eliminate this contradiction, but is rather only its more advanced form. The proposition that art has become theoretical can be inverted by saying that theory has become metaphor and is used as a symbolic act. Since the attacks of the early surrealists on normativity and the scientific intellectual tradition, this contradiction has been incorporated into literature. Oswald Wiener's attacks on a scientific, philosophical concept of truth and its claims to plausibility repeat the contradiction in a representative way.[8] Thus, on the one hand, people still openly or covertly cling to a Platonic, Hegelian aesthetics; on the other, modern literature and art have undermined the authority of such an aesthetics. Rüdiger Bubner's statement is true: "The radical self-liberation of artistic production from the traditional ontological corral and the methodical overcoming of every canon has left the possibility of theory hopelessly in the dust." [9]

But theory was always already lost with respect to that process of aesthetic perception in which the aesthetic value judgment is formed. Without exception, all models for literary evaluation proposed by German or other literary studies are deficient because they fail to pursue this state of affairs as a problem. Instead, they reduce the aesthetically relevant reaction to an analytic, processing, reflective act in the face of an objectively given work of art, however suspect one might find the hermeneutic situation of such a description. [10] In contrast, I propose the following. The aesthetic reaction that leads to a value judgment is always a synthetic act that can be divided into different phases, the first of which is finally overtaken by the last. We call the first and methodologically most relevant phase "anticipation." We anticipate the final judgment through the process of sympathy. This sympathy is not based on any recognized formal property that carries aesthetic value, nor on the recognition of previously encountered ideas. It is an event between subject and object in which the entire diffuse complexity of the subject comes into play in an anticipatory way. This first phase of anticipation, which can be described only as an intuitive, imaginative act, derives directly from the observation that long before we reach an intellectually grounded judgment we enter into an elemental value relationship that not resting on any of the criteria we will subsequently discover. The problem of these two steps was recognized early on, for instance in Quintilian's formulation, "*nescio quid,*" or in Pascal's "*je ne sais quoi.*" [11] The moment of the value judgment that cannot be fixed conceptually was also present in Dubos' concept of sentiment, which Gottsched developed further. [12] Nonetheless, sentiment and value judgment were not consistently paired in the German aesthetics of the eighteenth century, and the argumentation about rules was eclipsed by Bouhours' dainty aesthetic of the "surprising." The anticipation we speak of here must be distinguished from three comparable proposals in order to become fully clear. We have to differentiate it from Ingarden's idea of the "aesthetic experience" or the "aesthetic originary emotion,"[13] from Iser's "articulated moment of the reader,"[14] and finally from Gadamer's "hermeneutic circle."[15]

Ingarden's Aesthetic Experience

Ingarden's idea of the aesthetic experience or the originary aesthetic emotion is promising for the development of an aesthetics of reception but ultimately retains its attachment to the ontological concept of the work of art. In that view, the inherent quality of the work leads one to desire and possess the arousing quality, so that the final phase of the aesthetic experience corresponds to the *unio mystica*.[16] In contrast, anticipation describes a declaration of the subject's sovereignty in the presence of all its living, practical interests. For that reason, even the further phases of aesthetic perception do not produce a "neutralized" moment of positing, as Ingarden, in reliance on Husserl's abstract "phenomenon," believes.[17] This phenomenological attempt to understand the relationship of the whole to its parts suppresses the decisive feature of the experience of anticipation, which is the paradox it presents to epistemology: To form a judgment, we must become acquainted with the totality of the work, that is, experience the possible coexistence of several layers of meaning. But we encounter these layers of meaning only after the first anticipation has taken place, which for its part already makes a decision about meaning.

Iser's Articulated Moment of the Reader

The articulated reader's moment of Iser designates a perception of structure in a textual linguistic sense. But this is not achieved by the aesthetic reaction at the moment of anticipation. Iser does emphasize that in the single moment of reading, synthetic activities take place; he thinks of these, however, not as valuing acts, but rather as a functional structuring of the text.[18] Those who consider structural analysis and criticism as a single process have always overlooked the anticipatory phase. S. J. Schmidt correctly made a sharp heuristic distinction between the evaluation of a particular, individual work and the structural analysis of textual linguistics, which divides the work into its parts and always proceeds analytically.[19] In a manner of speaking, anticipation knows both more and less: it has no data to check, but it does have a sense of the whole.

Gadamer's Hermeneutic Circle

Gadamer's hermeneutic circle seems to take anticipation into account. But the hermeneutic circle is based on the assumption of an eternal meaning hidden in the work of art. The "miracle of understanding" expressly excludes a critical relationship to the object of understanding.[20] True, Gadamer's hermeneutics reclaimed the concept of subjective self-reflection for interpretation, and he posited the self-experience of the subject in the place of the art work as object. Still, what we reencounter in a work is the tradition that gives rise to the criteria of evaluation, so that their application amounts to the affirmation of aesthetic, philosophical, and ethical norms. Or as Habermas put it: "Gadamer transformed his insight into the biased structure of understanding into a rehabilitation of bias as such."[21] Gadamer himself confesses the impotence of judgment where "the distance of time has not given us sure criteria,"[22] and that shows the extent to which the hermeneutic circle amounts to a reversal of what I have suggested above is anticipation.

Only after we have succeeded in eradicating the normative dictates of the three comparable models of the formation of aesthetic judgment can we speak of a pure anticipation on the part of the subject. Within the phenomenological tradition, which was the first to discover the anticipatory character of perception,[23] this schema of experience is closest to Lukács' early idea of the "reality of experience"[24] with which he criticized the intellectualism of the "interpretive" work of art. In the experience of art, Lukács says, there is "no maxim of normative position,"[25] so there is no "differentiation as to value or truth,"[26] but only the perception of "quality" and "intensity."[27] This rejection of the analytic illusion and the reference to the synthetic act of "qualitative" particularity and uniqueness, the rejection of the "universal, abstract, conceptual" as merely a "necessary evil,"[28] shows awareness that every experience of intensity is always an "experience of one's own intensity."[29] In contrast to Gadamer's phenomenological discovery of the "expression,"[30] young Lukács concentrates on the anarchy of the intentionality of consciousness. He is thus able to avoid hypostatizing a fixed experience of "value," which would eliminate the progressive intentional act that we circumscribe with the concept of anticipation.

Anticipation, it becomes clear, presumes an aesthetic of imaginative perception to which H. R. Jauß once contributed a crucial distinction. In his treatise on "negativity and identification,"[31] since expanded, he distinguishes "between a first and second layer of aesthetic experience."[32] The first, imaginative layer is strictly separated from the second, "reflective" layer.[33] His simultaneous polemic against S. J. Schmidt,[34] however, cannot obscure the deficiency of his interesting theorem. Instead of elucidating the historicity of the first layer, he has recourse to the Aristotelian concept of catharsis in the sense of a timelessly relevant doctrine of emotion.[35] That leads him to the concept of identification with the hero,[36] which, from a hermeneutic point of view, is useless for modern texts; it reintroduces the whole old catalogue of norms.

None of the currently competing literary theories of the aesthetic experience explicates the concept of anticipation. The one who comes closest to this explication is Paul Feyerabend in his "Outline of an Anarchistic Theory of Knowledge." He described his idea of anticipation as understanding "after the event,"[37] as "unmethodological foreplay."[38] According to Feyerabend, just as a "clear and distinct understanding" never precedes the "formulation and institutional expression"[39] of new ideas and theories become "clear and 'reasonable' only *after* incoherent fragments of them have been used for a long time,"[40] anticipation presents a complete whole in an instance to be succeeded by many moments of analysis. Such epistemological anarchy in response to the compulsion of methodology corresponds to a surrealistic observation of André Breton's that laconically and precisely sums up anticipation: Breton ascertained that a certain woman or a certain idea made an impression on him, but he was unable to say exactly what impression.[41] In the same way, literature first makes a general impression on us, independent of our later recognition of the kind of impression it has made.

The introduction of the concept of anticipation excludes the values of conservative, ontological interpretation as well as the dialectic reduction by the critique of ideology, which supposedly determines the process of judgment. Anticipation does not replace them with the empty autonomy of the free-associating, imaginative subject. We must ask what verifiable data will make the act of anticipation not random and arbitrary but something we can comprehend.

II

Our next question is in what context theory is possible. Because we have to assume that the subject of anticipation is not an abstract reader, an artificial recipient, but instead an intellectual subject defined through a historical consciousness, we must rely on operative data within anticipation that are both complex enough not to let anticipation become simply a selective reflection and specific enough to give a continuing direction to the subject's intention. If we reduce the complexity of all influences that effect sympathy or antipathy to what we can understand, as sound methodological practice requires, we hit upon a codex that we could call the history of consciousness of the modern age, perpetuated in the act of reading. By history of consciousness we do not mean the piling up of scientific knowledge or philosophical tradition, but the secret line of the "incommensurably" constituted aesthetic constructs themselves, whose conflict with normative rules has become dramatic since the avant-garde. This history of consciousness provides the data that can become effective in the act of anticipation and either correspond to the text before the reader or exceed or underestimate it. The history of consciousness enables us to evaluate an aesthetic text without using traditional norms, without having to rely on the tautology of immanent valuation.

Our reference to the avant-garde as a term of comparison or *deus ex machina* would remove both difficulties in the process of aesthetic judgment:

  1. The consciousness acting in anticipation would not be structured by traditional norms but would experience a regulation that is analogous to the intentionality and openness of the modern text.
  2. The weakness of all models of aesthetic valuation, including the seductively developed solutions of textual linguistics, is that they do not imply the historicity of the subject making the literary judgments. This historicity is completely masked in Iser's and Jauß's reception theories as well as in all phenomenological, semantic, and textual linguistic theories of aesthetics. In traditional value theories, whether it is the "value consciousness of the present" (H. E. Hass)[42] or the "continuum of reflection"[43] or the "stages of human existence

and consciousness"[44] (Emrich), the historicity of the judging subject is dissolved in vague existential terminology or understood as immanent in the historicity of the text itself. By contrast, the reconstructed avant-garde offers a dual measure of progressive aesthetic consciousness (and its historicity). On the one hand, the level of consciousness of the text to be evaluated would have to prove itself in view of the level of awareness of the history of consciousness collected in the avant-garde. On the other, the evaluating subject's contemporary consciousness would test itself, that is, it would perform the necessary temporalization of its judgment. This is a necessary, not an arbitrary, criterion for the relevant criticism, as a glance at the historically reflective structure of judgment in critics like Friedrich Schlegel and Walter Benjamin shows. Those two critics worked during historical turning points and became emphatically aware of their situation. They transposed the process of anticipation we have described from the level of an aesthetic experience of an individual construct to the level of historical intuition. For them, literary criticism was identical with becoming aware of the "tendencies of the age,"[45] the "revolutionary desire to realize the kingdom of God,"[46] as Friedrich Schlegel wrote. For both critics, criticism seems only a means to determine the utopian content of the present.[47]

The purpose of the model of criticism we have developed here also is to perceive the level of consciousness of the text that reflects its time in relation to our own determination of the present. The general data of such a perception have sufficient complexity to guarantee the anticipation in the first phase of aesthetic perception. The data themselves must come from the history of consciousness of the modern age, which came into its own in the avant-garde. Before we turn to the catalogue of data of the avant-garde, we must consider a possible objection that creates a problem particularly with respect to anticipation. Does resorting to the avant-garde mean that we are replacing the old catalogue of norms with a new one?[48] If so, does imaginative anticipation then become impossible, returning us ultimately again to the second, "reflective" layer of the process of judgment? We will demonstrate that the catalogue of data of the avant-garde is not to be confused with specific categories of forms that are indebted to this or that school.

To begin with, such a catalogue would establish the phenomenon of a secret, contrary history of consciousness. It would make visible a line of development from early surrealism to the actions and "happenings" of the recent past, a line that contradicts the traditional canon of the academic understanding of literature. The surrealist Pierre Mabille's 1939 polemic is still true, or is true again: criticism—journalistic as well as academic—has largely remained true to a classical standard of value that has rigidified into a convention.[49] As a consequence, what Jan Mukarovsky has called the "newest norm,"[50] which could function as a recurrence[51] of always newly offered innovation, does not even exist as a category of literary criticism, namely, the avant-garde as a form of consciousness. For this reason both journalistic and academic criticism of contemporary literature can obey an unconditional subjectivism that would fall apart when faced with comparable works of painting and plastic art. In this way, critics validate insignificant creations as long as these works pompously evoke what the zeitgeist has just whispered, as in the case of the exemplary forms of representational narration. The innovations of painters and sculptors have long had to measure up to what the consciousness of the avant-garde once posited, but literature has been able to evade this claim on it. The pragmatics of this contradictory situation force us to admit that much of what is currently published as literature and discussed by literary critics lies beyond the scope of aesthetic experience, which is our topic here. Those works are low-flying aircraft that come in under the radar screen. That gives us a first indicator of the value of a contemporary work of literature, a clue operative in the process of anticipation: texts that do not respond to the avant-garde boundary's challenges to consciousness are aesthetically and historically irrelevant. This criterion is not to be confused with the proposed criterion of "interpretative richness."[52] The latter is to be avoided, because what appears so rich to German studies and to belletristic criticism are precisely the most traditional and epigonal features of literature, as a study of the scholarly reception of the works of Thomas Mann or Max Frisch can show.[53]

The history of consciousness of the modern age as a reconstructed one would constitute merely the framework within which the formal value of innovations could be judged at all. Divorced from such a framework, innovations appear empty or as merely immanently verifiable data in the history of the development of literary aesthetic forms. They would produce a significant catalogue for the second, "reflective" phase of the process of judgment; such a catalogue would meet S. J. Schmidt's demand for a theory "of 'aesthetic' procedures for textualizing" a theory that would allow "us to derive each individual text as a specific selection from a repertory of generally determinate procedures of textualization and to delimit its aesthetic rank."[54] Aesthetic rank here means the objective participation in certain stylistic, metaphorical, or grammatical characteristics and not the aesthetic value of the unique, individual text. Nor can innovation divorced from the history of consciousness be enlisted for an "emancipatory" experience, as various theorists have asserted.[55] Innovation, as the most visible criterion of the avant-garde, has native claim to the prestige of historical progressiveness. But the validity of that claim can be decided only after the relevance of innovation has been accepted or rejected in the context of the *posthistoire* discussion.[56]

As I emphasized above, such a reconstructed history of consciousness as a framework for innovation, that is, as a heuristic category, takes the critic as intellectual subject into account in a particular way. (It seems to me that the real deficiency of Iser's model of reception is that it failed to decide this question.) This critic is neither the random curious reader nor the arbitrary type that Roland Barthes describes as the representative of "critical verisimilitude."[57] Nor is he Grimminger's participant in a community of academic disciplines and discussion, integrated, always intersubjectively mediated, defined by his method.[58] Instead, this critic is vulnerable to the heuristic paradoxes of posthistoricism. To be sure, with Grimminger, Mecklenburg, and Müller he will be able to distinguish between the horizon of expectations of general leisure consumption, to which some of the play theories of fictional action threaten to sink, and a scientific interest in the intersubjective meaning of literature.[59] But he also knows that this meaning of a literature that is preunderstood by its academic discipline, becomes questionable. Such a meaning could subject the text to ideological expectations that derive from the scientific debate about theory but are contradicted by the poetic text itself. In this sense, mediated by the academic discipline, the nihilistic historicism of a historyless state could comment on itself. Apel has described that possibility: "In fact, the human being who scientifically objectifies all binding truths and norms and gathers them into the simultaneity of an 'imaginary museum' of whatever meaning remains is like a creature who cannot acquire any particular qualities, a pure 'person of possibilities,' as Musil says, who cannot actualize his life."[60] But we must note that actualization was proposed in the concept of anticipation. The intention of the modern subject of consciousness that was just described anticipates its own spontaneity and tendency in the work. Analogously, but now on the level of the historical moment, a piece of contemporary literature functions as a whole in regard to the future, which has yet to eventuate. Only in this tension of anticipatory time can literature be experienced in an immediate sense. The judging subject validates this tension as still being in effect. But is this tension still produced by the innovation of the avant-garde? Is its aesthetic value more than that of one work among many competing kinds of texts; does the work perform the emphatic temporalization to this historical moment; that is, does it do anything to define the "present moment," which we have assumed to be the cognitive interest of literary evaluation?

The answer to this question will decide the extent to which the reconstruction of the avant-garde I have proposed verifies our present consciousness. As far as I can tell, up to now only Peter Bürger has posed this question in the sense I mean here, namely that of a heuristic category.[61] In the meantime, the debate about the concept of the avant-garde[62] has also created a compelling alternative for the valuation model I propose here. Either the classical avant-garde can be reanimated,[63] or its actualized reception proves to be illusory and would then fall prey to that enlightened cultural pessimism that will finally direct the avant-garde, as the last of the Indians, into the waiting reservation.[64] If the latter is true, then the category I advance here—anarchic-emphatic anticipation conceived of as dual—is obsolete and what remains are the various simulation techniques that rely on analysis and the textual patterns evoking the play of fantasy. We could situate their aesthetic valence precisely on the scale of textual linguistics and the aesthetics of reception; even the criterion of an exceeded "horizon of expectations"[65] would retain merely a technical, formal quality without any reflection on the age. The poeticity of a text, thus freed of its historicity, would correspond to the situation of a postautonomous art as decreed by Gehlen and also envisioned by Habermas.[66] In that view, after a therapeutic determination of its meaning, all that would remain for art is a kind of evolved fitness program.[67]

Let us exclude for the moment this possible alternative, the reduction of the historical subject and a concept of meaning divorced from the subject, as Gadamer and Luhmann conceive it.[68] If we presume that it is possible to animate the avant-garde, however, then we immediately face the question whether such an animation is possible in any other way than through voluntarism. It is apparent that even Walter Benjamin's discovery of surrealism amounted to nothing more than positing an emotional subject and the mere "belief in an immanently compelling reasonableness of the historical process."[69] The same voluntarism is evident in contemporary attempts to animate the avant-garde, especially in the proposals of Dolf Oehlers.[70] The gap that has opened between Bürger and his critics demonstrates how the concept of "self-criticism of the present,"[71] which Bürger uses as Mecklenburg recently did,[72] can be distorted through the methodology. Bürger sees in the concept only the means of objectively understanding past epochs of art,[73] but it would be a matter of using Benjamin's distinction and converting "objective content" into "truth content,"[74] of compelling a "new birth" in which "all ephemeral beauty disappears and the work asserts itself as a ruin."[75] In our context, ephemeral beauty would be a merely formalistic conception of "innovation." It must be replaced by an "engaged cognition," as Apel argued: "In order to achieve the constitution of meaning, consciousness, which by its nature is 'excentric,' must engage itself centrically, that is, as physically present in the here and now. Every constellation of meaning, for instance, refers back to an individual perspective."[76] Bürger reduced this "here and now" to the mere objective content of the avant-garde, the formal, aesthetic external characteristics of a particular school, of montage, collage, and fragment, but he did not discuss the principle of surprise and the event with respect to its contemporary possibility. This instrumentalist formalism also causes him to miss—as his critics have pointed out[77]—Benjamin's discovery of the baroque allegory as a prefiguration of the modern fragment. Benjamin's allegory cannot be understood schematically by means of the modern technique of montage. Instead, it is a formal category belonging to the philosophy of history.[78] But if avant-gardist innovation loses its profane historical dynamic, then it makes no sense to relate it back to the baroque allegory, and the repetition of its external characteristics remains empty. Then it becomes impossible to decide what is arbitrary innovation and what is necessary, and we are left with the bleak picture that Wellershoff sketches. On the one hand, we have therapies of discharge through aesthetic acts, on the other, the "desolate freedom abandoned by meaning" and "futureless facticity."[79] Such a perspective takes the classical strategies of the avant-garde, shock and surprise, only as means of demonstration and the exhaustion of these effects in the artistic happenings and earthworks of the 1960s then becomes an argument against the possibility of reanimation.[80]

What answer is possible here? The quantifying reconstruction of the avant-garde as process is no answer to the dilemma of sheer voluntarism. We must posit another reconstruction, one based on a psychotic-imaginative experience of avant-garde techniques, which our power of association is only now in a position to permit. Only now has the gesture of the avant-garde, once misunderstood as pure provocation and therefore exhausted, been overtaken by the cognitive intentionality immanent to it. Only now can we read such texts by not only reconstructing their method but also by ascertaining their utopian character through exegesis.[81] In such a process, we reach the "temporal point of the present," which ought to be the goal of reanimation. That is not the result of a mere voluntaristic positing, and it cannot be achieved by accumulating all formal categories within the work. It is a complex, anthropological dimension, always linked to objects and in need of the presentification of discovery. Such a view of the avant-garde as history of consciousness would then not amount to a catalogue of norms but would yield criteria that would already operate within anticipation, criteria no modern text should fail to meet. Giving these criteria concrete names is left for a later pragmatic study, but it has already become clear that a series of officially favored literary texts do not stand up to the reconstruction of the history of consciousness that we have sketched here. It is only logical that this proposal, mediating between a theoretical starting point and the intuition of incommensurability, means that we cannot approach an emancipatory theory by determining the temporal point of the present[82] either from the standpoint of a political history of philosophy or theoretically. "Present moment," once again, means nothing other than a form of anticipation that is not yet aware of the whole.

NOTES

1. Wolfgang Kayser, "Literarische Wertung und Interpretation," in *DU* 4 (1952).

2. Its most important representatives are Wilhelm Emrich, *Zum Problem der literarischen Wertung*, Akademie der Wissenschaften und der Literatur zu Mainz, Abhandlungen der Klasse der Literatur 3 (1961); Emrich, "Wertung und Rangordnung literarischer Werke," *Sprache im technischen Zeitalter* 12 (1964); H. E. Hass, "Das Problem der literarischen Wertung," *Studium Generale* 12 (1959); M. Wehrli, *Wert und Unwert in der Dichtung* (Köln: Hegner, 1965); F. Lockermann, *Literaturwissenschaft und literarische Wertung* (München: Hanser, 1965); E. Lunding, "Das Wagnis des Wertens," *DU* 19 (1967); W. Müller-Seidel, *Probleme der literarischen Wertung* (Stuttgart: Metzler, 1965).

3. See Siegfried J. Schmidt, "Text und Bedeutung," in Schmidt, ed., *Text, Bedeutung, Ästhetik* (München: Bayerischer Schulbuchverlag, 1970).

4. Hans-Georg Gadamer, *Truth and Method,* 2d ed. (New York: Crossroad, 1989).

5. Peter Szondi, "Über philologische Erkenntnis," in Szondi, *Hölderlin-Studien Mit einem Traktat über philologische Erkenntnis,* 3d ed. (Frankfurt/Main: Suhrkamp, 1977).

6. Norbert Mecklenburg, *Kritisches Interpretieren: Untersuchungen zur Theorie der Literaturkritik* (München: Nymphenburger Verlagshandlung, 1972); N. Mecklenburg and H. Müller, *Erkenntnisinteresse und Literaturwissenschaft* (München: Nymphenburger Verlagshandlung, 1974); J. Schulte-Sasse, *Literarische Wertung,* 2d ed. (Stuttgart: Metzler, 1976); F. Nemec, "Literaturkritik in der Literaturwissenschaft: Das Problem der literarische Wertung," in Jörg Drews, ed., *Literaturkritik—Medienkritik* (Heidelberg: Quelle und Meyer, 1977).

7. Siegfried J. Schmidt, *Ästhetische Prozesse Beiträge zu einer Theorie*

der nichtmimetischen Kunst und Literatur (Köln: Kiepenheuer & Witsch, 1971).

8. Oswald Wiener, "Subjekt, Semantik, Abbildungsbeziehungen: Einige Probleme des Schriftstellers," in S. J. Schmidt, ed., *Text, Bedeutung, Äesthetik*, p. 3.

9. R. Bubner, "Über einige Bedingungen gegenwärtiger Ästhetik," *Neue Hefte für Philosophie* 5 (1973).

10. Even Mecklenburg agrees. See *Kritisches Interpretieren*, pp. 50ff.

11. Pascal, *Pensées*, Art. VI, 43.

12. See Alfred Bäumler, *Das Irrationalitätsproblem in der Ästhetik des 18. Jahrhunderts bis zur Kritik der Urteilskraft* (Darmstadt: Wissenschaftliche Buchgesellschaft, 1975), p. 75.

13. Roman Ingarden, "Das Ästhetische Erlebnis," in Ingarden, *Erlebnis, Kunstwerk; Wert Vorträge zur Ästhetik 1937–1967* (Tübingen: Niemeyer, 1969), p. 3.

14. W. Iser, *Der Akt des Lesens* (München: Fink, 1976), p. 186.

15. Gadamer, *Truth and Method*, pp. 235–344.

16. Ingarden, "Das Ästhetische Erlebnis," pp. 3, 5.

17. Ibid., p. 4.

18. Iser, *Der Akt des Lesens*, p. 179.

19. Schmidt, "Text und Bedeutung," p. 47.

20. Gadamer, *Truth and Method*, p. 258: "Understanding is not to be thought of so much as an action of one's subjectivity, but as the placing of oneself within a process of tradition, in which past and present are constantly fused."

21. Jürgen Habermas, "Zu Gadamers *Wahrheit und Methode*," in *Hermeneutik und Ideologiekritik* (Frankfurt/Main: Suhrkamp, 1975), p. 48.

22. Gadamer, *Truth and Method*, p. 265.

23. See H. Anz, "Erwartungshorizont: Ein Diskussionsbeitrag zu H. R. Jauß' Begründung einer Rezeptionsösthetik der Literatur," *Euphorion* 70 (1976): 402.

24. G. Lukács, "Die Kunst als Ausdruck und die Mitteilungsformen der Erlebniswirklichkeit," *Neue Hefte für Philosophie* 5 (1973): 6. At issue is a concept from the first chapter of the unpublished work, "Philosophie der Kunst," written between 1912 and 1914, which is still strongly influenced by the phenomenological method.

25. Ibid., p. 9.

26. Ibid.

27. Ibid.

28. Ibid., p. 19.

29. Ibid., p. 21.

30. Gadamer, *Truth and Method*, p. 198.

31. Hans Robert Jauß, "Negativität und Identifikation: Versuch zur Theorie der ästhetischen Erfahrung," *Poetik und Hermeneutik* 6 (1975): 263–339. The expanded book version is called *Ästhetische Erfahrung und Literarische Hermeneutik*, vol. 1 (München: Fink, 1977).

32. Ibid., p. 302.

33. Ibid.

34. Ibid.

35. Ibid., p. 304. See also S. J. Schmidt, "Ästhetische Identifikation als bewußter Umweg," *Poetik und Hermeneutik* 6 (1974): 546.

36. Jauß, "Negativität und Identifikation," p. 305.

37. Paul Feyerabend, *Against Method* (London, New York: Verso Press, 1988), p. 24, note 1.

38. Ibid., p. 27.

39. Ibid., p. 25.

40. Ibid., p. 26.

41. André Breton, "Manifeste du Surréalisme," in Breton, ed. *Manifestes du Surréalisme* (Paris: Gallimard, 1971), p. 22.

42. Hans Egon Hass, "Das Problem der literarischen Wertung," *Studium Generale* 12 (1959): 754.

43. The phrase is W. Emrich's, adopting a concept of F. Schlegel's, in "Wertung und Rangordnung literarischer Werke," *Sprache im technischen Zeitalter* 12 (1964): 982.

44. Emrich, *Zum Problem der literarischen Wertung*, p. 41.

45. F. Schlegel, "Fragmente," in Schlegel, *Kritische Schriften*, ed. Wolfdietrich Rasch, 3d ed. (München: Hanser, 1971), p. 48.

46. Ibid., p. 50.

47. On the concept of the present in the romantic experience of modernity, see Jauß, "Literarische Tradition und gegenwärtiges Bewußtsein," in Jauß, ed., *Literaturgeschichte als Provokation* (Frankfurt/Main: Suhrkamp, 1970), p. 51. See also Jauß, "Schlegels und Schillers Replik auf die 'Querelle des Anciens et des Modernes,' " in Jauß, ed., *Literaturgeschichte als Provokation*, p. 83.

48. This is Emrich's question in "Wertung und Rangordnung literarischer Werke," p. 976.

49. P. Mabille, "Das Auge des Malers," in Günther Metken, ed., *Als die Surrealisten noch Recht hatten: Texte und Dokumente* (Stuttgart: Reclam, 1976), p. 63.

50. Jan Mukarovsky, *Kapitel aus der Ästhetik* (Frankfurt/Main: Suhrkamp, 1975), p. 63.

51. See Schmidt, "Text und Bedeutung," p. 51.

52. The phrase is Wehrli's.

53. The work of Thomas Mann is exemplary as a play area for epigo-

nal academic criticism. In his case the criterion of "interpretative richness" reveals itself with particular clarity. What is rich is the intellectual tradition in whose ironic refraction the interpretation characteristic of German studies can encounter itself (see Mecklenburg's critique of Mann's "administration of ideas," N. Mecklenburg, *Kritisches Interpretieren*, p. 81). As measures of value, what counts are symbol, myth, quotation, but also genre-specific characteristics, that is, formal and contentual indications for cultural richness of reference. This identification of cultural referents and artistic value manifests itself also in the treatment of the better contemporary authors. A case in point is the analysis of Max Frisch's works. Even a critic as experienced as Hans Mayer judges the novel *Mein Name sei Gantenbein* positively because it fits the model of *homo ludens* (see *Über Max Frisch*, ed. Walter Schmitz [Frankfurt/Main: Suhrkamp, 1971], 2: 323). This relationship to the tradition shows itself also when scholars interpret modern narratives from the point of view of genre theory. Günther Grass' *The Tin Drum* is a case in point here. Critics see it as belonging into the tradition of the baroque picaresque novel, without elucidating the literary significance of such a conclusion, see W. Seifert, "Die pikareske Tradition im deutschen Roman der Gegenwart," in Manfred Durzak, ed., *Die deutsche Literatur der Gegenwart: Aspekte und Tendenzen* [Stuttgart: Reclam, 1971], p. 192). Unfortunately, cultural references and the intellectual tradition as criteria of evaluation have gained enormous theoretical credibility in German studies through Gadamer's hermeneutic approach.

54. Schmidt, "Text und Bedeutung," p. 55.

55. For instance, Habermas, Wellershoff, and S. J. Schmidt. Compare Mecklenburg and Müller, *Erkenntnisinteresse und Literaturwissenschaft*, p. 109.

56. Habermas does not decide about this alternative but claims nevertheless that avant-garde art is being progressively depleted of its semantic content (see J. Habermas, *Legitimationsprobleme im Spätkapitalismus*, 4th ed. [Frankfurt/Main: Suhrkamp, 1977], p. 120). On the situation of the *posthistoire* of literary studies, see Mecklenburg and Müller, *Erkenntnisinteresse und Literaturwissenschaft*, p. 115.

57. Roland Barthes, *Criticism and Truth*, trans. K. Keuneman (Minneapolis: University of Minnesota Press, 1987), p. 34.

58. R. Grimminger, "Das intellektuelle Subjekt in der Literaturwissenschaft," in Jürgen Kolbe, ed., *Neue Ansichten einer künftigen Germanistik* (München: Hanser, 1973), p. 45.

59. See Mecklenburg and Müller, *Erkenntnisinteresse und Literaturwissenschaft*, p. 55.

60. Karl Otto Apel, "Szientistik, Hermeneutik, Ideologiekritik: En-

twurf einer Wissenschaftslehre in erkenntnisanthropologischer Sicht," in Habermas, *Hermeneutik und Ideologiekritik*, p. 30.

61. Peter Bürger, *Theorie der Avantgarde* (Frankfurt/Main: Suhrkamp, 1974), p. 26.

62. See W. Martin Lüdke, ed., *'Theorie der Avantgarde': Antworten auf Peter Bürgers Bestimmung von Kunst und bürgerlicher Gesellschaft* (Frankfurt/Main: Suhrkamp, 1976).

63. See Dolf Oehler's "Hinsehen, Hinlangen: Für eine Dynamisierung der *Theorie der Avantgarde*, Dargestellt an Marcel Duchamps 'Fountain,' " in W. M. Lüdke, ed., *'Theorie der Avantgarde,'* pp. 143–65.

64. See Habermas, *Legitimationsprobleme im Spätkapitalismus*, p. 166.

65. The horizon of expectations of readers or critics is exceeded when the repertoire of norms with which they are familiar is replaced by a new, fictional norm that cannot be reduced to a discursive meaning. See Iser, *Der Akt des Lesens*, pp. 15, 116–33. That can happen in two ways. The technical, formal way is when the new code can be decoded as a play on a familiar literary and ideological system of norms. The temporally reflective way occurs when the innovation can no longer be compared but can only be described as an emphatic quality, as James Joyce undertook to portray in the persona of Stephen Daedalus. See Umberto Eco, "Joyce und D'Annunzio: Die Quellen des Begriffs der Epiphanie," in K. Reichert and F. Senn, eds., *Materialien zu James Joyces 'Ein Porträt des Künstlers als junger Mann'* (Frankfurt/Main: Suhrkamp, 1975), p. 280.

66. Habermas, *Legitimationsprobleme im Spätkapitalismus*, p. 111.

67. Wellershoff, *Die Auflösung des Kunstbegriffs* (Frankfurt/Main: Suhrkamp, 1976), pp. 21, 84.

68. Contrary to the transcendental tradition, which seeks the concept of meaning in relation to a subject and thus undermines the idea of objective reality, Luhmann states: "The concept of meaning is primary, to be defined without reference to the concept of a subject, because the subject as a meaningfully constituted identity presupposes the concept of meaning" (Niklas Luhmann, "Moderne Systemtheorien als Form gesamtgesellschaftlicher Analyse," in Jürgen Habermas and Niklas Luhmann, *Theorie der Gesellschaft oder Sozialtechnologie* [Frankfurt/Main: Suhrkamp, 1971], p. 59).

69. See Bubner on Benjamin's reception of surrealism. See also Bubner, "Über einige Bedingungen gegenwärtiger Ästhetik," p. 59.

70. See especially Oehler, "Hinsehen, Hinlangen," p. 145.

71. Bürger, *Theorie der Avantgarde*, p. 27.

72. In his lecture "Die Rhetorik der Literaturkritik" and in his *Erkenntnisinteresse und Literaturwissenschaft* (p. 115), Mecklenburg de-

manded a literary criticism within the framework of a "theory of the present age" (see Jörg Drews, ed., *Literaturkritik–Medienkritik*, p. 45).

73. Bürger, *Theorie der Avantgarde*, p. 28.

74. Benjamin makes this distinction at the beginning of his essay on Goethe's novel *Elective Affinities* (see Walter Benjamin, *Gesammelte Schriften*, ed. Rolf Tiedemann and H. Schweppenhäuser [Frankfurt/Main: Suhrkamp, 1972], 1: 125).

75. Benjamin, "Ursprung des deutschen Trauerspiels," in Benjamin, *Gesammelte Schriften*, 1: 358.

76. Apel, "Szientistik, Hermeneutik, Ideologiekritik," p. 10.

77. See A. Hillach, "Allegorie, Bildraum, Montage, Versuch, einen Begriff avantgardistischer Montage aus Benjamins Schriften zu begründen," in P. Bürger, *Theorie der Avantgarde*, p. 106. See also H. B. Schlichting, "Historische Avantgarde und Gegenwartsliteratur," ibid., p. 237.

78. See Hillach, "Allegorie, Bildraum, Montage," p. 106.

79. Wellershoff, "Die Auflösung des Kunstbegriffs," p. 89.

80. See Bürger, *Theorie der Avantgarde*, p. 83.

81. An excellent example of such a reading is Oehler's analysis of Duchamp, "Hinsehen, Hinlangen," p. 147. His category of "uniqueness" and the reference to the "extra-aesthetic possibilities" should be contrasted with what Bürger calls the "eternally identical gesture of protest."

82. See Mecklenburg and Müller, *Erkenntnisinteresse und Literaturwissenschaft*, p. 54. See also Peter Bürger, *Aktualität und Geschichtlichkeit: Studien zum geselllschaftlichen Funktionswandel der Literatur* (Frankfurt/Main: Suhrkamp, 1977), pp. 134, 156 note 76, 176. For Mecklenburg and Müller as for Bürger, the actualization of the point of view of the present is directed at the cognitive interest in "nonhierarchical communication" (Bürger) or in the a priori of a "community of communication for scientists" (Mecklenburg and Müller). They avoid the dilemma about which Bürger warns, namely, the one of becoming "arbitrary" or "solipsistic" (Mecklenburg and Müller, p. 55), but they fetter literature with those normative bonds which it is the nonidentical element of art to negate. See also, as a logical consequence, Bürger's ideological, moralizing critique of Proust (*Aktualität und Geschichtlichkeit*, p. 164) and Valéry (ibid., p. 173), which fails to take into account the cognitive accomplishment of derealizing portrayals of reality.

3

The Prehistory of the Sudden: The Generation of the "Dangerous Moment"

Since the definition of the novella as an "unprecedented event," a certain narrative method has characterized the style of the German short story and has been particularly significant as a criterion of the aesthetics of reception for romantic stories and the stories that follow the romantic style. It has become clear, however, that the temporal structure of suddenness cannot be derived solely from the formal features of this narrative method. In the context of modern prose, the concentration of temporal consciousness on a "dangerous moment" means a denial of the continuity of temporal consciousness. The narrated event claims a particular dignity that suspends the continuity of narrated time. This event-character of what is narrated implies that the history of the age is received as a sequence of unanticipated events.[1] In this view, no utterance is relevant for longer than the moment in which it is uttered.

Before we turn to the literary symptom of the reduction of time to a point in time and try to show that the "dangerous moment" was only a particular expression of the moment that modern literature had discovered at the beginning of the century, we must explain the conceptual framework of the temporal structure of the sudden. That framework was created by Nietzsche's aesthetics and Kierkegaard's criticism and was extended in the 1920s by the works of Max Scheler, Carl Schmitt, and Martin Heidegger. It does not matter much whether all participants in this inquiry were able to perceive the problem in its entirety or whether these writings directly influenced each other. What does matter is whether a language of the sudden bursts out of the conceptual framework that was established by phenomenological philosophy and thus is not defined in such intellectual analogies. Comparing philosophers of suddenness with its writers will allow us to distinguish the unique suddenness of the writers.

It is well known that Nietzsche's works had a significant influence on the generation of the 1890s. Both the ethics of the noble warrior and the aesthetic suspicion cast on reason derive from them. So Nietzsche's influence—always preeminently a stylistic influence—must also be considered in the formation of the structure of suddenness. Carl Schmitt's "decisionism" seemed to show an elective affinity for suddenness as well, while Heidegger's and Scheler's early ontological determinations of time at first glance seem more removed from the aesthetics of perception.

I. Nietzsche's Sudden Style

In discussing the aesthetic phenomenon of "terror" we must refer to Nietzsche's central interpretation of the concept. The effect of terror arises—as Nietzsche, continuing Schopenhauer's description, asserts—because the "principle of sufficient reason" suffers an "exception" when the human being "is suddenly dumbfounded by the cognitive form of phenomena." Suddenness is the temporal precondition of such a perception. Semantically, suddenness is also the stylistic figure in which the subjectivity of eschatological expectation of the "decisive event" comprehends itself "in a *great separation.*" In the preface to *Human, All Too Human,* Nietzsche described such a situation of expectation that can be viewed as a model of eschatological expectation since it fully develops the semantics of the sudden:

> For such bound people the great separation comes suddenly, like the shock of an earthquake: all at once the young soul is devastated, torn loose, torn out—it itself does not know what is happening. An urge, a pressure governs it, mastering the soul like a command: the will and wish awaken to go away, anywhere, at any cost: a violent, dangerous curiosity for an undiscovered world flames up and flickers

in all the senses. "Better to die than live *here*," so sounds the imperious and seductive voice. And this "here," this "at home" is everything which it had loved until then! A sudden horror and suspicion of that which it loved; a lightning flash of contempt toward that which was its "obligation"; a rebellious, despotic, volcanically jolting desire to roam abroad.[2]

To recognize the structure of suddenness in our perception of events, we must disregard causal explanations, renounce the traditional concept of knowledge, give up trying to explain things with the concepts of cause and effect; we must pursue "description," as Nietzsche says in his *Gay Science*.[3] For "the suddenness with which many effects stand out misleads us; actually, it is sudden only for us. In this moment of suddenness there is an infinite number of processes that elude us."[4] The structure of suddenness in perception is thus relativized through a critique of cognition. But that does not lead Nietzsche to a logical reassertion of the general and the coherent; instead, he contemplates from a metaphysical perspective the "flux"[5] that constitutes itself out of moments of suddenness.

We cannot pursue Nietzsche's philosophy of the "great separation" from the positivism of the nineteenth century.[6] His philosophy produced the intellectual-historical constellation leading to the conceptual framework for those theorems on the philosophy of existence that shaped the generation of the "dangerous moment." Instead, we are interested in the structure and style of "decisionist" speech itself, its horizon of expectations. Both together yield the raster through which all elements of the modern style of suddenness can become perceptible: the moment, curiosity, the undiscovered world, horror, suspicion. The concepts needed only the innovative shape they received through the challenge of the 1920s. Let us remember that it was the "restless minds," the "loners," the "brothers in horrifying night watches," who were called the representatives of sudden decision. Without wishing to restrict the clear parallels to futurism, Nietzsche anticipated this connection as well. His strong linguistic influence on early futurism is perceptible everywhere, although Marinetti fought against such an imputation of dependence.[7] Nietzsche anticipated the type of a pure intellectual revolutionary who practices hypothetically what only the "great separation" will accomplish in history. These are the "free spirits"[8] of tomorrow and the day after tomorrow, "brave fellows and specters."[9] He measured precisely the claim of anti-ideological freedom and the leap beyond any conventional content when he says that one must send the fellows "to hell" when they "get boring."[10] This is not the *ennui* of Baudelaire and his romantic predecessors, for whom Nietzsche certainly had a taste. Rather, it is the lack of *ennui*, of sensitivity to sensation.[11]

"Boredom" was the decisive objection of writers like Jünger to the spreading "dominance of reason." The aesthetic justification of existence developed in Nietzsche's *Birth of Tragedy* is the a priori principle that also grounds the annunciation of the death of God as the "greatest recent event,"[12] that is, the advent of modern nihilism. The fantasy of catastrophe develops a semantics of the apocalyptic structure of the "sequence of breakdown, destruction, ruin, and cataclysm that is now impending."[13] It reserves a special form of knowledge for this process. It is a "spectacle" that only those "few" perceive whose eyes register a "suspicion" that is "strong and subtle enough."[14] Both sensory perception and elitist reserve yield the constellation that also appears, under new political and ideological conditions, among the younger thinkers. In judging the connection between Nietzsche's style of suddenness and this new prose we must take into account that this was not a systematic reception. Rather, the eclecticism of the modern writer concentrated on words and concepts whose philosophical and ideological penumbrae of meaning interested him only as an element of poetics at first. With such an associative method, single sentences taken out of context receive the same significance as a longer piece of prose. We need not explain that Nietzsche's style of suddenness had an effect even outside the context of the philosophy of culture. It operated through the aphoristic, interesting turn of phrase, for instance, when Zarathustra says, "—for I must tell you everything lest your hearts harden against me for departing suddenly." "Do you know the fright of him who falls asleep?"[15] The one who suddenly departs or the "fright of falling asleep" imply enough metaphorical meaning to serve for the new angst of perception. Nietzsche's aggressive and eccentric self-interpretation in *Ecce Homo* as someone whose name will be linked to a "decision that was conjured up *against* everything that had been believed"[16]—someone who is "not human" but "dynamite,"[17] someone who wants to have his "four meditations out of time" assessed as "four attempts at assassination"[18]—this self-interpretation obtruded especially upon the individual anarchistic disposition of Ernst Jünger's early style. It would have been a random omission and, given the semantic results we can now see, a completely unlikely event for Jünger and others like him *not* to apply Nietzsche's sentences from the preface to *Human, All Too Human* to themselves and to those who seemed to be their spiritual cousins—that is, those "free spirits" whom Europe will have "among its sons of tomorrow and the day after tomorrow" and of whom Nietzsche said: "I already see them *coming*, slowly, slowly."[19]

II. Kierkegaard's Demonization of the Sudden

Kierkegaard's sharp, aesthetic discrimination valued the problematic dimension of the sudden so highly that he raised it to one of the central categories of his theology of the demonic. In his work *The Concept of Anxiety*, published in 1844, he writes: *"The demonic is the sudden."*[20] One definition of the demonic is thus "when time is reflected upon."[21] Another definition is "inclosing reserve," that is, the effect of the negating behavior of individuality.[22] According to Kierkegaard, communication is an "expression for continuity, and the negation of continuity is the sudden."[23] Kierkegaard here anticipates in a critical sense the two aspects of Nietzsche's nihilistic expectation. He sees the suspension of continuity exactly as what it represents in Nietzsche's aesthetic apocalypse, namely, as the closing off of the individual person against the rest of humanity in a solipsistic act and as the renunciation of any system of laws.[24] The continuity this "inclosing reserve" possesses is only apparent. Kierkegaard compares it to the "dizziness that a spinning top must have, which constantly revolves upon its own pivot."[25] Within his theological framework Kierkegaard further defines the sudden as something "afraid of the good"[26] and thus like the demonic. He describes it as a characteristic of "Mephistopheles,"[27] but also recognizes immediately its primary aesthetic relevance, namely, that the evil qualities must be comprehended as phenomena. The effect of the sudden on "the observer"[28] provides the framework actually determining it, and for that reason Kierkegaard explains this aesthetic effect by means of Satan and his appearance:

> If one wants to clarify in a different way how the demonic is the sudden, the question of how the demonic can best be presented

may be considered from a purely aesthetic point of view. If a Mephistopheles is to be presented, he might well be furnished with speech if he is to be used as a force in the dramatic action rather than to be grasped in his essence. But in that case Mephistopheles himself is not really represented but is reduced to an evil, witty, intriguing mind.[29]

In contrast to this manner of vaporizing the devil, Kierkegaard proposes another way of presenting him, by means of mime:

> The most terrible words that sound from the abyss of evil would not be able to produce an effect like that of the suddenness of the leap that lies within the confines of the mimical. Even though the word were terrible, even though it were a Shakespeare, a Byron, or a Shelley who breaks the silence, the word always retains its re- deeming power, because all the despair and all the horror of evil expressed in a word are not as terrible as silence. Without being the sudden as such, the mimical may express the sudden. In this respect the ballet master Bournonville deserves great credit for his represen- tation of Mephistopheles. The horror that seizes one upon seeing Mephistopheles leap in through the window and remain stationary in the position of the leap![30]

Almost offhandedly, with this reference to the phenomenal character of the "demonically sudden," Kierkegaard succeeded be- fore the fact in grasping the structure of suddenness in works of symbolist and decadent literature and art as well as in the modern works emulating them, at least those works in which the image of horror and its iconographic elements predominate. He had also undertaken this task in a sketchy way in his *Diary of a Seducer*, published a year earlier, in 1843. We should note the figure of the actor, the mime, to which Baudelaire's and Nietzsche's aesthetics will also give a role. We must mention particularly that Kierke- gaard calls the decisive effect of such an ambush of "sudden hor- ror"[31] muteness. This early anchoring of the perceptual category of suddenness in an analysis of aesthetic phenomena contains in a nutshell all essential elements of the modern aesthetics of "horror." Thus from the inception of its comprehension as a category, the sudden was subordinated to an aesthetic process of appearance. Of course, Kierkegaard discusses this observation in a theological context.[32] In the moment of its release from a theologically defined framework, the category of the sudden lost its unambiguously negative content. The sudden is a process that is directly coupled with the discovery of theological evil as a purely aesthetic quality and of its transformation from its theological determination to the highest goal of postromantic aesthetics: this "evil" removed from theology was hypostatized in Baudelaire's poetry.

Kierkegaard and Nietzsche, each at a historically advanced moment of the romantic process of secularization, diagnosed the sudden as a central perceptual category of modern consciousness. The suspension of the consciousness of time as an experience of continuity and the intrusion of a "moment" of appearance had already been anticipated in the romantic narrative (E. T. A. Hoffmann, Poe), but that does not detract from the inventiveness and theoretical relevance of positing it as a category. The romantic moment of a sudden appearance, moreover, gave a mythic dimension to the reflection on time.[33] This dimension was replaced in Kierkegaard and Nietzsche by a dimension of aesthetic effect that was at the same time also psychological.

III. The Intuitionist, Ontological, and "Decisionistic" Interpretation of the Sudden

It is remarkable that the concept of the sudden is used increasingly where the language of the early phenomenological school, the school of Max Scheler, is still strongly influenced by the metaphorics of existential philosophy. Oswald Spengler is the preeminent example of the rhetoric of existential philosophy; his Nietzschean stylistic gestures are always in evidence. In his late piece, *Der Mensch und die Technik* (Human beings and technology), he writes about the development of the human hand:

> It must have developed *suddenly* in comparison to the tempo of cosmic currents, like a bolt of lightning, an earthquake, like everything decisive in the history of the world, epochal in the highest sense. In this matter too we must separate ourselves from the views of the previous century as they have been contained in the idea of "evolution" since Lyell's geological research.[34]

Geological strata are distinguishable only because they are separated by *"catastrophes,"* and the *"types of fossil animals"* are distinguishable only because they *"appeared suddenly."*[35] Spengler speaks an emotional truth when he states emphatically: "The history of the world strides from catastrophe to catastrophe."[36]

In his *Vom Umsturz der Werte* (The toppling of values, 1919) and *Die Sonderstellung des Menschen* (The special position of human beings, 1927), Max Scheler used the category of the sudden to develop his intuitionistic, phenomenological theory:

> Shame, too, is the sudden awareness and intrusiveness of the *finite* side of our nature in the midst of performing intellectual or spiritual acts in which we believe that we are realizing eternal, divine laws, laws that have nothing to do with the finiteness and paucity of the *starting point* of these very acts—on which we suddenly look *back.*[37]

With the help of the idea of suddenness, Scheler tries to present the evidence of his theory of "productive thinking":

> This thinking that is not reproductive but rather *productive* is always characterized by *anticipation*, the *prior possession* of a *new*, never experienced state of affairs (prudentia, providentia, cleverness, cunning). The difference between this and the associative memory is obvious. The situation to be understood, which must be taken into account in practical behavior, is not only new in its type and atypical, but it is also, and especially, new to the *individual*. Such an objectively meaningful behavior moreover results *suddenly* and temporally *before* new attempts at testing and independently of the *number* of previous attempts. In the expression too, especially of the eye, this suddenness shows itself, for instance in the way the eyes light up, which W. Köhler graphically interprets as an expression of the "aha" experience.[38]

In 1920 the Neo-Kantian Heinrich Rickert attacked the intuitionistic theory of the cognitive act, in particular Scheler's theory. His objections develop Scheler's intuitionism very well, despite their negativity. Particularly the category of the new and that of discovery are recognized as specific to the intuitionist:

> At least the intuitionist will not doubt that perception must teach him something new, and that demonstrates that perception alone yields no cognition. Or does anyone question that we need thought to discover anything new? In a certain respect every experience is "new," to be sure, and to that extent a principle of selection seems unnecessary. But the new in this sense has no theoretical meaning.[39]

Scheler's talk of suddenness is without casuistic and stylistic refinement and invites speculation about worldviews rather than philosophical or aesthetic interest. For that reason, Heidegger's ontological analysis of suddenness must be sharply distinguished from Scheler's intuitionism. Scheler endows the zeitgeist with an arbitrary harmoniousness that could be interesting only by virtue of its stylistic qualities. Heidegger's analysis, however, is of systematic significance and must be compared to Kierkegaard's and Nietzsche's analysis of the sudden. This is clear especially in two characteristics of his reflection on the problem. In *Being and Time* (1927) he elevates the "now" to an eschatological, significant 'now' and thus arrives at a new terminology for Husserl's "now-point." He also ties the perceptual category of the sudden to the concept of alarm [*Erschrecken*].

Let us start with the latter, since the term *alarm* touches on the topic of avant-garde literature. It will become clear that Heidegger's philosophical analysis of the phenomenon of fear and the function of suddenness within that analysis show a marked similarity to Jünger's central concept of "the crash of sheet metal" and the representation of "terror" that he derives from it. However, this is only a similarity in their inquiry; the way the two men approach the phenomenon they seek through language points up an informative difference between the poet and the philosopher. Our interest in this difference grows out of the hermeneutic assumption that literary texts cannot be grasped in a relevant way by means of extra-aesthetic concepts. We see here a great affinity for the dissolution of the perception of time as continuous and its replacement by the perception of time in the significant "point," so that the perceptible distinction becomes all the more important for our inquiry into the possibility of a purely literary "horror."

In *Being and Time*, chapter 5, section 30 "Fear as a Mode of State-of-Mind," Heidegger writes:

> There can be variations in the constitutive items of the full phenomenon of fear. Accordingly, different possibilities of Being emerge into fearing. Bringing-close close by, belongs to the structure of the threatening as encounterable. If something threatening breaks in suddenly upon concernful Being-in-the-world (something threatening in its "not right away, but any moment"), fear becomes *alarm* [*Erschrecken*]. So, in what is threatening we must distinguish

between the closest way in which it brings itself close, and the manner in which this bringing-close gets encountered—its suddenness. That in the face of which we are alarmed is proximally something well known and familiar. But if, on the other hand, that which threatens has the character of something altogether unfamiliar, then fear becomes *dread* [*Grauen*]. And where that which threatens is laden with dread, and is at the same time encountered with the suddenness of the alarming, then fear becomes *terror* [*Entsetzen*].[40]

We do not know whether Jünger read *Being and Time* in the years when he was developing the topic of "sudden alarm" in connection with his aesthetics of perception. Whether he did or not, the analogy in the presentation of alarm is striking. Heidegger's and Jünger's text share the perspective of formulaic intensification of various modes of horror [*Schrecken*].[41] In Heidegger, fear [*Furcht*] becomes alarm, then dread [*Grauen*] and terror [*Entsetzen*], the most extreme intensification. Jünger also differentiates terror or the terrifying, as the greatest intensification of horror from dread [*Grauen*], anxiety [*Angst*], and fear [*Furcht*].

Both texts share an assumption—and in our context this seems even more significant—that the phenomenal form of terror is bound to the fact that suddenness has the "character of an encounter." In the passage from the first version of the "Abenteuerliches Herz," Jünger does not use the word *sudden.* But *suddenly* contains the same temporal structure that is implied in the shock of the "deadly plunge." If Heidegger's distinction of the individual modes of appearance of fear were continued in prose works of a similar structure, that is, in further stagings of the terrifying moment, then we could confirm an identity of views between him and Jünger. However, if we bring Heidegger's definition of terror into play in this context, an important difference from Jünger emerges in addition to the difference between systematic and metaphorical language we have already noted. In Jünger, the punctual intentionality that discharges itself reflects preeminently an aesthetic event. Time becomes exclusively an aspect of its psychic reception by the subject. To be sure, Heidegger reduces the history of the human race to "*Dasein*'s possibility of Being-a-whole and the Being-towards-death."[42] But such ontologizing also means that a generalization occurs in the abstracting conclusion that distances the specific intentionality of the here and now for the aesthetics of perception. To illustrate this in more detail, we will consider Heidegger's concept of temporality, especially his exposition of "the ordinary conception of time."[43] The significance of the now is not in the "ambush-like intentionality of a single aesthetic" act but, on the contrary, in the presentification of both the "now-no-longer"[44] and the "now-not-yet."[45] This is where the now differs from the "ordinary" conception of time. Heidegger presents the structure of the now as follows:

> *Significance* belongs to the structure of the "now." We have accordingly called the time with which we concern ourselves *"world-time."* In the ordinary interpretations of time as a sequence of "nows," both datability and significance are *missing.* These two structures are *not* permitted to "come to the fore" when time is characterized as a pure succession. The ordinary interpretation of time *covers them up.* When these are covered up, the ecstatico-horizonal constitution of temporality, in which the datability and the significance of the "now" are grounded, gets *leveled off.* The "nows" get shorn of these relations, as it were; and, as thus shorn, they simply range themselves along after one another so as to make up the succession.[46]

The now of pure aesthetic intentionality shares with Heidegger's determination of the "ordinary conception of time" the absence of "future." That does not mean that the aesthetic moment lacks a utopian horizon. In contrast to the "vulgar concept of time," utopia is a vital element of the aesthetic moment. But this utopian element is identical with the intentionality itself and no longer reflects the future. One can say that in accordance with the aesthetic conception of sensation,[47] Jünger's "shock" of perception reverses the philosophical concept of the now that Heidegger developed with reference to Plato. Without the claim of the concept, focusing only on direct perception, Jünger's now corresponds perfectly to that "theoretical nothingness" of which Rickert spoke,[48] if one rejects the false pejorative evaluation, which is not necessarily implied for aesthetics by Rickert's term. Jünger's and Heidegger's concepts of the now meet in an ecstasy that each writer grounds differently. The two are different forms of the opposition to a formalistic conception of time, which Heidegger diagnosed in Hegel's idea of time, which was based on Aristotle.[49]

The special intentionality of Jünger's suddenness seems to be closest to Carl Schmitt's concept of the "state of exception." Schmitt developed that concept in the first and third chapters of his *Politische Theologie* (Political Theology), published in 1922. The connection between the two concepts becomes clear in the following sentence: "The exception in jurisprudence is analogous to the miracle in theology."[50] Just as Schmitt undoes the rationalistic eviction of the "state of exception" from modern political theory, Jünger's various portrayals of the horror that "suddenly" emerges signify that the time reason can anticipate and the norms set by reason are to be rescinded. Jünger's aesthetics of perception, concentrated on the appearance of the shock, is illuminated by a sentence of Schmitt's: "The exception is more interesting than the rule. The rule proves nothing, the exception proves everything."[51] However, in Schmitt's adaptation of the theological "exception" the reference to "the general" disappears. The logical contingency relationship is replaced with a reversal that is supposed to make the "exception" autonomous: the exception "confirms not only the rule but also its existence, which derives only from the exception. In the exception the power of real life breaks through the crust of a mechanism that has become torpid by repetition."[52]

Of course, in the theoretical context in which we have discussed it up to now, the problem of suddenness does not lose the idea of continuity. Continuity is retained in the theoretical engagement with the problem of suddenness as a previously set condition, unless such thinking were to become completely irrational. However, once it is no longer the concept but a preconceptual semantics that is active, the challenge of the particular to the general, that is, the annihilation of continuity by the ecstatic moment, takes on an intensified form. This is what happens in modern art and in modern literature. The modern period provides the relevant context for Jünger's staging of the moment. The texts by Scheler, Heidegger, Kierkegaard, and Schmitt, which we have used for comparison, have demonstrated the power of the idea of suddenness in ontological and "decisionistic" thought. These texts have provided epistemological aspects of the temporal structure of suddenness. Now it is necessary to describe the "dangerous moment" with its poetological problems. I said above that the "dangerous moment" is only a specific variant of the ecstasy of the moment that is so striking in modern poetry. I will now demonstrate this in greater detail.

In the "Sizilischer Brief an den Mann im Mond" (Sicilian letter to the man in the moon), Jünger writes that "things" are like "riddles" to the man in the moon, the nocturnal observer, surfacing like the "moments of an indeterminate expectation" in which one listens to the "voice of the unknown." This perceptual experience, which is not meant as a simple mood but as an approach to the "being," to the "hidden," concludes and is interpreted with the sentence: "Language has taught us contempt for things." Unknowingly, Jünger thereby touched on the aporia of literary modernism that had been manifest since the 1890s and that opened a chasm between poetic language and its referent, a chasm that existed well into the first decades of the twentieth century. It was the crisis of consciousness of the literary person to whom words seemed too used up to say anything that had not yet been said. The larger context of consciousness fell into ruin as linguistic context; it became the unsayable. Only individual "moments" could feed the illusion that their linguistic presentation was adequate. This hope was concerned, to be sure, not with an objective grasping of the moments, but with the presentation of the moment in a context that had become disjointed and unreadable. The presentation became identical with the most extreme subjectivity. The case of the young Hofmannsthal, the "Lord Chandos" crisis has become famous and has entered literary history as the prime example of such alienation of language.

We will not discuss the complex conditions surrounding the origin of that crisis. The scholarly debate about them is still going on.[53] There is still some doubt about the source of the crucial impulse that triggered Hofmannsthal's epistemological relativism—the same relativism we also encounter in Musil and Rilke—so that Hofmannsthal "suddenly confronts the phenomenon that he would earlier not even have believed possible," namely, "that the words with which he deals no longer obey him."[54] Hoffmansthal undertook to perceive "something completely unnamed and perhaps also unnameable" about phenomena in his fictional "Letter of Lord Chandos" (1901–02).[55] It seemed to him that there is no objective, consistent external reality but that reality presents itself in an illusorily objective way in the moment in which it is perceived.

Wunberg elucidated this line of thought with sentences from Hofmannsthal's journals, where we read: "We have no consciousness
beyond the moment, because each of our souls lives only for a
moment. Memory belongs only to the body. It seemingly reproduces the past, that is, it engenders a past that is similar in
mood."[56] Wunberg believes to have discovered the lasting influence of the Viennese psychologist Mach in this justification of the
relativity of values—the young Hofmannsthal attended his lectures
at the University of Vienna. Mach believed that the senses do not
deceive us. What they show us is neither false nor true. The only
thing one can say about them definitively is that they trigger
various "feelings and perceptions" given various stimuli.[57] Mach's
conclusion that the human ego is a fiction is the final consequence
of this theory.[58]

Wunberg sees here the theoretical background of the Lord
Chandos crisis, which resulted in the poetological reification of the
moment. His belief, for which he presents good evidence, has
some plausibility. We must note, however, that the discussion
about the epistemological relevance of the here and now was a
general and central theme of psychologically oriented epistemology
at the turn of the century. In his first work, the 1900 piece entitled
*Die Transzendentale und Psychologische Methode: Eine grundsätzliche
Erörterung zur philosophischen Methodik* (The transcendental and
psychological method: A basic discussion of philosophical methodology), Max Scheler dealt with the question of whether the here
and now of the "state of consciousness" was an "originary datum."[59] Scheler rejected that possibility. However, while
Troeltsch had attempted to solve the problem of the relativity of
values with reference to Kant, Scheler concluded that with the
exception of the principles of formal logic there was no "absolutely
fixed, self-evident datum." "Feeling given in a moment"[60] could
therefore also not constitute such a datum. Scheler's critical presentation of the psychological method illuminates precisely the
poetological structure of Hofmannsthal's work as well as that of
Jünger's moment. From the book by Theodor Lipps, *Tatsachen des
Seelenleben* (Facts of the life of the soul), Scheler critically quotes
the passage that could explain Hofmannsthal's crisis:

> My here and now is the last pivot for all reality, and thus for all
> knowledge. If we assume that the connection with this point is

disrupted, the continuity of personality destroyed, the rest of the world of experience would be a fiction for us in which we make ourselves comfortable, whose contents we can really believe for whole moments, but which would constantly dissolve into nothingness like a lovely, internally consistent dream at the moment of awakening.[61]

The theoretical impulses that moved Hofmannsthal—if there really were any and if he had really needed them—could have been quite various, as the discussion of Scheler and Lipps shows. The question Scheler raises here and then negates is also Hofmannsthal's question—to what extent reality, or whatever asserts itself as reality, can prove itself in the face of the "momentary state of consciousness."[62] Hofmannsthal answered this question with reference to psychological epistemology, thus anticipating the only answer other poets have given since; though their answers had varying nuances, they were in principle identical to Hofmannsthal's. Hofmannsthal's reaction was an avant-garde act and cannot simply be extended to the general situation of literature around 1900.[63] On the other hand, we must understand that Hofmannsthal's awareness of the problem was not only a symptomatic event in the thinking of a young, highly gifted person; rather it had been prepared long since in the tradition of aesthetic theory of the nineteenth century. In addition to Ruskin's significant contributions to English aestheticism and the individual values of the artistic theory shaped by his work, it was Walter Pater who consistently focused on the transient nature of the moment. As Wolfgang Iser has shown, for Pater "the situation" triumphed over "continuity."[64] As early as Pater, reality presented itself without a context, so that only the "extraordinary," "the stimulating effect of things," was able to waken our interest.[65] Iser pointed out the revolutionary import of the "mood," its "potential to evoke a penumbra" "beyond a theoretical or logical understanding of existence."[66]

Pater as forerunner—not only for the problematic nature of mood for the young dandy Hofmannsthal but also for Jünger's conception of a magical language—shows up in the "Sizilischen Brief" quoted above. The lonely "I" randomly perceives objects that form a context only under the wonderful mood generated by observing the moon. It is a "rapture" of "discovery," a "strange lightninglike birth," things "unprecedented for me in this moment," that structures what is perceived here. Iser's interpretation of Pater's style also applies to the later perspectivism of the moment. His interpretation is substantiated by Jünger's "Sicilian Letter." In this perception the object triggering the perception seems almost to be annihilated. Instead of an analysis, Pater offers a sequence of pure impressions that have escaped being yoked to data. The imagistic elements possess something surprising: "the insane gleam of the sun, the tyranny of the moon, delirious scarlet flowers, and the summer as poison in the blood are metaphors."[67] Iser concludes that Pater's aesthetics accomplishes the consecration of the new and surprising to the "other."[68] At the same time, Iser draws the conclusion that Pater's aesthetics once and for all supersedes Hegel's definition of the beautiful as "the sensuous appearance of the Idea." The beautiful has begun its "retreat into pure phenomenalism."[69]

Hofmannsthal's crisis of consciousness, which has long been interpreted in too great an isolation from its context, is only the first, spectacularly expressed, poetological problem in a chain of further crises that were evoked by the perception of the moment. Jünger's moment must also be separated from the overly narrow view of it as "decisionistic." In other words, decisionism and the avant-garde are in a closer relationship than has been seen up to now.[70] The theoretical context that previously interested us is, however, insufficient to define this more closely. Instead, we must also consider the literary realization of the moment in Hofmannsthal's early work. Particularly in three of his stories the surprising moment appears as a turning point of events, as the pivotal point of the narrative. These stories are: "Das Märchen der 672. Nacht" (The fairy tale of the 672d night), "Reitergeschichte" (Story of a cavalryman), and "Das Erlebnis des Marschalls von Bassompierre" (The experience of Marshall Bassompierre). The surprising moment must be taken literally here. Each of the three narratives is structured by a mysterious or terrifying phenomenon that the hero—the merchant's son, the Marshall, or the cavalry sergeant—perceives in a glance, for just a moment. Leitmotifs prepare the reader for this mysterious or terrifying phenomenon of a moment; thus, from the very beginning the glances others cast at the hero as well as the hero's glimpses of another person are given significance. What is suddenly perceived or perceptible in that moment remains, however, pointedly unexplained and submerged in the sphere of enigma. It is instructive to enumerate these moments.

The story "Das Erlebnis des Marschalls von Bassompierre" has a
series of sudden scenes that focus on the expressions of human
faces. Though their theme is different, they confirm what is also
true for the structure of the "Märchen der 672. Nacht," namely,
that the reader receives the sensation of a series of moments that
do not connect to a context in the sense of psychological realism.
In the "Reitergeschichte," the moment structure has its most com-
plicated form, which allows the author to break through the earlier
hermeticism and in which the silence of the images is more elo-
quent than in the other two stories. Analogously, the central
moment is prepared by a series of incidental moments. The difference between this and the two other stories is that here two
moments structure the narrative process as events. As he reconnoi-
ters the territory, the protagonist notices a rider beyond a bridge,
at the same distance from the bridge as he is.[71] The strange rider
has the rank of cavalry sergeant and a horse unlike any other in
the squadron "except for the one on which he himself was sitting
at the moment."[72] The stranger and the protagonist approach each
other at an identical speed. The vision of the stranger, which we
recognize as the phenomenon of the doppelgänger, solidifies into
an image:

> and now, as both horses, one from either side, rode onto the bridge
> at the same moment, each with the same whitestockinged front
> foot, the cavalry sergeant, with a fixed gaze, recognizing himself in
> the other figure, pulled his horse up like a deranged man and
> stretched out his right hand with fingers spread toward the figure,
> whereupon the other also pulled up and stretched out his right hand
> and was suddenly no longer there.[73]

Without showing signs of fear or shock, the cavalry sergeant then
takes part in the battle following this scene. At the end of the
battle, the squadron assembles and the captain in charge orders the
release of horses taken as booty. This second moment contains the
following elements of perception. The captain

> raised . . . his veiled glance to the sergeant, who sat unmoving
> before him in the saddle and looked fixedly into his face. While
> Anton Lerch's unwavering gaze, in which now and then something
> dejected, doglike, flared up and then disappeared again, might
> express a certain kind of devout trust, the product of many years of
> military service, his consciousness was almost not at all filled with

the immense tension of this moment; it was flooded with a multi-
plicity of images of an alien kind of comfort.[74]

This passage is followed by a psychological justification for dis-
obeying the order. The expression of the sergeant is the opposite
of the reaction of the captain:

> But whether something similar transpired in the captain, or
> whether it seemed to him that the whole silent, spreading danger of
> critical situations coiled itself in this moment of mute insubordina-
> tion, is unknown. With a casual, almost foppish gesture he raised
> his arm and, his upper lip curled contemptuously, he counted to
> three. The shot rang out and the sergeant fell, struck in the
> forehead.[75]

This momentary image is complemented by the information that
the sergeant had

> not yet hit the ground when all the noncommissioned officers and
> men had released their plundered horses by a tug on the reins or a
> kick, and the captain, calmly seeing to his pistol, was able to lead
> his squadron, still trembling from a lightninglike blow, against their
> enemies, who seemed to be rallying in the obscure, twilit dis-
> tance.[76]

Two things make the structure of these two moments in the
"Reitergeschichte" more complex than those in the other stories.
First, the expressive image does not stand isolated within a course
of events that is as unreal as the image. Instead, the hero is
integrated into actions that are comprehensible, in which other
people participate. In the two other stories, the hero is the sole
perceiver of incomprehensible visions. In the "Reitergeschichte,"
however, the integration of the mysterious moment into the context of a realistic course of events even provides a psychological
motivation for the behavior of the main characters. In contrast,
the typical description of the moment that has its roots in *fin-de-
siècle* decadence is characterized by its renunciation of psychological motivation. There the expression of a face, for instance, is
always a little irritating, because it is stylized into an empty expression. The unease this provokes has its source in the absolute
and definitive renunciation of an explanation. In contrast, both
moments of the "Reitergeschichte" contain explanatory motives.

They allow the reader to think that the sergeant either suffered an optical illusion when he saw the doppelgänger or that his senses were overwrought, or readers can justify the sergeant's life-endangering and therefore irrational refusal to carry out the order with accurate social and psychological observations. This integration of the moment into a context of explanation does not, however, rob it of its suddenness nor of the terrifying suspension of the reality principle associated with that suddenness. On the contrary: only the firm anchor to a narrative course that remains comprehensible gives the moment here its uncanny intentionality. The reader receives a signal that something within reality is out of kilter, that at any time we can expect the intrusion of the incomprehensible.

The second thing that sets this story apart from the other two is that here there is a correspondence between the two moments. To be sure, it is only poetological, not to be grasped from the perspective of narrative technique or logic. The well-founded, but still improbable and therefore terrifying act of the captain points back to the appearance of the doppelgänger. It is beyond doubt that the second moment really took place, because the sergeant is killed. The first moment, the reality of which one could very well doubt, thus regains some intentional capacity, even if that means only that the reader can no longer evade the question of that moment's meaning. This is how these two moments are structurally interdependent. In addition, there is the stylistic device familiar from the other two stories: strange identities and similarities are established. The meeting between the sergeant and the captain, like the meeting between the sergeant and the doppelgänger at the bridge, is a face-to-face, threatening confrontation. What remains blank in the case of the first moment—there is no hostile confrontation although the reader expects one—is filled in in the second moment. The sergeant is killed. His opponent is not the doppelgänger, whose facial features are not described, who rides toward the sergeant with an empty or a mirror-identical visage; instead, it is the sergeant's real opponent whose facial features are described precisely. Nonetheless, the captain seems to have some relationship to this doppelgänger. The "immense tension of this moment" finds release in the captain's shot. The shot also releases the unresolved tension of the previous scene, and gives it its appellative power. The reader is now able to establish connections, which is impossible with a completely hermetic work. The connection that is created is the relationship between a comprehensible and an incomprehensible moment.

Wunberg made a fruitful observation on this point. Starting out with Goethe's definition of the novella as an "unprecedented event that actually took place," he points out that this definition fits only the shooting scene, not the doppelgänger scene. The scene of the shooting is "unprecedented" and actually took place. The scene with the doppelgänger is only unprecedented. The "unprecedented" and what actually took place no longer coincide.[77] The structure of the story challenges its genre and is the formal indication that narrativity in the sense of continuity is no longer maintained. The unprecedented event is reduced to a moment that does take place but whose content, if measured by the yardstick of realistic expectations, remains ambiguous. This "moment" can also not be interpreted as the "most terrifying now," which always retains a dialectical reference to history, as Emrich showed with respect to the sudden images of the romantic period, especially Eichendorff's.[78] There, as Emrich demonstrated, the forms of representation of suddenness, "quiet," "thunderstorm," "lightning," the "scream," have an "existentially salvific function that leads to true being."[79] In the case of Eichendorff, there is not only the mysterious "now" but rather " 'the present' is the critical, negated image of its historical age, whereas 'presentiment' leads from the images of the age that we view to a ground of time, to an origin as well as goals."[80]

Emrich's existentialist interpretation of the romantic moment is particularly interesting in our context because it can be discussed only with reference to the romantic moment but has nothing to say about the modern moment. This sheds additional light on the difference between Heidegger's theoretically founded, ecstatic concept of the now and Jünger's suddenness: the modern writer— to the extent that he is not shielded by his world view, that is, occupied with ideology—has already left behind traditional models for understanding reality. Hofmannsthal's moment is one of the first proofs for this negative, theory-free vulnerability of the reflecting modern artist who has broken out of traditional certainties. The epiphany of the moment is the only thing of substance remaining to such a writer. It cannot be interpreted "symbolically" and does not point beyond itself, but instead it calls into question every sort of anticipated continuity.

This absolutizing of the now to an appearing moment, to the poetological structure of the epiphany, characterizes all of modern literature. Maurice Blanchot points out the "alluring charm of the pure instant" in Virginia Woolf's work.[81] He calls the experience of the moment "the insignificant abstract glimmer which cannot last, remains nothing, and returns to the void it illuminates."[82] These, as Blanchot quotes, are the last remaining "moments of being."[83] Virginia Woolf's modernity lies in her refusal to weight the moment with anything that points beyond itself, in her sense for the extreme point and for "horror."[84] Here it is clear how far she is from a traditional and—despite his ironic breaches—somewhat naive writer like Thomas Mann. Mann was unburdened by doubts about what Freud called the cultural norm, and therefore he developed very early on a distance from the "decisionistic" character of the artistic avant-garde.[85] He defined the object that is significant for him as follows: "An intellectual, that is, a significant, object is 'significant' by virtue of pointing beyond itself, being the expression and exponent of something that is intellectually universal."[86] Later, under the influence of fascist hegemony in Europe, he took a more sophisticated attitude and increasingly took into account what deviates from the norm. Gunter Reiss pointed out that Mann, when he described Joseph's dangerous individuality in the *Joseph* novels, accentuated Joseph's deviation from the "more usual" and still constantly tried to reestablish the appearance of universality.[87] In his novel *Dr. Faustus*, even the "symbolic" "unity between the particular and the general" disappears.[88] That indicates Mann's clear-sightedness concerning the dangers of isolating the individual from the context of the general, something that fascism, as he saw it, promoted.[89] The isolation of phenomena in *Dr. Faustus* is a stylistic signal of the awareness of a crisis and a portrayal of this crisis. With deep concern, Thomas Mann thus ultimately took into account the most radical hypostatization of that which does not refer beyond itself. Virginia Woolf's empty "moment" reflects just this loss of the universal. Its transitoriness can be redeemed only by lifting it out of time. Thus it retains the dignity of the unreal phenomenon.[90]

James Joyce broadened the modern motif of the epiphany to a

poetological theory, as Theodore Ziolkowski has explained in an important essay.[91] His results confirm the poetological structure of the sudden moment that we have worked out here. According to Ziolkowski, the epiphany in Joyce's works arises out of three elements: from the "whatness" or "soul" of things, which cannot be derived either from a higher power (revelation) or from a philosophical or archetypal authentication; from the present "moment" of contemplation, which must be distinguished from Proust's associational technique of remembering; and finally, from a particular "brilliance."[92] Ziolkowski believes that Joyce's work is formed in such a way that it "virtually consists of such moments of sudden illumination."[93] This illumination is "born of the spirit of the age and is encountered in exactly the same form, although not so consciously articulated, in certain German writers between the periods of Impressionism and Expressionism."[94] As examples, Ziolkowski names Hofmannsthal, Musil, Rilke, Barlach, Döblin, and Hesse.[95] The perspectivistic and stylistic characteristics of these authors are their typical reaction of "astonishment" and the perceptual category of the sudden.[96]

It has become clear that the moment appearing suddenly, which can take on the character of an epiphany, does not only leave behind the tell-tale trace of Jünger's "decisionistic" style. Instead, Jünger's moment belongs into the larger context of the crisis in the idea of continuity and in the idea of reality that was no longer taken for granted, a crisis that had already become acute in the 1890s. The emphasis on the imagistic aspect of every perception, the optical surface reality of things that Hofmannsthal described in his Lord Chandos letter and that Kafka presented in the "Beschreibung eines Kampfes" (Description of a struggle)[97] implies a mystification of reality. The irreality that arises here is no psychic projection but an event in the transempirical realm. It is covered by the category of the "completely other."[98] Dialogue ceases, and there is only the feeling of being struck by the figures or phenomena that "appear." Such an attempt to imaginatively rescue objective reality by bringing it both to an extremely subjective and a transempirical level incontestably is open to ideological occupation.

This seems to be the point where analogous but different developments of reacting to the challenge of a receding reality begin. The artist reflects critically on the negativity of this loss, while the ideologue, who argues from the perspective of a worldview, uses the strategy of compensation. That is, the latter tries to replace the needed but destroyed connections with new, parareligious contents. I can only sketch this process here; it is not fully elucidated but has been recognized in principle.[99] The difference between the ideologue and the artist should be emphasized all the more because in their political behavior during the 1920s and 1930s some representatives of the irreal style demonstrated a marked affinity for some of the various ultraconservative or even fascist ideas.[100] We must distinguish between the artist who seeks irrationality and its poetological forms in the sudden moment and the epiphany and the inventor of irrational ideological concepts. This distinction seems obvious and emerges as a pretheoretical certainty from the difference in their language. As we have examined the function of the moment in the work of several modern writers, it has become clearer that it first seemed that the autonomy of a language shaped primarily by aesthetic concerns with respect to the concept of the sudden is different from philosophical attempts seemingly directed toward the same goal—and this difference is not merely one of method.

We can now see that the literary, aesthetic hypostatization of the moment in the artistic act can be free of a primary ideological load. The aporia of consciousness formulates itself more authentically in an artistic context. The same cannot be said without reservation of the ontological and "decisionistic" determination of the sudden. To be sure, the various sudden forms of portraying reality that we have compared are not contemporaneous. The literary examples originated mostly in the period before 1920 (except for Jünger's texts). But they have furnished examples for the awareness of crisis in literary decadence and have demonstrated Jünger's intellectual heritage by means of the central topos of the moment.

Of course, and this is especially true of Hofmannsthal and Virginia Woolf, the artists also clearly demonstrated the style of alienation by use of atmosphere and symbol, in which the highest reflection of literature and art encounters itself. The "moment" is felt, but it is not a signal. The distancing from vital experience, as for instance from the political area, could not be greater. This is the critical difference between the writers of the epiphany and Jünger's moment, which is also a sign of the anarchic leap and which is an intuition, albeit a hermetic one, of future political events.

In this diagnostic function Jünger's style of suddenness achieves its literary quality and converges directly with texts of early French surrealism. To point out this relationship is not merely to write a scholarly footnote. Instead, it places Jünger's early work in clearer perspective. That is all the more urgent because the multiple connections linking him as an eclectic writer to works of the early aestheticism may explain stereotypically employed motives and structures but do not adequately elucidate the perspectivism of the sudden as giving an intuition of the epoch. The passages from Heidegger and Carl Schmitt quoted above correspond to this perspectivism, but in terms of method they remain unsatisfactory as points of comparison or reference because of their differing semantics. The perspectivism of the sudden must be discussed in a literary context that also reflects the historical moment. This would be possible if we considered the as yet unexamined analogies between the style of suddenness in Jünger's early work and in texts of the young Breton and Aragon.[101] Then the Janus-face aspect of the sudden as a concept between progressive and regressive expectations would emerge more clearly. Before we conclude our discussion of the background of the ontological category of the sudden, it must be stressed that the fascist rejection of the idea of continuity coincides with the emphasis on the sudden.[102] What Gershom Scholem wrote about Walter Benjamin must be adopted as a methodological principle: "He developed an extraordinarily precise and fine sense for the subversive elements in the work of great authors. He was able to perceive the subterranean rumble of revolution in authors whose world view bore reactionary features."[103]

In itself, the reference to Jünger's connection to surrealism is not surprising. Quite the opposite. Earlier scholars have described Jünger's style as surrealistic. However, that description was more a metaphor than a reasoned, substantiated comparison between Jünger's works and the French surrealist texts.[104] The affinity between Jünger's aesthetics of perception and surrealism as well as the difference between the two can be shown only in direct comparison with the surrealist texts. The result of such a comparison would produce a more precise evaluation of Jünger's perceptual "horror."

NOTES

1. The term event is not used here either in a textual linguistic sense or as it is used in the history of philosophy, e.g., in the debate about the question of story, event, and narrative. See Reinhart Koselleck and Wolf-Dieter Stempel, eds., "Geschichte—Ereignis und Erzählung," *Poetik und Hermeneutik* 5 (1973).

2. Friedrich Nietzsche, *Human, All Too Human: A Book for Free Spirits*, trans. Marion Faber with Stephen Lehmann (Lincoln, Nebraska and London: University of Nebraska Press, 1984), p. 6.

3. Friedrich Nietzsche, *The Gay Science*, trans. Walter Kaufmann (New York: Vintage Books, 1974), p. 172.

4. Ibid., p. 173.

5. Ibid.

6. On this topic see Karl Löwith, *Nietzsches Philosophie der ewigen Wiederkehr des Gleichen* (Hamburg: Meiner, 1956), p. 31.

7. See Christa Baumgarth, *Geschichte des Futurismus* (Reinbek: Rowohlt, 1966), p. 127.

8. Nietzsche, *Human, All Too Human*, p. 5.

9. Ibid.

10. Ibid.

11. Compare Nietzsche's complaint about the lack of a sense of nuance in German in *Beyond Good and Evil*, trans. Helen Zimmern (London: Allen & Unwin, 1967), p. 41.

12. Nietzsche, *Gay Science*, p. 279.

13. Ibid.

14. Ibid.

15. Friedrich Nietzsche, *Thus Spake Zarathustra*, trans. Walter Kaufmann, in *The Portable Nietzsche* (New York: Viking Press, 1954, 1982), p. 257.

16. Friedrich Nietzsche, *Ecce Homo*, trans. Walter Kaufmann (New York: Vintage Books, 1969), p. 326.

17. Ibid.

18. Ibid., p. 277.

19. Nietzsche, *Human, All Too Human*, p. 5. Löwith points out Nietzsche's prophesy and sees in Jünger one of those nihilists without discussing Jünger's affinity for Nietzsche's style (Löwith, *Nietzsches Philosophie der ewigen Wiederkehr*, p. 228 note 13).

20. Soren Kierkegaard, *The Concept of Anxiety*, trans. Reidar Thomte

with Albert B. Anderson, *Kierkegaard's Writings* (Princeton: Princeton University Press, 1980), 7: 129.

21. Ibid.

22. Ibid.

23. Ibid.

24. Ibid., p. 130.

25. Ibid.

26. Ibid., p. 131.

27. Ibid.

28. Ibid., p. 130.

29. Ibid., p. 131.

30. Ibid.

31. See Walter Rehm, *Kierkegaard und der Verführer* (München: Rinn, 1949), p. 286.

32. Rehm does little to work out the aesthetic relevance and the modern semantics of the concept of suddenness. Instead, he elaborates on the theological-existential thematics: "He recognized that the demonic could get a person into its power involuntarily, in a hideous way, through the ambush of suddenness, and could use him as a 'stimulus,' as a 'goad' in the false direction, moving him not against the false reformers but using him as a false reformer" (*Kierkegaard und der Verführer*, p. 462).

33. See Wilhelm Emrich: "Fouqué, Eichendorff, Brentano, E. T. A. Hoffmann and others try over and over to present the intrusion of old historical worlds (a palace in rubble, a ruin, a fallen castle, etc.) into the present, in the sense that suddenly and surprisingly the castle, the lost time, etc., arises again just as it was, . . . and in its present wholeness the difference between the ages suddenly disappears" ("Begriff und Symbolik der Urgeschichte in der romantischen Dichtung," in Emrich, ed., *Protest und Verheißung: Studien zur klassischen und modernen Dichtung* [Frankfurt/Main: Suhrkamp, 1960], p. 42).

34. Oswald Spengler, *Der Mensch und die Technik: Beiträge zu einer Philosophie des Lebens* (München: Beck, 1931), p. 27.

35. Ibid.

36. Ibid., p. 28.

37. Max Scheler, *Vom Umsturz der Werte*, 2d ed. (Leipzig: Der neue Geist Verlag, 1923), 1: 42.

38. Max Scheler, "Die Sonderstellung des Menschen," in Keyserling, ed., *Mensch und Erde* (Darmstadt: Reichl, 1927), p. 186.

39. Heinrich Rickert, *Die Philosophie des Lebens: Darstellung und Kritik der philosophischen Modeströmungen unserer Zeit* (Tübingen: Mohr, 1920), p. 17.

40. Martin Heidegger, *Being and Time*, trans. John Macquarrie and Edward Robinson (San Francisco: Harper & Row, 1962), pp. 181–82.

41. On the parallels between Freud's and Hermann Broch's discussion of horror, see K. H. Bohrer, *Die Ästhetik des Schreckens* (München: Hanser, 1978), p. 92.

42. Heidegger, *Being and Time*, p. 278. On this reduction see Jakob Taubes, "Geschichtsphilosophie und Historik: Bemerkungen zu Kosellecks Programm einer neuen Historik," in Reinhart Koselleck and Wolf-Dieter Stempel, eds., *Geschichte—Ereignis und Erzählung* (München: Fink, 1973), p. 495.

43. Heidegger, *Being and Time*, p. 472.

44. Ibid., p. 473.

45. Ibid.

46. Ibid., p. 474.

47. Ibid., p. 475.

48. Rickert, *Die Philosophie des Lebens*, p. 61.

49. Heidegger, *Being and Time*, pp. 482, 484, 485.

50. Carl Schmitt, *Political Theology: Four Chapters on the Concept of Sovereignty*, trans. George Schwab (Cambridge, Mass.: MIT Press, 1988), p. 36.

51. Ibid., p. 15.

52. Ibid.

53. See Wunberg, *Der frühe Hofmannsthal: Schizophrenie als dichterische Struktur* (Stuttgart: Kohlhammer, 1965), pp. 11ff.

54. Quoted in ibid., p. 109.

55. Hofmannsthal, *Prosa II* (Frankfurt/Main: Fischer, 1979), 9: 14.

56. Quoted in Wunberg, *Der frühe Hofmannsthal*, p. 31.

57. Quoted in ibid., p. 34.

58. Quoted in ibid., p. 31.

59. Max Scheler, *Die Transzendentale und Psychologische Methode: Eine grundsätzliche Erörterung zur philosophischen Methodik* (Leipzig: Durr, 1900), p. 165.

60. Ibid., p. 179.

61. Quoted in ibid., p. 148.

62. Ibid., p. 149.

63. See Wunberg, who should be supported in this evaluation, as opposed to other interpretations. Wunberg, *Der frühe Hofmannsthal*, p. 11 note 1.

64. Iser, *Walter Pater: Die Autonomie des Ästhetischen* (Tübingen: Niemeyer, 1960), p. 205.

65. Ibid., p. 47.

66. Ibid., p. 57.

67. Ibid., p. 81.

68. Ibid., p. 45.

69. Ibid., p. 87.

70. Hans Magnus Enzensberger emphasized this correspondence but his analysis of it was too one-sided and polemical (see Enzensberger, "Die Aporien der Avantgarde," in Enzensberger, *Einzelheiten* [Frankfurt/Main: Suhrkamp, 1962], pp. 311ff). Peter Bürger solved the problem with reference to critique of ideology; see Bürger, *Der französische Surrealismus: Studien zum Problem der avantgardistischen Literatur* (Frankfurt/Main: Suhrkamp, 1971), pp. 35, 68. His *Theorie der Avantgarde* (Frankfurt/Main: Suhrkamp, 1974) does not discuss this. On the relevance of the classical avant-garde for an aesthetics for the present time, see the essays in the volume *Theorie der Avantgarde: Antworten auf Peter Bürgers Bestimmungen von Kunst und bürgerlicher Gesellschaft*, edited by W. Martin Lüdke (Frankfurt/Main: Suhrkamp, 1976), especially the essay by Dolf Oehler, "Hinsehen, Hinlangen: Für eine Dynamisierung der Theorie der Avantgarde, Dargestellt an Marcel Duchamps 'Fountain,'" pp. 143–65.

71. Hofmannsthal, "Reitergeschichte," in Hofmannsthal, *Die Erzählungen* (Frankfurt/Main: Fischer, 1979) 7: 57.

72. Ibid., p. 58.

73. Ibid.

74. Ibid., p. 61.

75. Ibid.

76. Ibid., p. 62.

77. Wunberg, *Der frühe Hofmannsthal*, p. 63.

78. Wilhelm Emrich, "Eichendorff: Skizze einer Ästhetik der Geschichte," in Emrich, *Protest und Verheißung*, p. 16.

79. Ibid., p. 22.

80. Ibid., p. 11.

81. Blanchot, *The Sirens' Song: Selected Essays*, trans. Sacha Rabinovitch (Bloomington: Indiana University Press, 1982), p. 89.

82. Ibid.

83. Ibid.

84. Ibid., p. 90.

85. In a letter to Karl Kerényi dated September 15, 1946, Mann wrote about expressionistic activism, which he had turned against because of his romantic-protestant-nationalist attitude between 1914 and 1918 (see Thomas Mann, *Briefe 1937–1947*, ed. Erika Mann [Frankfurt/Main: Fischer, 1963], p. 506).

86. Quoted in Gunter Reiss, *Allegorisierung und moderne Erzählkunst: Eine Studie zum Werk Thomas Manns* (München: Fink, 1970), 87. See

also Thomas Mann, *Der Zauberberg*, in Thomas Mann, *Gesammelte Werke in zwölf Bänden* (Frankfurt/Main: Fischer), p. 904.

87. Reiss, *Allegorisierung und moderne Erzählkunst*, p. 89.

88. Ibid., p. 89 note 88.

89. Ibid., p. 92.

90. See Iser, *Walter Pater*, p. 185.

91. Theodore Ziolkowski, "James Joyces Epiphanie und die Überwindung der empirischen Welt in der modernen deutschen Prosa," *Deutsche Vierteljahresschrift* 35 (1961): 594–616. On the concept of epiphany in Joyce see chapter 9 of this volume, "Utopia of the Moment and Fictionality."

92. Ziolkowski, "James Joyces Epiphanie," p. 602.

93. Ibid., p. 605.

94. Ibid.

95. Ibid., pp. 606–16.

96. Ibid., pp. 610–13.

97. In this connection see Peter Kobbe, *Mythos und Modernität: Eine poetologische und methodenkritische Studie zum Werk Hans Henny Jahnns* (Stuttgart: Kohlhammer, 1973), p. 172.

98. Ibid., p. 99.

99. See Helmuth Plessner, *Die verspätete Nation: Über die politische Verführbarkeit bürgerlichen Geistes* (Stuttgart: Kohlhammer, 1959), pp. 82–105.

100. See Walter Heist, *Genet und andere: Exkurse über eine faschistische Literatur von Rang* (Hamburg: Claassen, 1965). See also Alastair Hamilton, *The Appeal of Fascism: A Study of Intellectuals and Fascism, 1919–1945* (London: Blond, 1971).

101. These analogies have been unexamined in part because surrealist texts have been largely unknown in Germany. German translations of Breton's and Aragon's early works were not available until the 1960s. In 1960 a translated version of *Nadja* by Max Hölzer appeared in the series *opuscula*, published by Neske. It was not until 1969 that Rudolf Wittkopf's translation of Louis Aragon's *Le Paysan de Paris* was published by Rogner & Bernhard, with an afterword by Elisabeth Lenk. That was followed by two further works from Aragon's early years: *Anicet oder das Panorama* (1972) and *Libertinage: Die Ausschweifung* (1973), both translated by Lydia Babilas and published by Werner Gebühr. We should note that Aragon withdrew his authentic foreword to *Libertinage* in 1924 and insisted on having the work published with one from 1964, in which the ecstasy of the original foreword was replaced by a distanced explanation of that early phase. In 1973 Rogner & Bernhard published Breton's *Die kommunizierenden Röhren*, translated by Elisabeth Lenk and Fritz Meyer.

This work was written at a later period (1932). The theoretical works on surrealism have also been difficult to find in German. Maurice Nadeau's *Geschichte des Surrealismus* (Reinbek: Rowohlt, 1965) marks a beginning. For important documentation see Günter Metken, ed., *Als die Surrealisten noch recht hatten: Texte und Dokumente* (Stuttgart: Reclam, 1976).

102. See J. P. Stern, *Hitler: The Führer and the People* (Berkeley: University of California Press, 1975), p. 45ff.

103. Gershom Scholem, "Walter Benjamin," *Neue Rundschau* 76 (1965): 19.

104. Karl Otto Paetel, for instance, writes of the "core of these somehow 'surrealist' books" (*Ernst Jünger, Weg und Wirkung: Eine Einführung* [Stuttgart: Klett, 1949]; p. 87). H. J. Lang sees surrealist technique in the deformed world of the *Gläsernen Bienen,* a late work of Jünger's. Lang's prejudice against surrealism relativizes this conclusion: "Ernst Jünger does not intensify the surrealistic attitude to total meaninglessness, as the surrealists do. His auditory surrealism is not without symbolic reference, however horrible it is" (Lang, "Wesen und Funktion des Traumhaften in Ernst Jüngers Werk," Ph.D. dissertation, Freiburg i. Br., 1960, p. 306). This attempt to shield Jünger from charges of being a surrealist by pointing to symbolic references, which characterize his late work, reveals the weakness of that attempt. The first concrete references to a substantiated connection between Jünger and early surrealism (see Bohrer, "Surrealism und Terror," in Bohrer, *Die gefährdete Phantasie* [München: Hanser, 1970], pp. 32–61) met with surprised interest or rejection of this thesis. See Elisabeth Lenk, *Der Springende Narziss: André Bretons poetischer Materialismus* (München: Rogner & Bernhard, 1971) p. 216 note 7; Hanns Grössel, "Im Jahre Fünf nach Breton," *Merkur* 25 (1971): 1002. It was Alfred Andersch who pointed to the surrealistic character of Jünger's early prose. In his "Amriswiler Rede auf Jünger" (Amriswil speech on Jünger), he characterized the prose of *Das abenteuerliche Herz* and *Blätter und Steine* as surrealistic, but with a caveat that restricted the concept: "When I read them for the first time, I was not yet in a position to recognize that I saw myself confronted in this prose with a global movement of the intellect about which we say nothing if we toss the word 'surrealism' into the air" (reported in *Frankfurter Rundschau,* June 16, 1973, p. 7). Andersch later expressed this insight more deeply and with a more certain instinct:

> Did he know Breton, Eluard, Aragon, Péret, Soupault, Tzara, when he wrote *Das abenteuerliche Herz?* Whatever the answer, these dream visions, these magical descriptions are the only book of surrealism in Germany. . . .Their sadism (read: In den Wirtschaftsräumen), which also marks the French movement, annihilates any-

thing comfortable and is aimed against any sentimental illusion. ("Achtzig und Jünger," Merkur 29 (1975): 248)

Thomas Kielinger took up the question of Jünger's surrealism again with reference to Andersch's remarks, but furnished no concrete answer. He correctly refers to connections between Jünger's surreal perspectivism and the modern German literature of consciousness (Musil, Bloch, Benjamin) but it is unsatisfactory that he uncritically equates Jünger's point of view, which is not dialectic, with the dialectic method of early French surrealism. That inadequacy erases his promising beginning (Kielinger, "Der schlafende Logiker," Merkur 29 [1975]: 930–46).

4 | The Fear of the Unknown: On the Structure of Mediation of Tradition and Modernism

The fear of the unknown—how well known is it? It is most familiar, perhaps, as a catch phrase in science fiction films and thrillers. And in those products of fantasy only the pitiable victims experience it; it is foreign to us, the enlightened. After all, our everyday life contains nothing unknown that is frightening. Quite the opposite. The course of our days is infinitely predictable, and is not premeditation the law of every act within society? Nothing is so improbable as the sudden discovery of something unexpected. And still, the phrase "the fear of the unknown" seems to be a self-evident metaphor for an elemental human condition. That is why Hamlet's famous soliloquy still has immediate effect when he says that only "the dread of something after death, the undiscovered country from whose bourn no traveler returns" stays the potential suicide's hand. The unknown—the word if not the experience—hides a mythic remnant that reason cannot dissolve. And when the unknown really does appear, then it still occasions fear, even hostility, precisely because it was unexpected.

But it no longer frightens in the form of myth, of death, or in any other uncanny disguise from the great beyond, as it did in Edgar Allan Poe's stories. It now appears from within the familiar, as when someone, a colleague from work or a guest, suddenly disrupts the rules of conversation and not only looks intently at his or her conversational partner but craftily takes the partner at his or her word. That gives rise to one of those unpleasant moments we usually classify as "embarrassing," because we are irritated that someone has said something unpredictable, not in keeping with the rules. As a matter of experience, it is usually not educated, sensitive people who provoke such unpleasant moments, but children—and artists. Artists probably provoke them to greater effect, because when they deviate from the norm, a freely acknowledged reputation and a psychological deviation that is not acknowledged collide with each other. When artists provoke in this way, they use their words not as a vehicle of communication but as a means of alienation. In fact, they do not even use their words; they merely accommodate them, for example, when they fail to speak of art like an educated person and speak instead of reality. Without meaning to sound polemical, that is the difference, isn't it, between someone who is educated about art and someone who creates art. What could be more comfortable than a lecture about, let's say, the history of the Renaissance, the forms of expressionism, the techniques used at happenings, or the fear of the unknown? The speaker, who is a scholar or at least knowledgeable about art and literature, makes what is unknown about the Renaissance, expressionism, happenings, or the unknown into something known by subsuming what is aesthetically exciting and basically inexplicable under a cultural concept and placing it in a historical context.

On the other hand, what could be more frightening than if this comforting context were denied to us? Say, a question, a phrase that does not refer to the cultural context we already understand but instead directly expresses experience, life? This happens already in the preparation for aesthetic production whenever a piece of reality becomes visible that has not yet been authenticated by a moral or intellectual code. The deep shock that can result is then hidden behind the mask of violated convention. Perhaps it was something like this on a higher stage of reflection that prompted Goethe to reject the young Kleist, something that Goethe called the "confusion of feelings." Schiller, on the other hand, considered "confusions" to be among the most instructive chapters in the history of humanity, even if the subject matter was the story of a crime.

In the cultural sphere, confusion of feelings, the failure of the expected to appear, is both taken for granted and scandalous. We can also discover this in the difference between irony as a socially mediated attitude and wit as subjective ability. Irony counts on cultural norms. Wit breaks through them, if it is sharp, in a subversive, dangerous way. It is no accident that from the nineteenth century on, the witty person, the artist, always appears as an extreme figure in an environment that does not understand him or her—as a criminal, for instance, in the works of E. T. A. Hoffmann, E. A. Poe, Baudelaire, and Oscar Wilde. If we demythologize these uncanny figures and read the word "crime" correctly, we arrive at the real threat they pose: the artist-criminals break through cultural norms because they do not repeat tradition as a structure in every moment of their acts. If a modern writer, such as Oswald Wiener, takes part in a scholarly discussion, then each of his words, each of his sentences, torpedoes the prevailing academic consensus, unmasking it as false parables. The creative structure cannot be reduced to a grammar of aesthetics.

If we look for the cause of this conflict between cultural norm and new discovery, then we see: the creative person lives entirely in the present; the scholar lives entirely in the past. By being wholly in the present, the creative person has literally forgotten every taboo. Heinrich von Kleist was forgetful in this sense; that is, he was completely uninhibited. A sensitive observer once called Kleist's lack of inhibition cynicism, and that is exactly what we mean here: it is the cynicism of someone who is concentrated in each moment, who simply forgets previous arrangements. Put paradoxically, the artist is no friend of art but its true opponent, that is, the opponent of the kind of art that predominates up to his or her arrival.

This provocation, which is inherent in every creative act, lies not only in the work's provocative message. Rather, it is contained already in the work's pure presentness, which can elicit a "confusion of feelings" if no known structure can immediately be recognized. This provocation results in a rejection of tradition, a rejection that seems to the scholar, but not to the creative artist, like a violation of the moral order of the world.

The most significant German aesthetician to date, Friedrich Nietzsche, drew the polemical conclusions from all these observations. At the apogee of a reactionary swing, he addressed the educated German bourgeoisie in his essay "On the Use and Abuse of History":

> Consider . . . the inartistic or half-artistic natures whom a monumental history provides with sword and buckler. They will use the weapons against their hereditary enemies, the great artistic spirits, who alone can learn from that history the one real lesson how to live, and embody what they have learned in noble action. Their way is obstructed, their free air darkened by the idolatrous—and conscientious—dance round the half-understood monument of a great past. "See, that is the true and real art," we seem to hear; "of what use are these aspiring little people of today?"[1]

Nietzsche there described, with preternatural clarity, what has since become the core of classicistic, historical, and realist misunderstandings of art:

> But if . . . the artist [be] put on his defense before the court of aesthetic dilettantes, you may take your oath on his condemnation; although, or rather because, his judges had proclaimed solemnly the canon of "monumental art," the art that has "had an effect on all ages," according to the official definition. In their eyes there is no need nor inclination nor historical authority for the art which is not yet "monumental" because it is contemporary.[2]

Nietzsche reduces the lover of tradition and opponent of the present to one sentence: "For they do not want greatness to arise; their method is to say, 'See, the great thing is already here!'"[3]

When he discovered historicism, Nietzsche also discovered the conflict between the artistic present and artistic tradition, a conflict that has given us no peace since. Thus, nothing could be more wrong than the comfortable notion that this conflict was created by the moderns themselves, by the avant-garde, whereas art is really something eternal. This is not a conflict between the aesthetic methods of Joseph Beuys and Caspar David Friedrich, between Arno Schmidt and Novalis. Instead, the conflict is between the art of yesterday, classified as "valuable" and thus tamed, and the art of today, classified as valueless because it cannot be tamed. At issue is the denial of a conflict between the present, which the spirit of tradition has denied, and tradition, which has been cut off from the spirit of the present and thus been cheated out of this spirit. Before Nietzsche analyzed this dilemma we have inherited, using the example of the merely historical understanding of art, the conflict had already been formulated in the epochal battle about the exemplary nature of the ancients, the *querelle des anciens et des modernes*, a battle in which Friedrich Schlegel, Schiller, and Hölderlin took part. Heinrich Heine continued the battle in his criticism of universal history and its failure in view of the "interests of the present." Stendhal continued it too, in his famous definition of the beautiful as no longer the transcendent but the entirely present and actual. Finally, Baudelaire gave us the first definition of modernity, in which the polar opposition of old and new is resolved in the knowledge that what is romantic today will soon be yesterday's romanticism, thus definitively establishing the idea of the transitory nature of art.

If we sum up the discussion about the ancients and the moderns culminating in Baudelaire's concept of modernity, we see the modernist view that eternity is constantly fleeting, always in motion and can never be grasped. Then it becomes clear how provincial all attempts are to regress to a consciousness preceding the *querelle des anciens et des modernes* and to establish a stabilized concept of the beautiful, as it were, and thus to eliminate the dialectical opposition between the consciousness of the present and the past, the structure that is the condition of art. Instead, this opposition must be taken as the universal structure of art, regardless of its style. And that is why even today we cannot do without the concept of the "present," which has become indispensable since the time of romantic aesthetics—notwithstanding all the talk about history having reached the end of its course and *posthistoire* prevailing once and for all. Even if this thesis about history were factually correct, for the artist one thing would still remain of the structure on which art is conditioned: the artist, in experiencing reality—and not just the quotation of it—as no one else does, must constantly reach new decisions. Therefore we must declare the concept of the present the aesthetic category that emphatically gives us sure footing in this precarious inquiry. And for the same reason we cannot avoid referring to Walter Benjamin's definition of the present in order to see what is left for us if we do not blindly accept his messianic rhetoric. His definition of the present is in the sixteenth of his theses on the philosophy of history and reads as follows:

A historical materialist cannot do without the notion of a present which is not a transition, but in which time stands still and has come to a stop. For this notion defines the present in which he himself is writing history. Historicism presents the "eternal" image of the past; historical materialism supplies a unique experience with it. The historical materialist leaves it to others to be drained by the whore called "Once upon a time" in historicism's brothel. He remains in control of his powers, man enough to blast open the continuum of history.[4]

Like Heine and like Nietzsche, Benjamin attacked the universal historical deficit of the historical perspective. But his contradiction gives us a guywire on which we can pull ourselves to a systematic position. Benjamin discovered the "constructive principle,"[5] as he called it, to stop fleeting time and fill this stop with his own moment. He called this constructive principle both materialistic and messianic, because the "cessation of happening" is a "revolutionary moment in the fight for the oppressed past."[6] Benjamin wants to rediscover tradition in the light of a revolutionary future with a clearly political goal. His emphatic understanding of the present as anticipating such a future in a messianic sense helps Benjamin in this undertaking.

The utopian Ernst Bloch transferred Benjamin's category of the now completely into a utopian context by warning that the messianic content of the present moment "would be placed senselessly on one point if it is not defined within an objective 'anticipation.' "[7] Bloch was correct in sensing the phenomenological element in Benjamin's punctualism, in which the continuum of history comes to a stop. That is not only a conceptually compelling aspect of Benjamin's construction of the moment; as an aesthetic element, it is still more obvious in his linguistic style. That is why Bloch, suspicious, insisted on the historical context, on the tendency of history.

This is not the place to attack this "tendency" although we may question what it might be. Still, we want to hold fast to the concept of the present *without* the utopian horizon and say: this moment, this now-point belongs to the anticipatory structure of every aesthetic attempt, every draft of ourselves. Without such a now-point an aesthetic act necessarily becomes pure imitation, an act of restoration, whether reproducing epigonously with deceptive guises what has already been created or coopting it as cultural heritage. This coopting need not consist in recapitulating the past from the victors' point of view, to use Benjamin's phrase. The restorative coopting takes place every time the past robs the moment of its self-understanding and prevents it from becoming self-reflective, thus keeping it from doing what people do when they irritate others by saying what is unexpected, what has not yet been integrated. The pointlike nature of the now is thus not, as the utopian Bloch believes, simply meaningless. Rather, only that punctuality guarantees the unconventional meaning of the now, especially its openness to the unknown.

We must shield Benjamin's idea of the present from too naive an interpretation by the utopians in order to preserve its strategically indispensable "constructive principle." That is possible only if we do what Bloch warned us against: we must emphasize the powerful position of Benjamin's now and reactivate its phenomenological capability. That does not amount to a simple repetition of Dilthey's "now-point" or of Husserl's "horizon" in the sense of a quasi-mystical attempt to resubstantialize life itself. But it is reminiscent of Husserl's insight into the anticipatory structure of every moment of our perception. We must not only realize, in a psychological sense, the potential of every moment in relation to time as a whole; we must also grasp it systematically. Then it becomes self-evident how false the view is that the history of art has become the objectivity of art history, in which the so-called great works have their fixed ranks and which can serve as a basis for describing and criticizing the future of art. One does not need a utopian perspective to grasp the utopian element of every aesthetic act. The punctual nature of the hermeneutic consciousness itself points this out. Even as conservative an aesthetician as Gadamer admits that the only criterion for contemporary art is the moment, "that electric contact," which, as he says, sometimes distinguishes a contemporary work and is experienced in a moment, in the fulfillment of an apprehension of meaning transcending all conscious expectation. One can also say: it is not necessary to force the principle of hope onto the now; that principle is always preconceptually part of the now. This paradoxical conception of punctuality is not a subjective evasion. It is the condition of aesthetic perception in the modern and postmodern age. We cannot make do without Benjamin's concept of the present, even if we do not share all of his and Bloch's conclusions about the philosophy of history or utopia. After all, our purpose is not to reconcile hermeneutics and materialism, but only to determine the significance of the unknown for the aesthetic moment.

Then we will also understand that the so-called avant-garde is not something historically finished and dated, but it is only what we make of it with the exegetical risk of our contemporary moment. The talk of the end of the avant-garde purports to apply only to a certain phase of the newer development of art, Vostell and Beuys, let us say, but in truth its aim is to reconstruct the doctrine of eternity and to annihilate the moment we have just described. The doctrinaires of eternity are methodical in presenting their point of view, which amounts to a discussion of only the formal aspects of the avant-garde: montage, collage, and the fragment. Now these three formal techniques of modern painting and literature seem so indispensable because they are what prevents the false illusion of an aesthetic reconciliation, that is, a reconciliation of the reader or observer with reality through the harmonization of the latter in art. Especially montage, as we know, has uncomfortably prevented that comforting synthesis, that direct interpretation of meaning. For that reason scholars have largely explained the enigmatic character of modern art by recourse to the aesthetic accomplishments of those formal means thanks to which a large segment of the public can still exclaim, half a century after the appearance of the first products of modernism: I don't understand it! If we explain modernism or the avant-garde so one-sidedly in terms of its formal techniques, then eventually these techniques come to repeat themselves. That brings about what people have termed the aging of the avant-garde. But from the beginning, the formal aesthetic definition of the avant-garde was based on a very understandable error—the erroneous assumption that in art and literature the law of modernity, that is, of progress in history, was expressed through constant innovation. This application of a technological, positivistic idea of progress to the rhythm of appearance of new works of art was a mistake. Works that are modern in a formal, aesthetic sense need not embody a "progressive" idea; the truly innovative, on the other hand, cannot be reduced to the formal techniques of collage, montage, and use of the fragment. From the beginning of this century, the radicalism with which artists have staged the new, the incomprehensible, and—let us not hesitate to name it—the unknown has gone far beyond mere formal techniques. Let us put it this way: the new, the incomprehensible, the unknown does not simply equal the most advanced style; instead, it is what fits the moment.

To prove that formal techniques exhaust themselves over time does not prove anything. In keeping with the importance of the moment as a criterion of modernism, formal techniques can vary greatly. The historical misunderstanding that keeps repeating itself is to imagine postmodern art as a merely technical repetition of the avant-garde and thus to dismiss it as something outworn. With the fathers of the avant-garde, Marcel Duchamp and André Breton, to take just the line of surrealists, it was probably less a matter of the famous "shock" as an innovative surprise than of a sort of epistemological wit that we can interpret as the realization of the emphatic moment. This epistemological wit at this emphatic moment originates when an observer or a reader is put into a perceptual situation where the unique character of what he or she sees or reads shakes up the dominant perceptual norms and values. In *The Birth of Tragedy*, Nietzsche, referring to Schopenhauer, speaks of "the tremendous *terror* which seizes man when he is suddenly dumbfounded by the cognitive form of phenomena because the principle of sufficient reason, in some one of its manifestations, seems to suffer an exception."[8] Nietzsche called this experience the Dionysian aspect of art. To date, we have failed to examine this dimension of depth in the avant-garde, say in Duchamp's provocation, because it was classified too early as formalist anti-art and was relegated to an objective history of art and style and to the idea of art prevalent in those disciplines. We might still discover that Duchamp's laughter has never yet been heard. Shock is disturbing not only because it provokes us but also because of the up to now unknown aspect of what it expresses, an aspect that confuses us. Shock is not a matter of ever more eccentric new eccentricities; it is a result of contents of consciousness that have not yet been processed. Otherwise what the avant-garde originated would become a mere craft. Duchamp's cynicism lies in his epistemological wit. It is the same cynicism as that of Heinrich von Kleist, of Oswald Wiener, of Kurt Schwitters. It is yet to be realized in the mind of the academic disciplines and, indeed, in all of our minds.

In order to stress the great importance of cynicism or of this epistemological wit for the meaning of the moment, we need only consider those modern artists whom the representatives of tradition like to praise: Henry Moore, let's say. He lost the quality of the moment because he was absorbed by the meaning that his objects attracted to themselves. He allowed himself to fit seamlessly into a cultural norm because his formal techniques were "modern." He rehabilitated art in the sense of the traditionalists, as a symbol, as a work of art. Duchamp's principles, on the other hand, are not only not outmoded, they are only now being discovered and made fruitful for a methodology of the unknown in philosophy and aesthetic analysis.

We now have a basis for understanding the moment as a key to the modern movement, a basis that is free of the metaphysical, symbolic, and ontological baggage that this moment still carries in Walter Benjamin's usage. We take special pleasure in explaining the actual dynamics of this moment with reference to Paul Feyerabend's epistemological investigations, because he himself styled them "anarchistic," and "anarchy" is one of the terms used nowadays to criminalize modern artistic practice.[9] Feyerabend demonstrated that there was no scientific rule, however clear and epistemologically well grounded, that had not at some time been broken. Now breaking a rule is not in itself the astonishing or irritating thing. Even the most rigid traditionalist will admit that breaking an old rule provides a possibility for revising it. What is irritating is the way this rule gets broken. The rule is not refuted from within the system of rules; rather, it is just ignored and simply passed over. It is not the case, as people often assume, that a "clear and distinct understanding"[10] precedes new ideas when they are to be formulated and applied. Instead, theories become "clear and 'reasonable' only *after* incoherent fragments of them have been used for a long time."[11] They are not foreseeable, they become reasonable suddenly, in a moment. Their reasonableness is anticipated in a playful moment.

Let us make the anticipatory quality of the pretheoretical, intuitive phase somewhat clearer on two levels: by means of the example of literary interpretation and the example of an imaginative act as such. The aesthetic-evaluative reaction that finally produces a value judgment is not an analytical act; it is always a synthetic act that is simply performed in different phases. The very first phase anticipates the final judgment, although we cannot necessarily give any reasons for that anticipation. This anticipation is not due to our rediscovery of preexisting ideas or even of formal aesthetic qualities that we favor. If that were the case, we would not do justice to the uniqueness of the present work and would be behaving in a very conventional way. The real approach is an intuitive, imaginative decision in which we enter into a basic value relationship long before we arrive at any intellectually justifiable judgment. This anticipation of understanding can be distinguished from the suggestions of phenomenological aesthetics, which sound similar (see chapter 2 in this volume), whether they refer to the "originary emotion," the articulated moment of the reader, or simply the hermeneutic circle. In these postphenomenological explanations of the moment of aesthetic enlightenment or aesthetic comprehension, the emphasis is always on the work of art itself, which appears ontologically, and on the application of aesthetic, philosophical, and moral norms. The anticipatory moment, on the other hand, does not contain these norms; rather, subjectivity and unknown objectivity meet in it. Young Lukács, with his idea of "lived reality," most closely approximated this pure anticipation. He criticized the intellectualism of the "interpreted" work of art and believed that in the experience of art there was "no maxim of a normative position." Therefore, this experience contained no "difference in value or truth" but only the perception of unique quality and specific intensity. This rejection of the analytical illusion is directed against both the values of the conservative understanding of art and the values of the Marxist orthodoxy whose main representative Lukács later became. Lukács' shift shows how close the reactionary-bourgeois and the orthodox-Marxist worship of the good, the true, and the beautiful have always been.

In contrast to the analytic illusion of these two schools of thought, the anticipatory moment contains the knowledge that any experience of intensity is always also the experience of one's own intensity. To sum up: the general impression that "this is art" has an effect independent of the knowledge of the specific content we are experiencing. And the stronger this impression is, the greater chance a modern work of art has to be understood on its own terms, without being made subject to preconceived ideas.

This paradoxical insight into the enigmatic character of art is explained even more strikingly in literary texts themselves. It was Nietzsche, once again, who pointed out to us the confession of the rationalist Friedrich Schiller, who said that the "preparatory state before the act of poetic creation" contains not "a series of images, with thoughts arranged in causal order," but rather a "musical mood": "In the beginning, my mood is without a definite, clear object, this is formed later. A certain musical mood of the spirit precedes, and the poetic idea follows."

We need not belabor the fact that Schiller's dramatic style, and most especially his aesthetic writings of the 1790s, grew not out of the tradition he knew but rather out of the emphatic moment of the French Revolution, which elicited a sudden change of consciousness. No pattern, no topos, no grammar, no quotation, however much intellectual precedent one may cite, can explain that change. The thing itself is not derived from anything else, it is simply there, and thus the category of the moment, of the new, of the unknown, cannot be ignored even where our scholars of the classical period so enthusiastically collect examples for their preoccupation. Only the romantic imagination, however, comprehended the anticipatory moment as a leap into what a few moments before had been unknown in such a way as to nurture an actual aesthetic of the unknown and our fear of it. Friedrich Schlegel's essay, "Über die Unverständlichkeit,"[12] is a unique, early coming to terms with the representatives of the norm, as though he suspected the devastation they would one day effect especially in the German debate about art and the politics of art. Heinrich von Kleist, in his essay "Über die allmähliche Verfertigung der Gedanken beim Reden," gave us the best description of the function of the moment as discovering and anticipating what is still uncomprehended, unknown.

> I believe that many a great orator, in the moment when he opened his mouth, did not know what he wanted to say. But the conviction that the circumstances and the resultant arousal of his spirit would create for him the necessary plenitude of thoughts made him bold enough to make a beginning, trusting to luck. I am thinking of that "thunderbolt" of Duke Mirabeau with which he laid low the master of ceremonies after the last monarchistic convention of the King was dissolved on June 23. The King had recommended that the

états should dissolve themselves, and the master of ceremonies
returned to the meeting room in which the *états* were still assembled
and asked them if they had heard the King's order. "Yes," answered
Mirabeau, "we heard the King's order." I am certain that with this
gentle beginning he was not yet thinking of the bayonet with which
he closed: "Yes, sir," he repeated, "we heard it." One sees that he
still does not know what he wants to say. "But what gives you the
right," he continued, and now suddenly a spring of monstrous
imagination opens up, "to tell us about orders here? We are the
nation's representatives." That was what he needed! "The nation
gives orders and does not receive them"—now he is at the height of
boldness. "And let me make myself perfectly clear to you"—and
only now does he find the words to express the whole resistance to
which his soul is armed, "tell your King that we will forsake our
places only at bayonet point." Pleased with himself, Mirabeau then
sat down.[13]

It is likely that a political master of today would declare this
passage of Heinrich von Kleist's unconstitutional because Kleist
was bold enough to illustrate his case with a striking example of
lawbreaking, and he does it with overt satisfaction, even identification. It is as if Kleist is not only describing the gradual completion of an immense political thought but as if he himself is gradually discovering the important idea of the "momentary" structure
of creative processes and brings his own idea as well as Mirabeau's
to expression. What makes Kleist's presentation of the conventional version of the origin of the French Revolution so interesting for the structure of tradition and modernism is the fact that
he has Count Mirabeau do two things. On the one hand, Mirabeau does not simply reiterate a preexisting idea, that of the sovereignty of the people; he discovers the idea in an intuitive burst.
On the other hand, however, this advance into the unknown is
also subversive in a very literal sense. The coincidence of discovery of the unknown and of the forbidden as a structural element
of modernism could not be more clearly demonstrated—nor the
fear that this coincidence engenders. It does not even matter
whether Kleist himself was a consistent supporter of the French
Revolution. What matters is that he discovered the anticipatory
power of a moment. In similar fashion, he describes this event of
world history offhandedly by saying "It could be that it was, in the
last analysis, the trembling of an upper lip or an ambiguous fiddling

with a cuff that brought about the fall of the order of things in France."[14]

What is anarchistic about this discovered quality of the moment? In the sense of Paul Feyerabend's system to oppose systems, what is anarchistic is that this quality cannot be derived, however we twist it, from previous considerations or from the cultural tradition. It is without preconditions to such an extent that a sudden change of consciousness is needed for such a moment to happen. Such a change is a decision, whether we call it "existential" or the process of intuitive illumination. But this contradicts all ideas of how tradition is passed on to become a cultural norm. Feyerabend therefore reaches the following conclusion:

> To those who look at the rich material provided by history and who are not intent on impoverishing it in order to please their lower instincts, their craving for intellectual security in the form of clarity, precision, "objectivity," "truth," it will become clear that there is only *one* principle that can be defended under *all* circumstances and in *all* stages of human development. It is the principle: *Anything goes.*[15]

This explanation corresponds closely to the law of the joyously sensuous order in Rabelais' *Gargantua*, which has become a touchstone of anarchistic utopias. The single rule in Rabelais' monastery was: Do what you will!

With this sensuous and intuitive recommendation, the anarchistic critique of epistemology takes up what became a method for artists who oppose the norm, such as the Dadaists. Not only did the Dada movement develop no program or platform; it opposed any kind of program, but this did not prevent Dadaists from occasionally defending a program. That brings us once more to the epistemological cynicism we have mentioned, which is nothing other than a radical, merry frankness. It is cynical in the same sense as the sentence: "An anarchist is like a secret agent who plays the game of reason in order to undermine the authority of reason (or of the truth, of honor, of justice, etc.)."

Now we have arrived at the question of scandal, which has been our destination from the beginning of this discussion. These days scandal is presented to us as criminal but is in reality part of every imaginative, creative act. The connection between the momentary leap into the unknown and political anarchy is an optical illusion to which one succumbs if one lets oneself be lulled by conventional analogies instead of concentrating on the crucial difference. If we compare the imaginative, poetic, and epistemological leap into the unknown with political anarchy, this difference emerges in regard to the quintessential element of the poetic. The political anarchist cherishes an eschatological faith according to which the existing order must be destroyed so that human potential can be realized. He or she entertains a naive trust in the natural rationality of human beings and other certainties that the epistemological and poetic anarchists defy by being unconditionally opposed to one single thing: general ideas that have long since become clichés. Modern artists in fact destroyed these general ideas, and if it should turn out that the entire avant-garde was on the wrong track in its choice of methods, its imaginative accomplishment definitely was not. A return to the image of beautiful nature, to the reconciliation of ideal and life, which some thinkers currently hope for, is no longer possible. This meaning that art is supposed to provide for us is out of the question. The idea of the moment, which modernists from Kleist to Benjamin turned against tradition, has certainly limited our view. Still, that keeps us from the illusion that we are beholding eternity. In other words, the emphatic moment in modern art did not forget tradition. But when modernists quote tradition, then it is a quotation after the manner of Tom Stoppard's early comedies: it destroys tradition in order to create meaning in the present. Part of the structure of modernism is this polar tension, however it may manifest itself stylistically. It is a tension without piety, something like a patricide, so to speak. The old unequivocal meaning is replaced by ambiguity, the beauty that merely puts interesting drapery on something already well known is supplanted by a beauty that lets the unknown shimmer through.

But this unknown, which we take to be a criterion of modern art, what would it be if it were translated into the language of the old doctrine of beauty? What would the unknown be as the beautiful? Breton once defined the beautiful as the "convulsive," and Benjamin, the real discoverer of the surrealistic unknown, used the example of Goethe's *Elective Affinities* to speak about the "shock," the "unrest" of the heart that occurs when the comforting appearance of beauty passes.[16] The objective category in which Benjamin places this condition of transition and decline is that of the sublime. This understanding of beauty stands in contrast to the idea that beauty is simply truth made visible. But what was it again that Nietzsche said? "For art flees when you spread the tent of history over your deeds" rather than retaining "in prolonged shock the incomprehensible as the sublime." The incomprehensible as the sublime? Well, as we saw, modern art, which no history of style can encompass, has in fact stripped away the tent of history and become incomprehensible. The implosion of the sublime into the beautiful marks in fact the point at which classicism became romantic and modern art. According to Kant, people confronting the sublime look serious, intent, astonished, and shocked; and Satan has become the sublime figure of literature since Milton and Blake. The scandalous writings of the Marquis de Sade are satanic and sublime at once. Since then, astonishment and terror are the conditions under which we perceive modern art and literature. We do not need the charge of anarchy in order to see something dangerous in modern art. That charge reveals itself as a sham argument because its true goal is to replace the new and terrifying (say, Beuys or Thomas Bernhard) with the old and beautiful. The fact that the terrifying and subversive also belong into the aesthetic category of the sublime makes the fearful rejection of it all the more urgent to the opponents of the modern.

So scandal remains, and we insist on it. The rift that an emphatically experienced present moment causes between tradition and the future forbids us to assume normative rules or laws for current art. As Kleistian art or as the very latest art, art is by definition unlawful, subversive, without obligations. As with scientific knowledge, nothing is unimaginable for current art, nothing is forbidden, nothing can be forbidden. The fear of such art is understandable. But it must be revealed as fear and cannot be permitted to drape itself in sham arguments, like those we have tried to expose here. Instead of mounting such sham arguments, those who fear the unpredictable and unknown in every imaginative act should side with Plato, who banned art from his utopian republic as being dangerous to society. Then we will know where they stand: in an authoritarian state.

NOTES

1. Translator's note: The German text for this chapter does not have footnotes. Where I could, I have provided them. Friedrich Nietzsche, *The Use and Abuse of History*, trans. Adrian Collins (Indianapolis: Bobbs-Merrill, 1957), p. 16.

2. Ibid.

3. Ibid., p. 17.

4. Walter Benjamin, "Theses on the Philosophy of History," in Benjamin, *Illuminations*, trans. Harry Zohn (New York: Schocken, 1968), p. 262.

5. Ibid.

6. Ibid., p. 263.

7. Ernst Bloch, "On the Present in Literature," in Bloch, *The Utopian Function of Art and Literature*, trans. Jack Zipes and Frank Mecklenburg (Cambridge, Mass.: MIT Press, 1988), p. 218.

8. Friedrich Nietzsche, *The Birth of Tragedy* and *The Case of Wagner*, trans. Walter Kaufmann (New York: Vintage, 1967), p. 36.

9. The references are to Paul Feyerabend, *Against Method: Outline of an Anarchistic Theory of Knowledge* (London: NLB; Atlantic Highlands: Humanities Press, 1975).

10. Ibid., p. 25

11. Ibid., p. 26.

12. Friedrich Schlegel, "Über die Unverständlichkeit," in Ludwig Rohner, ed., *Deutsche Essays: Prosa aus zwei Jahrhunderten*, (Neuwied: Luchterhand, 1968), 2: 12.

13. Heinrich von Kleist, "Über die allmähliche Verfertigung der Gedanken beim Reden," in Rohner, *Deutsche Essays*, 2: 39.

14. Ibid.

15. Feyerabend, *Against Method*, pp. 27–28.

16. Walter Benjamin, "Goethes *Wahlverwandtschaften*," *Neue Deutsche Beiträge* (1924–25).

5 | Don Quixote's Mistake: The Problem of the Aesthetic Boundary

Since the 1920s, the heyday of phenomenological research, there has been little new insight into the nature of art. Instead, there have been variations of aspects that resemble each other. Dissimilarity, that is, theoretical and practical actuality, arises only when the person judging is motivated in a particular historical situation. This dissimilarity, that is, the new experience or theory of art—as we could pointedly put it—is nothing else than motivation appearing suddenly. That is why this motivation is suspected of self-deception. The revolutionary cultural theory of Herbert Marcuse was fifteen years old in 1968. For a long time it seemed to be much like Schiller's aesthetic theory. It became dissimilar to all that had gone before, that is, it became active in the present moment, when the students in their situation wanted it to be. The new reading of Kant's *Critique of Judgment*, which had been presented by Marcuse himself in such a stimulating and original way, was also not taken up again until the mid-1970s and then without any mention of Marcuse. This exegesis of Kant was dissimilar to the preceding one, but only because it was differently motivated. If Marcuse's reading had been included in the newly discovered framework for understanding Kant's doctrine of perception, then the difference between the earlier and the later exegesis would have become marginal. They would have become similar. Only one thing prevented this from happening: the different motivation behind each exegesis.

Are we being cynical about this subjective factor? No. We are merely saying: let us not use philosophy to legitimate the beautiful. Let us especially not look to Hegel's verdicts about the end of art when the conversation turns to higher matters. That is, let us not constantly subordinate art to knowledge about world history or the claim to it nor to the insistence on truth. We will have to part ways with the concept of progression and still not perceive stagnation as endless, changeless repetition. With respect to art, the dissimilar, the always new motivation, can be understood as the *sudden appearance*. This does not define what art is but tells merely how it affects us. We see the character of art as appearance as a function of its boundary, its delimiting role in regard to life and reality. And this without all the intellectual back and forth that wants to reassure itself about the concept but with the clarity that validates Plato's scandalous instinct when he wanted to ban art as mere appearance, while Hegel purported to save art as the "appearance of the Ideal." [1] Plato took art more seriously than Hegel and his current followers. In what follows, we will not discuss the "appearance of the Ideal" but talk of mere appearance itself, for that is the boundary of art.

The tendency to explain the mere appearance of art by means of something external to it is certainly related to the unique and strange ways in which appearance crosses boundaries. The unbounded promise of mere appearance in art is forfeit only when one tries to take it as being actually without limits, as a psychological, sociological, philosophical, or political insight. It is certainly no coincidence that several of the most imaginative Western European works of art were created within narrow limits, in confinement, exile, or prison: Sophocles wrote *Oedipus in Colonos* in Athens when it was under siege, Ovid wrote the *Metamorphoses* when he was exiled on the Black Sea, the Marquis de Sade invented his delusionary sexual system in the Bastille, Cervantes created his mad, wise knight in a Seville dungeon, Hölderlin's late work was written during his confinement in a tower. Where external circumstances are so reduced, fantasy obviously works to keep us alive, removes limitations, and posits mere appearance as reality.

It is precisely this appearance that captivates us in a work of art. It is not, as people repeat as though reciting a catechism, the reality that shines through the work or its ideological formulations that attract us. For what is it that makes *Don Quixote* a Western European literary myth? Cervantes' critique of the novel of romance or chivalry that was so popular in the sixteenth century and its destructive consequences for realistic behavior? The purported self-denunciation of the fantastical? Do we find satisfaction in the ironization of the irrational, so that aesthetic pleasure arises because at the end we witness how the deluded hero finally becomes reasonable and aware of his "false consciousness," to use a contemporary phrase? No—none of the above. I take pleasure in *Don Quixote* not because I recognize Cervantes' intent to unmask the illusions of the Spanish upper class, but because—as we will see in a moment—I gradually come to identify with the fantastic element in the work.

It is certainly possible to criticize Don Quixote as a politically and ideologically negative symbol. Such a criticism would yield some information about the development of the European Enlightenment, but it would tell us nothing about the cause of our aesthetic fascination. When the hero charges windmills, he does so not because he has been driven mad by reading, but because something contrary to reality occurs to him. He acts according to the principle that appearances are not tautological; instead, he posits relationships and meaning. He says to Sancho Panza, the realist: "One cannot see the truth." His order of "knights errant" has the same spiritual referent as Ignatius Loyola's decision to found the Jesuits after he saw visions.

Don Quixote, whom Cervantes, in all seriousness, calls "wise," mistakes fantasy for the world only when he wants to, and when he does, he is absolutely consistent at staying within his system. It is Sancho Panza, the realist, who is deceived against his will. Sancho, the man of no imagination, is not deceived about invisible things, but he sometimes fails to grasp what is visible. Don Quixote, on the other hand, is not deceived; he deceives himself. No one forces him; he forces the rules of his illusory appearance on others. And why do we follow him so long on his quests without tiring of them? Because it is not mere appearance that blinds him. The reality Cervantes describes is not, to all appearance, something different that could explain Don Quixote's error. The windmills are quite obviously windmills, and no trick of the light makes them look like something else. The appearance is the windmill, and it is Sancho Panza who completely accepts this appearance. This appearance is not deceptive, and Don Quixote does not fall victim to a false appearance. He sees, always and intentionally, something other than what is visible. Sancho Panza, on the other hand, takes the illusory island that he is supposed to govern as reality. He confuses, Don Quixote posits.

Let us assume that the narrator had not allowed us to witness the grotesque duel with the windmill and that we had to rely completely on the reports of either Don Quixote or Sancho Panza. We would take the report of the appearance and of the reality as two contradictory narratives; the windmills would be windmills, and the giants would be giants, and we would also have the assurance of each narrator that the other was mistaken. Our pleasure would lie in the comic sensation of the grotesque error. But our pleasure is in fact of another kind altogether: as the narrative progresses, we begin to suspect that the Knight of the Mournful Countenance has deeper reasons for exchanging visible reality for his fantasy. Thomas Mann commented instructively on the "fantastical wit" that Friedrich Schlegel saw at work in *Don Quixote*: "To have fantasy does not mean to think up something, it means to make something of the things around us." We follow this game of exchange between appearance and reality with great interest and are fascinated to see how different Don Quixote's ideas are from the real things.

Michel Foucault saw in this dissimilarity the boundary between Cervantes' time and the earlier era of certainty and correspondences.[2] We should add: the dissimilarity is the sign of the boundary phenomenon, that is, of art itself, a sign that unfolds in the paradoxical territory between appearance and truth, subjectivity and reality. To be sure, we discover this state of affairs as modern readers of an old story. The hero, Don Quixote, does not merely amuse himself with this appearance. Instead, in his characteristic, deadly serious way, he is in search of truth. He is so serious about this quest that he takes the figures of his own reading (which consisted—like Loyola's—of all the romances of chivalry that he could find) for real and becomes unable to distinguish between them and his own modest existence in La Mancha.

And he does one more thing: he wants to repeat the experienced appearance, the adventures of Arthurian and Spanish knighthood, in his own person. No, not repeat: he wants to extend his fantasy into his life. Don Quixote is thus the first member of the avant-garde; his behavior is a key event of the history of our conscious-ness. For this reason the spiritual anarchy of the nineteenth cen-tury declared Don Quixote to be its patron saint, and the French surrealists also honored him as their spiritual brother: he attempted the "impossible," as he himself says, the dissolution of the bound-ary between fantasy and reality, between the appearance of art and the truth of the promises it contains. Cervantes was a great writer because he ironically elevated this violation of boundaries to a theme and executed it with pathos. The surrealists, and the avant-garde in general, however, succumbed to a sentimental weakness when they crossed the boundaries and forced art out into the realm of life, declaring life to be art. They surrendered their best weapon at the moment when they could no longer bear the appearance of creating. This was repeated as a beautiful illusion in 1968, when people chanted, "Up with fantasy." This illusion is inherent in all theoretical attempts to determine the factor of subjectivity from beyond its own phenomenologically given boundaries, regardless of any concessions to immanence.

I did not discuss the case of Don Quixote in order to recall a touching story from our heroic cultural tradition but in order to expand the perspective I established at the outset. We must pay more attention to the boundary between art and reality than to the fall of boundaries, look more for art's appearance than for its truth. Otherwise, theoretical and creative work will become lost in the illusionary and vague, as it presently threatens to do. The danger is that we will either place the phenomenon of aesthetic appear-ance in the pure transcendence of utopian fantasy or reduce it to an alienated consciousness through an ideological critique—that is, subordinate it to the determinants of social, economic, or psychoanalytical, reception-oriented concepts and causality. We are dealing here with an objective, materialist form as well as with a subjective, idealistic one of removing boundaries. The concept of appearance is heuristically emphasized here not in Bloch's sense, according to which the mere appearance of the still unrealized is redeemed as the "reflection of what could be," that is, in view of a utopian horizon. That would result in one of those strategies for removing boundaries and would amount to incurring theoretical debts that we probably cannot repay, as all the emphatic utopian attempts of the last few years have demonstrated. Instead, we take appearance here to mean expressly what is unique to the aesthetic construct and legitimized by no logos and no social reference—the quality Friedrich Nietzsche discovered.

The subjective removal of the boundaries between the concept of art and life has taken place on three levels: in the dissolution of the concept of art or work, in the dissolution of the genres for the purpose of establishing a new *Gesamtkunstwerk* or total work of art, and finally in the relativization of the positivist, objective concept of science. These three different operations, which obscure the nature of art as a phenomenon, do not represent a mistake that could now be discovered and undone or at least be avoided in the future so that we can come to a better understanding of what art is. On the contrary: some operations cannot be undone but belong to our historical inventory. Part of this inventory is dropping the idea of a representational work, which we have inherited from the classical avant-garde. Another is the mix of art forms, to the point that we have an aesthetic definition of the trivial. In the realm of theory, this includes the current "logic of research," which does not separate subject and object but takes as its point of departure the effect of each on the other and the resultant blurring of ideas. The role of hermeneutics in the cultural disciplines is representative in this regard. Yet another operation that cannot be undone is the replacement of the concept of causality by that of probability.

On the other hand, we should condemn any purely subjective move to declare the world a narcissistic fantasy, to give up Cervantes' ambivalence and commit the error of his hero Don Quixote to extend art into life. Let us paint the following frivolous image: as long as we do not attack the windmills, they may remain giants. The character of art as appearance is also suppressed in the objective attempts to remove the boundaries between art and life; for example, when a work of art is censured or legitimated on account of the social world or causal relationships it reflects. The obstacles

to asserting the mere appearance of art, that is, its pure immanence, are historical and systematic; they are indeed considerable
obstacles, despite or because of Nietzsche and the English aesthetes.

These obstacles are weakest where they run along political-
moral or sentimental-utopian lines, and they are as old as the
modern concept of art itself. Following Kant, Schiller and the
romantics, especially Novalis, reflected emphatically on the relationship between morality and art and reached various conclusions
because of the difficulty of the problem. Schiller formulated the
boundary problem itself very clearly in his essay "Über den Grund
des Vergnügens an tragischen Gegenständen":

> The well-meant intention to pursue the moral good everywhere as
> the highest goal, which has produced and protected so much that is
> mediocre in art, has also done similar damage in the theory of art.
> In order to give artists a high rank, to win for them the favor of the
> State, the respect of all people, one drives them out of their own
> territory and forces on them a profession that is foreign and unnatu-
> ral to them. One imagines one is doing them a great service by
> imputing to them, instead of the frivolous goal of merely entertain-
> ing, a moral goal.[3]

In the aesthetic debate of his time, Schiller is speaking here half
to himself and half to theorists like Diderot. But has the dilemma
of that period actually changed much since then, considering that
Schiller himself coupled his idea of aesthetic education with a
political goal in his *Letters On the Aesthetic Education of Man?* At
this point, we must note that the period of late romantic aestheticism, after classicism and its tension between ethics and aesthetics,
failed to provide a satisfactory answer to the problem of the aesthetic boundary. Aestheticism failed despite its culmination in
Nietzsche's proclamation that the existence of the world could be
justified only as an aesthetic phenomenon—and despite the fact
that Nietzsche, along with the English aesthetes Walter Pater and
Oscar Wilde, was among the first to grasp and formulate the nature
of art as appearance in the sense we have in mind. As a result
of the past and present German flight into the reactionary and
apolitical—a preeminent part of that flight is the reverential or
academic reception of late romantic aestheticism—the French debate about engaged art was taken up quite late in Germany and
was sentimentalized. Our bad conscience made it impossible for

the German intelligentsia after World War II to demonstrate the same clarity with respect to the aesthetic boundary that was apparent in the representative confrontation between Sartre and Camus and also later in the *nouveau roman.* Nevertheless, its first lesson could have been learned then. Despite Camus' naive stoicism—with Sartre, we can call it a rejection of dialectic—Camus correctly identified the Achilles' heel of Sartre's position and that of his German epigones: their sentimentality, their failure to live with contradictions in theory or to attack them in practice, their attempt instead to overcome them through art. Camus reduced Sartre's position to a phrase: "Sartre or nostalgia for the universal idyll."[4] The phrase may not fit Sartre perfectly, but it fits our contemporary West German literature of bliss or shabbiness. In that debate, Camus repeated in different words what Schiller had already stated: "I prefer committed men to literature of commitment. Courage in one's life and talent in one's works—this is not so bad. And moreover, the writer is committed when he wishes to be. His merit lies in his impulse. But if this is to become a law, a function, or a terror, just where is the merit?"[5]

We cannot deny that the refusal of Camus, the former resistance fighter, to practice engaged art has a metaphysical foundation that we cannot, or can no longer, share: his heroic nihilism, his pathos of the absurd. In the best Sorelian manner, he called revolution "great thought."[6] But a proposition and a thesis does not become true or false because of what motivates it. The truth of a proposition is like the evidence of a phenomenon: to be tested in and of itself. And it turns out that Camus' attack on Sartre, on the German Hegelians, and on engaged art is a rejection of history and a reestablishment of nature and the beauty of nature.

This idea is so fruitful for our inquiry into the appearance of art and the boundary of art that we must discuss more extensively the concept of nature as opposed to history. From the beginning engaged art has guarded itself against irony by claiming to be the only kind of art. One no longer said: I want to reach this political goal or that moral goal with art. One simply said: art *is* the political, is life itself. The radical shift of early surrealism and Dada had displaced the boundary between art and nonart for the first time, with extreme consequences. Suddenly everyday experience itself appeared fantastic; the *objet trouvé* and montage destroyed the old concept of a work of art. And what happened in the 1960s in terms of ritual and kinetic art, in neosurreal wit, was a definite crossing of the boundary between art and life: suicide staged as a happening and a revolution presented as beauty, propelled the attempt to test the appearance of art for its existential truth and social effects. The aspect of this attempt that heightened and differentiated the intensified perception of social processes cannot be left out of any future concept of art. However, we should revise what resulted in a false understanding of utopia and makes the West German intellectual scene so dull today. What do the false utopians and chiliasts mean by utopia? They jump to the wrong conclusions by taking the promises immanent to art, the anticipation of the future that is peculiar to art, too literally and by insisting stubbornly that either the world must change here and now to fulfill these promises, or else all of art is worthless. They do not realize that the madness of a Rimbaud or an Artaud or a Nietzsche are to be taken seriously only as a style, as an ecstasy, as a semantic or theatrical event, or not at all. Instead, the false utopians understood the utopian concept and all its representative elaborations merely in their content, alternating between a vague claim to private happiness and claims of social perfectibility.[7] A cool examination at truly significant literary examples of utopian thought, such as *Robinson Crusoe,* would have showed that the aesthetic utopia—if the word is to have any meaning at all—does not consist in the sentimental feeling of happiness of the recipient nor in the promises of the work's contents, but solely in the formal arrangement of the aesthetic material. In the case of *Robinson Crusoe,* the formal arrangement is the narrative style of second-by-second relation of life-saving, alert perception, against all anticipation.[8]

It would also be false tact to ignore the fact that Bloch's metaphor of the "principle of hope" has much to do with that cheap, sentimental version of utopia that is now spreading like a weed. The reverse side of this cheap utopia is the outrage that responds to any doubts about a future of reason with moral and intellectual censure as well as the autobiographical reports of misery that are gaining respect under the cloak of the "authentic." Instead of the vague talk of utopia, which is the most current example of the fall of the boundary between art and life, we should hypothetically emphasize the opposition between art and utopia. Art has always been able, at the right moment, to prevent contradictions from being reconciled in a utopia and to keep a monolithic claim to truth, which turns utopia into an ideology, from replacing the error that is interwoven with time.[9]

Of course, the crossing of boundaries, be it political-moral, surrealistic-destructive, or utopian-sentimental, can always be understood and accepted under the affirmative general label of the "no longer beautiful arts."[10] The theoretical debate on this subject has yielded a valuable result for our decision about boundaries. Those who are ready to accept such a crossing of boundaries as a fact of the modern development of art do so only after they guard their position on the level of the history of style and philosophy by claiming that the anti-aesthetic position is anticipated in romantic art and in Hegel's philosophy, whether as the art of the ugly or as an intellectualization of image and word. Comforted by intellectual history, nothing about the "no longer beautiful arts" can disturb such people. Those who problematize a crossing of boundaries, on the other hand, do so by taking it not as something that has developed gradually but as something qualitatively new. And they are right. In fact, all the learned references to an aesthetics of the ugly, the obscene, and the terrifying—an aesthetics that began to develop as early as the eighteenth century—cannot undermine the argument that these theories never applied to extra-aesthetic phenomena. Rather, these theories only modified the traditional concept of beauty, intensified it, and made it more fundamental, as looking at the discovery of the sublime, ugly, and picturesque in Burke, Lessing, and Diderot would show us. And even if it suddenly becomes permissible in the nineteenth century to represent evil artistically, this is not a "boundary phenomenon" in our sense. Rather, in the figure of Satan the beautiful becomes the sublime. Kierkegaard calls the appearing devil the "sudden" and thus categorically anticipates the structure of modern artistic phenomena. Even where the ridiculous shows itself in the hideous, as in Goya's war paintings, no crossing of boundaries is involved but rather a mixture of once strictly separated genres, tragedy and comedy, a mixture for which the Spanish and the English artistic traditions have very early examples.

Odo Marquardt has attempted to legitimate the existence of the "no longer beautiful arts" by reference to a dictum of Hegel's.[11] According to Hegel, art loses its absolute position but at the same time gains unlimited liberties. Art's freedom to choose its material and themes goes hand in hand with its diminished importance. Marquardt sees modern art as the fulfillment of Hegel's prophecy. However, this highly authorized theory of the fall of boundaries implies that art is harmless, an implication we need not accept if we insist on the aesthetic boundary. This thesis, which is so popular in philosophical, particularly Hegelian, circles, completely overlooks two things: (1) The self-understanding of art was never more emphatic or fundamental than in the century following Hegel, and (2) art has never so attacked and damaged philosophy as a mediator of meaning and symbols as in the avant-garde.

The diminished relevance of art Marquardt asserts is actually just the opposite of what he thinks it is. Philosophy lost relevance while art gained significance. For that reason it is misleading to assume that crossing the aesthetic boundary requires a philosophical or historical legitimation. If the boundaries have fallen, then that fact itself is necessarily outside any normative certainty. Any legitimation basically follows the method of the false removal of boundaries and does not even really perceive what actually appears in art but derives it from something else or refers it to something else.

And the Hegel-inspired conclusion that there is no longer any difference between art and nonart is also incorrect. When proponents of the classical avant-garde made that claim, it was one of their epistemological jokes and maneuvers, which lose almost all of their aesthetic content when taken as dead serious or as serious in the philosophical or moral sense. Taken seriously in a Hegelian sense, the statement about the disappearance of the difference between art and nonart amounts, of course, to a denunciation of art as something subordinate. Emphasizing the boundary then means the very opposite of the philosophical understanding we have noted. It is only through closing the boundary between art and reality that the aesthetic appearance becomes visible; this appearance is the scandal of the beautiful. We can explain this with a sentence from Hegel's antipode in aesthetics, Nietzsche. With a bow to Schopenhauer, Nietzsche sees in the aesthetic appearance the "tremendous *terror* which seizes man when he is

suddenly dumbfounded by the cognitive form of phenomena because the principle of sufficient reason, in some one of its manifestations, seems to suffer an exception."[12] Nietzsche later modified
this purely phenomenological beginning under "the hammerblow
of historical knowledge."[13] In *Human, All Too Human,* the "book
for free spirits" that initiated his break with Richard Wagner—to
whom he had inwardly dedicated the *Birth of Tragedy*—he even
speaks of the arts aging and becoming intellectualized. Nietzsche
here uses an argument that touches directly on Hegel's aesthetics.

> Previously, the mind was not obliged to think rigorously; its impor-
> tance lay in spinning out symbols and forms. That has changed;
> that importance of symbols has become the sign of lower culture.
> Just as our very arts are becoming ever more intellectual and our
> senses more spiritual, and as, for example, that which is sensually
> pleasant to the ear is judged quite differently now than a hundred
> years ago, so the forms of our life have become ever more *spiritual*—
> to the eye of older times *uglier,* perhaps, but only because it is
> unable to see how the realm of internal, spiritual beauty is continu-
> ally deepening and expanding, and to what extent a glance full of
> intelligence can mean more to all of us now than the most beautiful
> human body and the most sublime edifice.[14]

In contrast to Hegel's conclusion, Nietzsche sees the ugliness of
the modern period as its legitimate expression, which does not
diminish its aesthetic rank or its intellectual importance. In juxta-
posing the "glance full of intelligence" with the "most beautiful
human body" and thus taking Schiller's concepts of the sentimental and the naive a step further, Nietzsche already indicated the
unique spiritualization of a future art and, indeed, the very criteria
of the aesthetic avant-garde. To be sure, as in Hegel, "thought"
has overtaken "symbols and forms," but these are no longer identical with art in general, as they were for Hegel. Instead, for
Nietzsche they characterize a "lower culture." As a result, the
historical aging of the arts does not entail a diminished importance
of the aesthetic. On the contrary, the aesthetic, becoming broader
and deeper, has taken on entirely new forms. The principle of the
exception is thus still valid.

Let us therefore not start with imported ideas but with our
phenomenological experience when confronted with artistic pro-

duction. That experience tells us: aesthetic perception takes effect
as joy, not as a recognition of value. The concepts effect, perception, and joy do not indicate a purely intuitive model of explanation, however. It was, after all, Kant who gave us explicit instructions to focus exclusively on the effect of the aesthetic phenomenon because there could be no constitutive concept of the beautiful
itself. We owe Rüdiger Bubner the helpful idea that Kant's concept
of the reflective power of judgment (as opposed to the determinative power of judgment) is closely related to a theory of natural
beauty to which the beauty of art is subordinated.[15] According to
Bubner, Kant saw the function of the reflective power of judgment
in the fact that it first merely became aware of something, of a
particular thing that could not be subsumed under a general category. The aesthetic experience does not become identified with a
concept of the understanding; it is not possible to grasp the thing
given intellectually.

This interpretation of Kant is easily verified when we consider
that aesthetic value judgments come about through anticipation
and not through an analytic process.[16] That is the reverse of
Hegel's position, and we now see why Hegel's solution had to fail
when confronted with the paradoxical character of art as mere
appearance. The deeper reason for Hegel's failure lies in his teleological understanding of history, which not only declared the experience of art as something secondary in the progress of the spirit to
itself but also entirely excluded the beauty of nature from aesthetics. For the aesthetic illusion we are talking about here has something to do with that elemental phenomenon we call the beauty of
nature; we already came across this in our discussion of Camus'
attacks on engaged art and the dialectical understanding of history.
To put it briefly, since Hegel's condemnation, Nietzsche's reverence, and, finally, Adorno's ambivalence toward natural beauty,
any renewed approach to the beauty of nature has been suspect as
rank ideology.[17]

Not every "authentic" understanding of modernism necessarily
results in a ban on the beauty of nature. Adorno's statement that
poems were impossible after Auschwitz and Brecht's thoughts on a
poem about trees in this historical era both reveal the unique
situation of German aesthetics in view of the terror of National

Socialism. This unique situation, however, cannot be generalized or dogmatized. In his attack on Sartre, Camus also had his eye on the dogmatic ban on the concept of nature:

> The whole effort of German thought has been to substitute for the notion of human nature that of the human situation and hence to substitute history for God and modern tragedy for ancient equilibrium. Modern existentialism carries that effort even further and introduces into the idea of situation the same uncertainty as in the idea of nature. But like the Greeks I believe in nature.[18]

Even in this polemic, Sartre took Camus' concept of nature seriously, in part because he recognized that Camus was continuing the great French tradition that had been hostile to history since Descartes. But Sartre also secretly admired Camus' adoption of "indifferent, empty nature" in Nietzsche's sense and his rejection of, as Sartre put it, the "dizziness of the soul and the idea."[19] This "dizziness of the soul," this sublime kitsch of ideas, threatens whenever politically justified skepticism regarding the beauty of nature deteriorates into a seminarian's hysteria. People then are reluctant to confront nature itself, whether it is beautiful or ugly. They fail to realize that the aesthetic boundary has something to do with this nature—for example, with the silence in Albers' pictures, with this being looked at by the natural world that both attracts us aesthetically and terrifies us.[20]

Now a way out has been found, a way to deal with the vexing concept of the beauty of nature and with nature itself without shirking one's duty of rationality: we can have recourse to Freud's theory of creative writing as pleasure. But this theory is only helpful if it does not lead us to fall victim to yet another strategy of removing boundaries—the newest one yet—and to assert that neurotic and poetic fantasy are the same or at least analogous. Freud never equated the two. On the contrary, he distinguished strictly between creative and regressive fantasy formations and stressed repeatedly that the psychoanalytical relationship between the daydream of a patient and the fantasy of an artistic image cannot explain the aesthetic phenomenon. Equating of the two kinds of fantasy is one of those current methods of obliterating the boundary between art and nonart, the boundary on whose existence we insist.

One cannot help but suspect that the sudden boom in research on creativity has a subterranean connection with the tendency to shy away from formal aesthetic criteria and to escape into the "authenticity" of autobiographical material. Only when this resistance against the softening of the boundary is clear can we use Freud's analysis of art, precisely because it simply spotlights the problem of the aesthetic boundary without tricks or lures and thus aids our interest in a natural substantiation for aesthetic fascination. First of all, Freud sees a relationship between art and neurosis because both are so-called redirection activities. Both the artist and the neurotic fantasize because they are dissatisfied and must process formerly repressed libidinal impulses. The fantasy of creative writing and of a neurotic's daydream are continuations, that is, redirections, of childhood play: "A strong experience of the present awakens in the creative writer a memory of an earlier experience (usually belonging to his childhood) from which there now proceeds a wish which finds its fulfillment in the creative work."[21]

One prominent contemporary misunderstanding of this sentence is the belief that we have gained something in a literary sense if we retell our own childhood. In contrast to such officious, sentimental, or engaged attempts, which have grown into a new genre in West Germany, Freud emphasized the indifference of the artist, for instance, Leonardo da Vinci's lack of sympathy in his observation of terrified candidates for execution.[22] This indifference is reminiscent of the aesthetic principles of the English theorist Ruskin, who was an inspiration to Proust and who instructed us not to let the sight of a dying man distract us from what was artistically relevant. Freud explains this cruelty of the aesthetic gaze with a reference to depth psychology that should preclude any misunderstanding of the problem of the aesthetic boundary. In order to clarify the difference between neurotic redirection activity and creative sublimation, Freud distinguishes various stages of repression. The repression that explains Leonardo's cruel indifference takes place in such a way that the repressed libido sublimates itself from the very beginning into "curiosity."[23] The sublimation thus does not result in the unresolved "compulsive brooding" that meanders off with no limits, as in the case of an intellectually competent but not creatively gifted daydreamer;[24] that is, the character of neurosis is missing. Instead, the drive can validate itself freely in the service of the intellectual interest.[25]

Freud here gives us an exact justification for our actions on both sides of the aesthetic boundary, and the present attempts to solve the aesthetic problem with a kind of psychoanalytical materialism have no reason to base themselves on Freud. Given the loquacity of recent West German prose texts, we can add that the neurotic "compulsive brooding," which Freud calls the unsuccessful stage of repression, leads to infantile confessions about one's life in which—to use Freud's words—"this brooding never ends" and in which "the intellectual feeling, so much desired, of having found a solution recedes more and more into the distance."[26]

If Freud seldom confused the psychic motivation for creative action with the creative act itself, that is certainly because of his profound respect for genius, which tradition instilled in him. He shared this respect with Marx, whose aesthetic ideas always retained the stamp of German classicism. When Freud tried to account for the aesthetics of an individual work with psychoanalytical methods, he failed miserably. This was the case, for instance, when he attributed the uncanny effect of E. T. A. Hoffmann's story "The Sandman" to the secret male fear of castration.[27] He also tried to analyze *Hamlet*, a drama, according to Freud, that viewers could enjoy only if they understood it as neurotics, that is, if they recognized in Hamlet the impulse they themselves also had repressed, so that it would cause them pleasure instead of dislike.[28] Despite these occasional analytical false interpretations of aesthetic causation, Freud still realized with phenomenological acuity that aesthetic pleasure ultimately lies in the nature of art as appearance. As Freud says in "Creative Writers and Day-Dreaming," our pleasure in poetry is related to our narcissistic interest in the hero. We enjoy the hero's invulnerability in the face of manifold dangers. This is also true of the invulnerability of his majesty the ego in a daydream. By contrast with a daydream, however, the poet softens the character of "egoistic daydreams" by altering and disguising it; he bribes us with the "purely formal—that is, aesthetic—yield of pleasure."[29] Freud calls the aesthetic yield of pleasure an "incentive bonus or fore-pleasure."[30] But when the artist softens his characters to the point of bribing our narcissistic need in an aesthetically permissible way, then he or she "lies," in a manner of speaking, that is, he or she creates that appearance that fulfills expectations while avoiding feelings of anxiety. Once again it seems—only with respect to this strand of the argument—that for Freud, art and nonart are not interchangeable. He does not address the actual "ars poetica."[31] His concept of "play" shows that Schiller's insights influenced him. He does not force art into a shabby role,[32] because he respects the aesthetic boundary.

We can certainly derive from Freud's theory the concept of literary redirection activity as a wish fulfillment, as American New Criticism[33] and Habermas' concept of the strategy of discharge did. But it is not permissible to make Freud a champion of the removal of the aesthetic boundary itself. The opposite is closer to the truth: to the extent that psychoanalytic interpretation plays itself out on the level of symbolic representation, as Serge Leclaire has convincingly shown, its structure gains the dignity of literary feeling. And in the rare cases when the structure of neurotic fantasy itself is actually poetic, as Leclaire demonstrated with the example of his "unicorn" dream,[34] then we can discern the poetry of the series of symbolic images only if we do *not* decode its psychoanalytic meaning, that is, only if we leave untouched the insights that the theory of the unconscious gives us and replace them with symbolic correspondences of greater ambiguity.[35] This ambiguity cannot be grasped with psychoanalytical methods; it requires the methods of the American neo-Aristotelian school, which has fallen into undeserved obscurity in Germany.

The ambiguity of a phenomenon corresponds on the subjective side to the concept of perception. If we once, long ago, ingenuously proposed this word as the final means of rescuing the aesthetic boundary, we propose it today with mixed feelings. After all, this word, too, has been pressed into the service of the strategists of removing the aesthetic boundary, who inflate it until it bursts, like their fetish, utopia. The stylish, "colloquial" recourse to "perception" instead of to "social relevance," as was common a just short time ago, is only one of the current uncertainties ignoring the historical conditions of the new joy in perception. How then can we free this word, *perception*, of its meaningless, inflationary, fattened fullness of meaning? How to trim it back to its operative functional value? Of course, we would have to insist on a strict phenomenological valence, regardless of which theory of "seeing" we have in mind. It is not a question of reestablishing the arguments that were formulated in the debates between Wölfflin and Panofsky or between Hofmannsthal, Mach, and Husserl. At most, it is a question of why that very first phenomenological discovery of the sensory object, even after many different attempts at demontage, can still be the systematic location where we can precisely determine the boundary between art and nonart.

In this undertaking we can do without a theory of "pure seeing" to the extent that this implies not just seeing but also a flight to the new trendy theories, the very thing it pretends to avoid. The sheer idealism of the old phenomenological starting point must be replaced with reflection on the present without damaging the strict phenomenological essence of our approach, as Sartre demonstrated in his early essay on imagination and as Foucault showed again with his phenomenology of the modern period. In any event, we should realize that everything the New Sensuality of the 1960s wished to accomplish was aimed at coupling dialectic reflection with phenomenological elementarism, whether we are talking about Andy Warhol, Arnheim, Umberto Eco, Laing, or the visitor's school of Bazon Brock, which, after all, was not merely a school of social perception. However, we cannot alleviate the aestheticist danger of that concept of perception by simply declaring it an organ of any random object. We are therefore right to be suspicious when perception is elevated to a utopia that is hailed as expanding our consciousness and sensitizing us with respect to appearances but that all too soon turns out to be merely a method for legitimizing what is insignificant and unarticulated.

The most convincing proposal comes, not coincidentally, from the psychoanalytical tradition. The psychoanalytical reaction model: "Say everything that occurs to you; absorb everything you hear" has been put forth as the model for a "utopia of perception."[36] Leclaire emphasized Freud's instructions regarding a particular technique of listening in psychoanalytic treatment.[37] The significance of Freud's technique of a freely hovering attention for such a "utopia of perception" is obvious. In both cases, the unregulated absorption of various word impressions helps prevent preconceived ideas from entering and censoring; as result, unconscious or unknown matters can be recorded. We can also recognize in this actualized terminology the well-known procedure of surrealistic technique of forming sentences in free association. (Freud himself never understood his surrealist students, and only at an advanced age, when he encountered the style of the young Salvador Dali, did he relinquish his aversion to surrealism.)

The difference between the surrealist and the neoutopian effect also reveals the disadvantage of the utopian crossing of the boundary between art and life: if surrealistic free association still conceals artistic pathos—if not of the work, then of its "making"—the "utopia of perception" amounts to the opposite: it cancels out the formal aesthetic conditions. Even if we use Rimbaud's style and his renunciation of ego control for comparison, we still find as a distinguishing criterion of his work a poetic field of meanings or of negated meanings. The prose of the new perception, however, runs the risk of literally becoming meaningless because it does not respect the aesthetic boundary. However seductive it may be to follow the "alienated gaze" of the author who perceives everything,[38] the accompanying secret interest in saving souls and the tendency to view literary practice from the standpoint of its function of spiritual liberation remain suspect. Freud's reference to a neurotic "compulsion to brood," a term that decodes in one fell swoop the wave of aesthetically unbounded writing in West Germany, shows us how easily sentimental misunderstanding can occur in this area. The metaphor of seeing, somewhat belatedly circulated, lacks substance to the extent that the ideological-critical attack on the concept of perception remains aesthetically numb.

Aesthetic perception is the equivocal form of apperception pure and simple. If its problem were only the veiling and unveiling of social conditions, for example, in the consciousness of the hero, then literary representation would be nothing more than the explication of already given political theories; it would degenerate into a mere façade, a Hegelian "appearing of the Idea." But the truth of fantasy is not simply a precursor of analytical truth, or, to put it more concisely, "Literary pleasure, on the other hand, derives from a misapprehension of its own source."[39] If ambiguous perception is the late bourgeois hero's form of reflection, then the perspective of the author often begins to coincide with that of his or her fiction.[40] Only for that reason is there any doubt about whether our aesthetic interest derives legitimately from an identification with this form of perception—that is, from being an accomplice of an obviously false consciousness—or from the discovery of the social causes.

To reach a decision here, we do not need to resort to modern examples of alienated perception. We can simply return to the example of false perception we discussed initially, namely, *Don Quixote*. If we were still reading this novel as it was undoubtedly read when it first appeared, namely, as a mere satire on the illusionary consciousness of the old Spanish nobility and on an unrealistic conception of fiction itself, then its effect would long since have dissipated. Moreover, it is doubtful whether this effect hinges primarily on the social-critical humor of the figure of Sancho Panza, as a sort of vehicle for rebellion against authority, in the joke as a social process. The more we distance ourselves from that sort of information imparted by the work, the more certain we can be that we are within the aesthetic boundary.

Flaubert was contemptuous of the leading scientific theories of the nineteenth century, heredity and environment. Fortunately for us, for that led him to perceive only "things," as he said. Applied to the problem of perception in *Don Quixote*, that means that as the novel's plot progresses, the author's sympathetic bond with his character grows stronger. Nevertheless, the author does not fall victim to the same deception of the senses; he does not charge windmills. Like Sancho Panza, he keeps his distance from them. But he is not Sancho Panza;, he is much closer to being Don Quixote. That is because something keeps him from being a complete partisan of critical humor. It is as though the reflective form of confused perception undermines the critical consciousness of the social contents. The absurd behavior of Don Quixote can no more be explained by means of our knowledge of social history than cultural anthropology or psychoanalytic reconstruction can explain the so-called enigma in the smile of Leonardo's figures. In the novel, Don Quixote's grotesque deception of the senses—which on a social and psychological level is certainly a metaphor for false consciousness—suddenly becomes an act of aesthetic perception. While this is not a perception of the appearance, it is nevertheless deceptive, as we saw at the beginning. In any case, it is this perception that keeps Don Quixote alive. For that reason—without phraseology this time—we can call that perception utopian. J. B. Pontalis quotes a sentence of Flaubert's, the author of another figure who confused reading and life: "Life is bearable only with a caprice, a whim. As soon as you give up your dreams, you die of sadness. You have to get a stranglehold on them and hope that they pull you along."[41]

Don Quixote, as the author explicitly tells us, dies of sadness. The fact that Don Quixote becomes sad at the moment when he understands his delusion and gives up his dreams, when he can no longer hold on to them so that they can pull him along, this gives this novel the aesthetic depth of an awareness of the aesthetic boundary. The death of Don Quixote is also the death of aesthetic perception, the beginning of the fall of the boundary. In view of this figure and what it secretly means for the ascending modern age, we recognize the aesthetic appearance as the aporia that is still unresolved. This figure makes Nietzsche's "appearance of the appearance" and our "originary desire" for it more comprehensible. To guard this mysterious boundary of perception means that we must perhaps charge the windmills, not only with Sancho Panza's comfortable smile at our backs but also with Socratic irony and, most terrifyingly, Hegelian knowledge.

Nietzsche called Socrates and Hegel the two great antipodes of aesthetic perception. Nietzsche, who discovered the new kind of "seeing," was the first aesthetician to understand and formulate the problem of appearance in modern art in contradiction to their systems:

> And as for our future, one will hardly find us again on the paths of those Egyptian youths who endanger temples by night, embrace statues, and want by all means to unveil, uncover, and put into a bright light whatever is kept concealed for good reasons. No, this bad taste, this will to truth, to "truth at any price," this youthful madness in the love of truth have lost their charm for us: for that we are too experienced, too serious, too merry, too burned, too *profound*. We no longer believe that truth remains truth when the veils are withdrawn.[42]

Any counterproposal for the ideological-critical reduction of the aesthetic can begin with these sentences.[43]

NOTES

1. On the following, see Rüdiger Bubner, "Über einige Bedingungen gegenwärtiger Ästhetik," Neue Hefte für Philosophie 5 (1973): 68.

2. Michel Foucault, The Order of Things: An Archaeology of the Human Sciences (New York: Pantheon Books, 1970), pp. 46ff.

3. Friedrich Schiller, Sämtliche Werke, ed. Gerhard Fricke and Herbert Göpfert (München: Hanser, 1975), 5: 359.

4. Albert Camus, Notebooks, 1942–51, trans. Justin O'Brien (New York: Knopf, 1965), p. 171.

5. Ibid., pp. 140–41.

6. Ibid., p. 5 note 3.

7. See the volume Die Phantasie an die Macht: Literatur als Utopie. Literaturmagazin 3, ed. Nicolas Born (Reinbek: Rowohlt, 1975). See also Gert Ueding, ed., Literatur ist Utopie (Frankfurt/Main: Suhrkamp, 1978).

8. Karl Heinz Bohrer, Der Lauf des Freitag: Die lädierte Utopie und die Dichter (München: Hanser, 1973), pp. 87ff.

9. See Karl Hielscher, "Über den Gegensatz von Kunst und Utopie," in W. Martin Lüdke, ed., Nach dem Protest: Literatur im Umbruch (Frankfurt/Main: Suhrkamp, 1979), pp. 222–40.

10. That was the theme of the work group "Poetics and Hermeneutics" in 1968. Published under the same title in the third volume of the series Poetik und Hermeneutik, ed. Hans Robert Jauß (München: Fink, 1968).

11. Odo Marquardt, "Zur Bedeutung der Theorie des Unbewußten für eine Theorie der nicht mehr schönen Künste," Poetik und Hermeneutik (München: Fink, 1968), pp. 380ff.

12. Friedrich Nietzsche, The Birth of Tragedy Out of the Spirit of Music, trans. Walter Kaufmann (New York: Vintage Books, 1967), p. 36.

13. Friedrich Nietzsche, Human, All Too Human, trans. Marion Faber with Stephen Lehmann (Lincoln: University of Nebraska Press, 1984), p. 42.

14. Ibid., pp. 15–16.

15. Bubner, "Über einige Bedingungen gegenwärtiger Ästhetik," p. 64.

16. See chapter 2.

17. See Peter Gorsen, Das Bild Pygmalions: Kunstsoziologische Essays (Reinbek: Rowohlt, 1969), p. 41.

18. Camus, Notebooks, p. 136.

19. Jean-Paul Sartre, "Antwort an Albert Camus," in Sartre, Porträts und Perspektiven (Reinbek: Rowohlt, 1968), p. 91.

20. See Gottfried Boehn, "Die Dialektik der ästhetischen Grenze:

Überlegungen zur gegenwärtigen Ästhetik im Anschluß an Josef Alber,"
Neue Hefte für Philosophie 5 (1973): 68.

21. Sigmund Freud, "Creative Writers and Day-Dreaming," trans.
James Strachey, in Freud, *The Complete Psychological Works* (London:
Hogarth Press, 1953), 9: 151.

22. Freud, "Leonardo da Vinci and a Memory of His Childhood,"
trans. Alan Tyson, in Freud, *The Complete Psychological Works* (London:
Hogarth Press, 1957), 11: 69.

23. Ibid., p. 80.

24. Ibid.

25. Ibid.

26. Ibid.

27. Freud, "The Uncanny," trans. James Strachey, in Freud, *The
Complete Psychological Works* (London: Hogarth Press, 1955) 17: 227–33.

28. Freud, "Psychopathic Characters on the Stage," trans. James Strachey, in Freud, *The Complete Psychological Works* (London: Hogarth Press,
1953) 7: 309–10.

29. Freud, "Creative Writers and Day-Dreaming," p. 153.

30. Ibid.

31. Ibid.

32. This is Odo Marquardt's thesis in his discussion in "Zur Bedeutung
der Theorie des Unbewußten für eine Theorie der nicht mehr schönen
Künste," in *Poetik und Hermeneutik* 3, p. 391.

33. Simon O. Lesser, "Die Funktionen der Form," in Joseph Strelka
and Walter Hinderer, eds., *Moderne amerikanische Literaturtheorien*
(Frankfurt/Main: Suhrkamp, 1970), p. 272.

34. Serge Leclaire, *Psychoanalyser: Un essai sur l'ordre de l'inconscient
et la pratique de la lettre* (Paris: Seuil, 1968), pp. 97ff.

35. On the concept of ambiguity or aesthetic ambivalence or overde-
termination, see Ernst Kris, *Die ästhetische Illusion: Phänomene der Kunst
in der Sicht der Psychoanalyse* (Frankfurt/Main: Suhrkamp, 1977), p. 23.
See also W. K. Wimsatt and H. C. Beardsley, "The Affective Fallacy,"
in Wimsatt and Beardsley, *The Verbal Icon* (Lexington: University of
Kentucky Press, 1954), pp. 22–40.

36. For instance, by Michael Rutschky, "Freud," *Literaturmagazin* 10:
Vorbilder (979): 160f.

37. Leclaire, *Psychoanalyser*, pp. 9ff.

38. See Rutschky, "Freud," p. 161.

39. The formulation is Jeffrey Mehlmann's, in "Zwischen Psychoanalyse und Psychocritique," in Mechthild Curtius, ed., *Seminar: Theorien
der künstlerischen Produktitivät* (Frankfurt/Main: Suhrkamp, 1976), p. 120.

40. On this problem, see Gert Mattenklott, "Der subjektive Faktor

in Musils Törleß," in Mechthild Curtius, ed., *Seminar: Theorien der Künstlerischen Produktivität*, p. 373. See also Umberto Eco, *Das offene Kunstwerk*, 2d ed. (Frankfurt/Main: Suhrkamp, 1973), p. 272.

41. J. B. Pontalis, "Flauberts Krankheit," in Alexander Mitscherlich, ed., *Psychopathographien: Schriftsteller und Psychoanalyse* (Frankfurt/Main: Suhrkamp, 1972), p. 259.

42. Friedrich Nietzsche, Preface to *The Gay Science*, trans. Walter Kaufmann (New York: Vintage Books, 1974), p. 38.

43. Käte Hamburger's new book, *Wahrheit und ästhetische Wahrheit* (Stuttgart: Klett-Cotta, 1979) tends in this direction. I was able to read it only after I had written my manuscript.

Part Two

6 | Aesthetics and Historicism: Nietzsche's Idea of "Appearance"

I

The concept of "appearance" or "semblance"[1] has always been ambivalent in colloquial language and in aesthetic theory. On the one hand, applied to reality in general, it means that we are dealing with something empty and deceptive, that a mere external semblance is hiding the true essence of a thing. And the highest form of such deception can occur in works of art. From the very first theories about the aesthetic phenomenon, it has been suspected of being a deception rather than truth. Even before Plato gave this distrust its first, privileged expression, by characterizing rhetoricians and poets as counterfeiters because they betray reality for the sake of creating an effect,[2] Hesiod wrote: "We know how to say many false things / that seem like true sayings, / but we know also how to speak the truth / when we wish to."[3]

Toward the end of the eighteenth century, the concept of appearance in the sense of something deceptive that falls short of the truth became topical again in the aesthetic debate about a theory of the beautiful. Recently, this concept has been radicalized in the critique of "commodity aesthetics," with far-reaching implications for the critique of ideology.[4] On the other hand, in the sense of "beautiful appearance," the concept means the immediate presence of the beautiful in art itself. Friedrich Schiller elaborated this idea, with its autonomous eminence for aesthetics in the modern period, in his 1795 essay "On the Aesthetic Education of Man" after having developed it indirectly in his earlier "Kallias Letters" of 1793. To be sure, Schiller did not completely relinquish the tension between the positive side of the concept and the pejorative idea of mere semblance. On the contrary, he rescued the idea of "beautiful appearance" by expressly granting it the dignity of a concept and admitting that it cloaked the truth.

As early as 1790, Kant distinguished in his *Critique of Judgment* between the semblance in poetry and the delusive fair semblance of rhetoric by arguing that poetry declared itself as mere "play" beyond any claim to truth.[5] As long as this ambivalence or dialectic of the concept of appearance remained unresolved, it continued to be a problem peculiar to aesthetic theory. It is only when this ambivalence is relinquished or when defensive rescue of appearance leaves the sphere of aesthetics proper and enters the moral realm that we approach the problem of aestheticism. In his early work, *The Birth of Tragedy out of the Spirit of Music* (1871), Friedrich Nietzsche provided a first, theoretical expression of that problem, and his treatment of it is the subject of our current investigation. We aim to make clear the historical change in the concept of appearance that Nietzsche brings about and its origin in his work as well as the hidden ambivalence inherent in the concept from the beginning as a tension between the claim to truth and the objection that the appearance exists only for effect. Our undertaking could thus provide a new point of departure for supporting the position of aesthetic autonomy.

In the twenty-sixth letter of the *Aesthetic Education,* Schiller recognized the problem that later became definitive for Nietzsche and formulated it more incisively than Kant:

> To the question, '*How far can semblance [Schein] legitimately exist in the moral world?*' the answer is then, briefly and simply this: *To the extent that it is aesthetic semblance*; that is to say, semblance which neither seeks to represent reality nor needs to be represented by it. Aesthetic semblance can never be a threat to the truth of morals; and where it might seem to be otherwise, it can be shown without difficulty that the semblance was not aesthetic.[6]

Schiller defends aesthetic "appearance" by restricting it completely to its aesthetic sphere, defining it in relation to its "frontiers," the "frontiers of truth."[7] Schiller, who was still a disciple of
Kant's *Critique of Judgment* at this time,[8] anticipated the as yet
unsolved problem of how to make a theory to account for the
experience of the beautiful; by honoring mere appearance as a
phenomenon "in the insubstantial realm of the imagination,"[9] he
emphatically shielded theory, the "essence," and "truth" from any
claims of this appearance. And if we consider the *Aesthetic Education* as a teleological-historical sketch, we realize how instrumen-
talism, which Schiller, as Kant's disciple, rejects for sake of the
individual aesthetic appearance ultimately finds its way back into
his system. In other words, his concept of appearance is only
temporarily free of purpose, of the claim to represent the truth
or essence.[10] The teleological framework of Schiller's *Aesthetic
Education,* which also shapes Friedrich Schlegel's 1796 essay,
"Studium," keeps the hidden explosive power of the concept of
appearance under the control of the category of universal history.
Thus tamed, the concept of appearance remains a function of the
moral progress of history, and aesthetics has ultimately not gained
anything with which to answer the question of what makes the
beautiful beautiful—for the time being, we are not distinguishing
here between the beautiful in art and the beautiful in nature.

Nietzsche was the first to move toward an answer to the above
question. He engaged in an operation of discovery, taking the
offensive and separating the concept of appearance from that of
truth. He thereby not only founded a consistent, ahistorical aestheticism; he also—and this is the more relevant point here—
understood aesthetic appearance in the sense of the rhetorical
tradition as the phenomenon of an effect. The ideological implications of this aggressive aestheticism must not blind us to the
accomplishment this phenomenological distinction represents. It
intensified the conditions and moved the question of the appearance of the beautiful beyond the scope of the question of truth. In
his essay on tragedy, Walter Benjamin bemoaned the "abyss of
aestheticism" and the loss "of all concepts" in Nietzsche's "genial
intuition about Greek tragedy,"[11] but in his manuscript notes for
his essay on Goethe's *Elective Affinities,* Benjamin wrote the enig-

matic phrase, "Nietzsche's definition of appearance in the Birth of
Tragedy,"[12] as if this definition could contain the inspiration of a
future aesthetics.

What is that definition? I would like to give an answer in two
parts: first, by systematizing the concept of appearance, and second, by explaining how it contradicts historicism. We will disregard Benjamin's own specific terminology of appearance for now as
well as any ideological-critical suspicions in order to understand
Nietzsche's actual insight in view of his precursors, that is,
Nietzsche's discovery of appearance as a phenomenon that coincides with its concept. One could judge rashly and assume that the
problems of the concept of appearance had been taken care of once
and for all in Hegel's famous definition of art as "the appearance of
the Idea," if not in Schiller's essay. But Hegel also conceived of
appearance without relating it to the Idea, as the mode of aesthetic
appearance itself.

> The one thing certain about beauty is, as it were, appearance for its
> own sake, and art is mastery in the portrayal of all the secrets of
> this ever profounder pure appearance of external realities. Especially
> does art consist in heeding with a sharp eye the momentary and
> everchanging traits of the present world in the details of its life,
> which yet harmonize with the universal laws of aesthetic appear-
> ance, and always faithfully and truly keeping hold of what is most
> fleeting.[13]

If we disregard for the moment the argument about the "details,"
about what is "momentary" and "everchanging," as a final relativization of art in the face of the "universal laws" and if we remember
that Schiller rejected for the artist the "fleeting moment" and the
pure present as deceptive "appearance" in his ninth letter of the
"Aesthetic Education,"[14] then we can see a surprisingly modern
turn in Hegel's taking seriously the "momentary" and "most fleeting." In discussing the "fugitive appearance" that becomes "sta-
tionary"[15] in art, Hegel's view comes close to the image of the
modern period Baudelaire formulated. Hegel's call for a "true"
portrayal of "the most fleeting," however, limits this boldness
again.

Plato, who wanted artists banned from his republic, prepared
the way in his *Phaedrus* for the understanding of the aesthetic

phenomenon at issue here, namely, to define art in the process of its verbal completion, in the process of appearance itself rather than as objects shaped and modified by the Idea. As the hallmark of "appearing" Plato chose not art or the beauty of art but instead distinguished the "beautiful" from "justice" (διχαιοσυνη) and "temperance" (σωφροσυγη), preparing the way for the phenomenological isolation that Nietzsche consciously completed in his attack on historicism: Plato writes that "in the earthly copies of justice and temperance and the other ideas which are precious to souls there is no light"(Φεγγοζ).[16] Only of "beauty" (καλλοζ) does Plato say that it is "shining in brightness" (λαμπρον).[17] It "shone in brilliance" (ελαμπεν),[18] Plato emphasizes, when it was still present in its true essential composition. Unlike"justice" and "temperance," beauty is connected to sight (οψιζ), "the sharpest of the physical senses."[19] And when Plato emphasizes that "beauty alone has this privilege" and therefore it is "the most clearly seen" (εκφανεστατον) to us,[20] he points to its special position, which is due to beauty's relationship to our senses, a special position whose organ is our eyes. To be sure, anyone who remembers true beauty at the sight of earthly beauty would fall prey to "madness" (μανια). But this argument about the Ideas is already acquainted with "enthusiasm" and the person who "shudders" and the old "awe"[21] of those times, descriptions of the condition of aesthetic perception that will be repeated in the rhetorical realm but Nietzsche will secure them categorially for the first time.

In *Phaedrus*, Plato captured the effect of the aesthetic appearance in phenomenological metaphors, which were known to preidealist and idealist aesthetics but which were not taken up, despite Winckelmann's acknowledgment of the beautiful as the particular and Schiller's and Hegel's concessions with respect to appearance.[22] Kant's verdict on the rhetorical element of appearance precluded that line of development.[23] Therefore, Nietzsche's treatment of the problem of appearance represents a kind of rediscovery, with a different metaphysical justification and at a much later point in history; consequently, it is fraught with the historical contradictions that this time factor produces. What Nietzsche rediscovered or rehabilitated was the rhetorical side of the problem of appearance.

II

Nietzsche developed the phenomenology of appearance using the example of Greek tragedy. Limiting himself to the works of Aeschylos and Sophocles and giving them a fresh interpretation by means of the artistic principles of the "Dionysian" and the "Apollonian," Nietzsche defined the specific affective mode of aesthetic appearance. His presentation of the tragic does not continue the clarification of the concepts fear and pity that had been undertaken following Aristotle's definition of tragedy. Instead, it analyzes a different psychological effect, that of the aesthetic-rhetorical epiphany. In discussing this effect, we must distinguish two aspects: the nature of appearance as phenomenon, which Nietzsche developed, and the mechanism of the appearance of appearance, as opposed to the appearance of truth, or the Idea, that he proposed.

The Nature of Appearance as Phenomenon

The nature of appearance as phenomenon is the temporal structure of its *suddenness* and is indicated by the repeated expressions relating to the concepts of seeing and sight. It becomes clear that what Nietzsche means is not the submersion of the seeing subject in the contemplation of eternal ideas or essences, but the predominance of what is actually perceived at the moment. The object seen in that way replaces what it represents. Nietzsche's theory centers on the nature of appearance as phenomenon and on the mode of seeing. In his description of the Dionysian experience, Nietzsche assigns the phenomenal character of appearance its aesthetically definitive features:

> In the same work Schopenhauer has depicted for us the tremendous *terror* which seizes man when he is suddenly dumbfounded by the cognitive form of phenomena because the principle of sufficient reason, in some one of its manifestations, seems to suffer an exception. If we add to this terror the blissful ecstasy that wells from the innermost depths of man, indeed of nature, at this collapse of the *principium individuationis*, we steal a glimpse into the nature of the *Dionysian*, which is brought home to us most intimately by the analogy of intoxication.[24]

Nietzsche borrowed the image of the "tremendous terror" from Schopenhauer's fourth book of the first volume of *The World as Will and Idea*.[25] We will consider Schopenhauer's purely metaphysical argument only with respect to Nietzsche's aesthetic application. To put it briefly, according to Schopenhauer we experience "terror"—he also speaks of "horror"—when we no longer see mere appearances in time and space that are subject to the principle of sufficient reason and instead perceive the essence of things. This deeper knowledge occurs only when we renounce the principle of individuation and become one with the "thing in itself," when we pull aside the "veil of maya"[26] that interposes itself protectively between our vision and the true nature of things, that is, the cruelty of being.

While young Nietzsche adopted Schopenhauer's pessimistic basic ideas about the cruel nature of being, he changed the relationships among the relevant concepts in characteristic fashion. In Schopenhauer, the concept of phenomenon as opposed to "thing in itself" meant false appearance. In this contrast, which grew out of Plato's doctrine of ideas and Kant's transcendental argument, visible reality is revealed as deceptive. Reality is penetrated here not in an aesthetic act but by means of "higher knowledge."[27] In Nietzsche, these relationships are reversed. The experience that cancels out the principle of individuation does provide a "view of the essential," but only of the essence of the Dionysian aspect. With respect to this view, the characteristics of the Dionysian are defined from the outset as aesthetic qualities. There is no more "thing in itself" here, no "true essence of things." Nietzsche assumes the existence of a final cruelty of being, but he is interested only in the initially given manifestation of this cruelty as it appears to us, that is, in the Dionysian act itself. In other words, the appearance that fascinates in the Dionysian experience, behind which there is no essence to discover, serves in the metaphysical thesis as an indicator for the cruelty of being. In his attempt to show this Schopenhauerian cruelty by the example of Greek tragedy, Nietzsche discovered that the appearance of this cruelty can be enjoyed.

Concerning Schopenhauer's understanding of being, we do not ask whether the "shudder" has to do with the cruelty being perceived or with the manner in which the perception of this cruelty comes about. We do not feel compelled to make such a specific differentiation of apperception. In Nietzsche's work, however, the particular conditions of perception gain phenomenological effect, which makes this perception an aesthetic rather than epistemological one. That is, this perception takes place *suddenly*, accompanied by the loss of the "principle of individuation" and by a terror combined with pleasure.

In our discussion we can only sketch the special function and valence of the concept sudden in the context of Nietzsche's writings. This concept centers the experience of the moment outside of reflected history in the most radical way and is the semantic sign most often used for Nietzsche's antihistoricism. Suddenness establishes that pointlike quality which allows us to conceptualize the new, the entirely other of the cultural alternative in a purely static way, to disregard the *course of time* that is a necessary part of our consciousness. Suddenness in the sense of a "self-identification of the actual now" (Derrida) is here not a logical or metaphysical concept but an aesthetic concept derived, as we will see, from the rhetorical tradition.

In the notes that were published under the title *The Will to Power*, Nietzsche writes: "*What is evil?* Three things: chance, the uncertain, the sudden."[28] At this late point in his posthumously published work, Nietzsche had already performed a cultural diagnosis and classified the sudden as a condition of the perception of fear in the archaic human being. He recognized it as having been superseded by the concept of Enlightment. In the context of the earlier essay on tragedy, however, such a relativization through historical consciousness was not yet possible, and the archaic regression doubtlessly contributes to the aesthetic element. The lost principle of individuation in Schopenhauer has both an epistemological and a metaphysical meaning. While Nietzsche borrows the words that represent those two realms, he frees himself of their given systems and uses them to establish an aesthetic situation. He does not wish to address the logical contradiction in a phenomenon but rather the collapse of reason in an act of strong emotion.

Although Kant had approached the idea of imagination as liberated by poetry, he kept it "accordant with a given concept."[29] Unlike Winckelmann, Nietzsche did not run aground on the concept; instead, he consciously renounced it. His "cry of horror" contains the experience of the "new," the "unheard of," the "never before experienced,"[30] even the "incommensurable,"[31] that is, here Nietzsche invents the concepts of modern aesthetics. Nietzsche categorially attributes intuitive perception to the loss of the principle of individuation. Friedrich Schlegel anticipated him in his *Gespräch über die Poesie* (Conversation on poetry) (1799), where he described the beginning and the future of poetry as "canceling out progress and the laws of rationally thinking reason and placing us again into the beautiful confusion of fantasy, into the original chaos of human nature, for which I know of no more beautiful symbol than the gaudy swarm of the ancient gods."[32] Anyone who understands the development of modern poetics recognizes in the early romantic protest against reason one of its central motifs and locates another in the rehabilitation of the beauty of nature. Nietzsche adopts both motifs completely and uses them to attack historicism's concept of history, as we will see later in greater detail.

The final element in the phenomenal nature of appearance is "pleasure" mixed with "terror." The first thing this element calls to mind is the mixed reaction to tragedy Schiller analyzed in his essay "Über den Grund des Vergnügens an Tragischen Gegenständen" (On the cause of pleasure in tragedy), a common theme of the late-eighteenth-century sensualist theory of art. It is not surprising to find the words *terror* and *horror* in a work about Greek tragedy. The analysis of tragedy up to then, however, was based on Aristotle's definition of tragedy as a mimetic representation that arouses pity and fear and thereby purges us of those emotions. The reception of Aristotle's definition has led to a great variety of interpretations of his key phrase, which we have cited here in Lessing's version.[33] Max Kommerell showed that the phrase requires interpretation and presented the history of this interpretation.[34] Here, however, Lessing's version is the only one that interests us. That is, we will look at Lessing's interpretation of the relationship between fear and pity, to show how Nietzsche used and altered an already existing cluster of concepts for his discussion of aesthetic appearance.

To begin with, we should recall that Lessing did not consider terror or fear as phenomena that actually manifested themselves. He spoke only of our "fear." Moreover, he understood this purely reactive terror as a mode of pity: "Terror in *the tragedy* is nothing more than the sudden surprise of pity," he wrote in a letter to Nicolai in November of 1756.[35] Lessing saw the purpose of tragedy as helping us to expand our capacity to feel pity.[36] Thus in a letter to Nicolai dated April 2, 1757, Lessing severely criticized several German and French translations of the Greek word "φoβoζ" as *crainte* or *terreur* or *Schrecken* ("terror"), and decided on *Furcht* ("fear") as the only reasonable translation, because, according to Lessing's argument, our experience of fear for the protagonist announces our pity.[37] Pity, which is not to be misunderstood as a didactic emotion, is the message of Greek tragedy and is Lessing's school of humanity. For that reason he also made a fundamental distinction between the atavistic terror, the horror that Richard III spreads, and the goals of bourgeois tragedy. Richard III does not arouse pity and arouses terror only "if by terror we mean astonishment at incomprehensible misdeeds, the horror at evildoing that exceeds our comprehension, if we mean the shudder that seizes us at the sight of intentional atrocities committed with pleasure."[38] This passage from the seventy-fourth piece of the *Hamburgische Dramaturgie* takes a negative approach to the characteristic signs of tragic terror. Nietzsche, in light of his different aesthetics, saw astonishment and incomprehensible misdeeds that exceed our comprehension as positive.

It characterizes the difference between Nietzsche and Lessing to point out that Lessing gives the accidental determinant of the sudden (seventy-fourth piece) no aesthetic status but merely employs the word in the service of a theory of pity based on sensation. Nietzsche, on the other hand, could develop his new theory because he disregarded the pivotal point of the traditional theory of tragedy as it had been handed down from Aristotle, namely, the calculation of the logical and psychological relationship between pity, fear, and catharsis; he ignored Lessing's humanistic, Enlightenment solution as well and instead replaced the traditional theory with a theory of purely aesthetic, rhetorical appearance. In the *Will to Power*, Nietzsche later remarked that Aristotle's great mistake was to describe pity and terror as "*depressive* affects,"[39] whereas tragedy is a "tonic," which only the "counterfeit of a systematizer" could fail to recognize.[40]

The impertinent attacks on a venerable explanatory model in Nietzsche's later years should not obscure his earlier discovery of the aesthetic structure as appearance. As part of this structure, Nietzsche also rejects the traditional definition of tragedy as action and replaces it with emotion.[41] He thus criticizes not only the narrative degeneration of Attic tragedy in Euripides but also any attempt to achieve a "painless condition" by means of the *factor of reflected time*. Nietzsche's view of the "*situation* of emotion" differs from that of Hegel, who understood it as a "collision"[42] that always introduces a new element of action, thus canceling out the pure moment of "emotion" in the course of time. Nietzsche considered the entire course of the tragedy as a phenomenon in which time has been eliminated.

The Appearance of "Appearance"

Recalling to Plato's problem, we could now object that the phenomenal nature of the Dionysian as the aesthetic phenomenon of appearance itself is mere accident. It does free appearance of the question as to what substance appears in it. Hegel disarmed the old objection that appearance is deceptive—and this objection arises if we do not state what is appearing—with the argument that appearance itself is essential to essence[43] and stressed that "Truth would not be truth if it did not show itself and appear."[44] In contrast to the "phenomena of the external world and its immediate materiality, as well as in relation to our own world of feeling,"[45] art is not mere appearance: "Art liberates the true content of phenomena from the pure appearance and deception of this bad, transitory world, and gives them a higher actuality, born of the spirit. Thus, far from being mere pure appearance, a higher reality and truer existence is to be ascribed to the phenomena of art in comparison with [those of] ordinary reality."[46]

The special nature of appearance as phenomenon is lost in this justification of art that pits appearance against essence, for, according to Hegel, even truth, to which Plato did not attribute the special "brilliance," "shows itself" and "appears." Thus, despite "partial" concessions, Hegel never grants appearance a specific dignity. He is always concerned with referring appearance back to an "essence" or the "truth." And this is what makes possible the historical relativization of artistic appearance: it is no longer the "highest and absolute mode of bringing to our minds the true interests of the spirit."[47] The symbolic period in which works of art were venerated as "divine"[48] is over. Now art must withstand "a higher touchstone and a different test."[49] This touch-stone is the "thought and reflection"[50] that surpass art, and—we can add—that means history.

Nietzsche renounced both Hegel's referring of appearance to truth and the touchstone of history. In a logically consistent way, he hypostatized the "appearance of appearance." The problem with this approach was to organize the insight that necessarily arose from his aesthetic experience without creating a simple tautology, as in: appearance is appearance. What can the "appearance of appearance" mean, as opposed to the appearance of the idea? This "appearance of appearance"—this is Nietzsche's first step—is like the effect of aesthetic perception that the "beautiful illusion of dream worlds"[51] leaves behind in the dreamer. Just as we have a sensation glimmering through the dream reality that it is *mere appearance*,[52] we enjoy the illusory nature of poetry. But reality itself—Nietzsche tells us, taking up the thread from Schopenhauer and Platonic philosophy—is appearance. Thus,in the relationship of an artistically receptive person to the reality of a dream—and here is Nietzsche's second step—we are dealing with an *"appearance of mere appearance."*[53] This "appearance of appearance" re-verses the value of the reflections in Plato's parable of the cave from negative to positive through an anthropological a priori. In the double illusion Nietzsche talks about, "danger and terror" still appear, but our awareness of dealing with an illusion makes them pleasant to us. This pleasure in the "illusion" or, as Nietzsche also calls it, this "primordial desire for mere appearance,"[54] is elabo-rated as a law of our psychological-anthropological structure, our unconscious mind, prior to and alongside our historicity.

The cultural-historical name for this appearance comes from Apollo, the "shining" or "appearing one,"[55] an association of two distinct qualities whose intertwining the young Wilamowitz picked apart in his famous attack on Nietzsche, *Zukunftsphilologie* (Philol-ogy of the Future). According to Wilamowitz, Apollo is the "shin-ing one," but he is not the god of "appearance."[56] Nietzsche began his work on tragedy with the distinction between the Dionysian and Apollonian principles, a distinction that, for all its influence on cultural analysis, did not originate with him.[57] The importance of *The Birth of Tragedy*, however, lies not in its cognitive contribu-tion to philology or to the history of religion but in its implicit aesthetic theory of "appearance." This theory is untouched by Wilamowitz's objections, for Apollo merely furnishes the symbol for the connection of the concepts of shining and appearance. This symbol could not be substantiated through the history of religion, but the theory that gave a positive meaning to mere appearance was unaffected. Nietzsche's thesis necessarily remained foreign to the classicistic world of the young Wilamowitz; therefore, in his concentration on the (incorrect) metaphorical means—i.e., the name Apollo—he overlooked the actual purpose of using the name, which was the phenomenological discovery of appearancee as the aesthetic event.

Apollonian appearance is also guaranteed by the principle of individuation, which dissolves in Dionysian rapture. The "delicate boundary" between Apollonian appearance and "crude reality" must never be overstepped[58] if the dream image is not to have a "pathological" effect.[59] From the very beginning, Apollonian appearance is prophylactically separated from "being" or the empirical idea of being. The fact that we need this appearance so desperately proves, according to Nietzsche's metaphysical assumption, that the "truly existent" is also the "eternally suffering," from which we are liberated only through "pleasurable illusion."[60] Following Schopenhauer's reasoning, Nietzsche relates aesthetic appearance to a metaphysically conceived "being." This being or essence, however, recedes behind the appearance, becomes its function, the function of redemption. Thus, Nietzsche reverses the metaphysical priorities. Not being but appearance now occupies the preeminent place of existential experience, and therefore Nietzsche can also speak of an "aesthetic metaphysics."[61] Now it is clear how Nietzsche potentiates appearance, or reduces Apollonian appearance "to the level of mere appearance."[62] Nietzsche derives appearance in dreams or in poetic experience from a primary appearance reflecting empirical reality, and in the process he moves the "primal unity" or the "truly existent"[63] completely out of our angle of vision. Nietzsche, who once spoke of his own "topsy-turvy Platonism,"[64] actually reverses the procedure of the Platonic parable of the cave. He wants to reach not the Ideas but their reflections! In this way he formalizes the ontic structure as a structure of mere appearance that finally become a substitute for being itself. There is no other being for us than appearance.

The example Nietzsche chooses to show the reduction of Apollonian appearance to "mere appearance" is Raphael's painting, *Transfiguration*. According to Nietzsche, the lower half of the canvas shows the reflection of "suffering, primal and eternal, the sole ground of the world."[65] That is the first, "mere appearance." From it, however, rises the actual Apollonian appearance, a "new visionary world of . . . appearances, invisible to those wrapped in the first appearance."[66] The subordination of being to appearance conceals an ideological implication, a sadistic motif that later proliferates in the literature of decadence: In order to experience beauty, we need the torment of others.

Nietzsche clarified the abrupt phenomenal character of aesthetic appearance in his discussion of the Dionysian mode. Although the Dionysian is first presented as diametrical opposite to the Apollonian, in the end it is the real and sole goal of Nietzsche's interest. For that reason, attempts to discover here the beginnings of an originally progressive but finally unsuccessful theory of history[67] overlook the actual contribution of the work. In contrast to the Apollonian artist, the Dionysian—Nietzsche uses the poet Archilochus as an example[68]—is at one with the "primal unity" and its "pain,"[69] and the Dionysian artist produces the image of the "primal unity." However, this is not the individual artistic product, because then this image would be merely a repetition of the world. Nietzsche wished both to establish the superiority of the Dionysian artist over the Apollonian in the former's unmediated experience of the pain of being and to preclude the subordination of the aesthetic product of this experience to being—which would, after all, simply cancel out his "aesthetic metaphysics." Therefore, Nietzsche constructs once more the doubled reflection of "appearance." The "reflection of the primordial pain,"[70] which is without images or concepts, redeemed by the effect of Apollonian "appearance" in dreams, produces a "second mirroring."[71] That second mirroring is the individual work of art. The Dionysian artist relates immediately to the torment of existence, although the relationship is mirrored in "appearance." From that relationship Nietzsche draws some final, weighty consequences for his aesthetics. The Dionysian artist does not find his way back to the principle of individuation, not even in the act of creating the individual work of art. His "I" echoes from the "abyss of [. . .] being."[72] But this being can be grasped only as Dionysian appearance, not as a "law." Nietzsche here turns against the romantic thesis of the subjectivity of the artist. Nietzsche's artistic "I" has an objective, not a subjective, basis, which is furnished by the Dionysian appearance that arises out of but cannot be reduced to a tragic conception of existence. One could say that the "touchstone" here is not reason in history but nature, and not nature's laws, but her pleasure.

Nietzsche concludes his theory of appearance in the fifth part of *The Birth of Tragedy* with the phrase: "for it is only as an aesthetic phenomenon that existence and the world are eternally *justified.*"[73] After our discussion here, that phrase should not be misunderstood as a metaphorical expression of *l'art pour l'art,* as has so often happened in the history of Nietzsche interpretation. Rather, this phrase means that we can accept and tolerate the world only as an aesthetic mirroring, because there is no deeper knowledge of the world than what we experience in the Dionysian act. This experience, however, is deeply horrifying. Therefore, the aesthetic phenomenon also has its own meaning that cannot be reduced to any meaning it might represent, because only as an aesthetic object does it speak of the contradiction of being. This finally conceded relationship of appearance to something else is fundamentally different in its logic from the traditional representation of being as "truth" by means of appearance. If we can speak of a dialectical method in Nietzsche at all, we certainly cannot do so in the case of the opposition of Apollonian and Dionysian, which is conceived of in ahistorical terms; rather, we find his dialectical method in the self-mediating structure of the concept of appearance. By separating appearance logically from being or truth, Nietzsche presented the modern phenomenon of aesthetic autonomy in a theoretical model that does not exhibit the flaw of neo-idealist, realist, or mimetic theories of art, that is, their quandary with respect to aesthetic "surplus value."

III

The explanatory model for aesthetic appearance divorced from being was bought at the price of the surrender of historical categories. In Nietzsche's writing critics have even seen the destruction of history as an anticipation of fascist aesthetics.[74] Walter Benjamin's suspicion of Nietzsche, noted above, becomes relevant here. At least the motif of tragedy fuels the suspicion that Nietzsche, in his archaic recourse to the myth of Aeschylos and his criticism of

Socratic reason and of the psychology of Euripides, established an aesthetic critique of culture and a philosophy of art that was intended to cancel out the present and future of the modern period. We will only briefly mention Nietzsche's attacks on democratic positions of his time, for instance on the quasi-progressive interpretation of the tragic chorus by A. W. Schlegel.[75] However, let us first answer the question whether the theory of appearance finally presuppose an attempt at "tragedism,"[76] that is, an attempt at reiterating tragedy, which had already become historically obsolete in Nietzsche's time.

As we have shown, Nietzsche was not at all interested in the plot inventory of ancient tragedy. He was only interested in the pathos of the sudden, terrifying appearance. In the radicalization of the psychic effects of this sudden phenomenon we can easily recognize an aesthetics of the "sublime," such as Edmund Burke developed in his early essay entitled "A Philosophical Enquiry into the Origin of our Ideas on the Sublime and the Beautiful" (1756). The theory of the sublime contains all the essential elements of the Dionysian "phenomenal" character of appearance, especially shock and suddenness.[77] German classicism failed to take up this reference to the mechanics of sensual effect, which derives from English sensualism, because it was too naturalistic. Kant's *Critique of Judgment*, however, and its category of the sublime were influenced considerably by Burke's aesthetics. Kant emphasized that the transcendental aesthetics of judgment should be limited to pure aesthetic judgments, that is, "examples are not to be selected from such beautiful or sublime objects as presuppose the concept of an end."[78] Otherwise, according to Kant, "the finality would be either teleological, or based upon mere sensations of an object . . . in the first case, not aesthetic, and, in the second, not merely formal."[79] The sublimity of the "starry heavens" or the "prospect of the ocean," according to Kant, must not originate in an interpretation that is guided by reason or morality but solely in the sensual power of the impressions of these phenomena. We must take them just as they strike the eye.[80] Nietzsche's theory of the phenomenon and appearance does not necessarily presuppose the concept of tragedy, but it does presuppose Burke's sensualist view of the sublime as the sudden.

The sublime was not a discovery of Burke's, but a concept in the rhetoric of antiquity. A work by Longinus entitled περιυψους[81] made the sublime a central concept of aesthetic theory. With its translation into French in the seventeenth and eighteenth centuries, the work became the most important essay on aesthetics after Aristotle's *Poetics* and the *Ars poetica* of Horace.[82] The specific elements we found in Nietzsche's aesthetic epiphany are already contained in Longinus' discussion of the metaphorical repertory of sublime discourse: "Sublimity, brought out at just the right moment, makes everything different, like lightning, and directly shows the 'all-at-once' capacity of the speaker"(1:4).[83] The metaphor of "lightning" and the "all-at-once," the momentum, that characterize the emphatic language of Nietzsche is repeated often in Longinus. Longinus supplements the metaphor of momentum with that of the "astounding" (22:4; 35:4). The noble pathos of the orator affects us if it is "there in the place where it must be" (8:4), the oratorical power of Demosthenes is compared to "lightning or a thunderbolt" (12:4); it has the strongest effect in the "powerful passages," "intense emotions," and "knowing when one ought to astound the audience" (12:5), Demosthenes "outthunders" and "outshines public speakers of all ages" as if with a "thunderbolt" (34:4).

Longinus' description of rhetoric leads us to the central distinction of the aesthetics of rhetoric, that of its relation to effect rather than truth: "What is beyond nature," as Longinus says, "drives the audience not to persuasion, but to ecstasy. What is wonderful, with its stunning power, prevails everywhere over that which aims merely at persuasion and at gracefulness. The ability to be persuaded lies in us, but what is wonderful has a capability and force which, unable to be fought, take a position high over every member of the audience" (1:4). This priority of emotional effect over objective argument or over the criterion of truth has been peculiar to the scheme of the rhetorical doctrine of affect since Aristotle, as Klaus Dockhorn has convincingly shown.[84] In the Aristotelian scheme of disposition of πραγμα, ηθος, and παθος, which continued to affect rhetoric through Cicero's *De Oratore*, παθος carries the actual rhetorical quality. This rhetorical quality can be diminished by ηθος, the reliability of the orator, and πραγμα, the detailed presentation of the matter. In Longinus' distinction between the wonderful and the stunning on the one hand and persuasion on the other, we find this arrangement repeated, with Longinus dissolving the classical balance between the emotional and intellectual function in favor of the stunning. The history of Aristotle's formula of ethos and pathos, which we can only touch on briefly here as far as it relates to our topic—but which Dockhorn discusses at length—reveals that Longinus was the only thinker to subordinate ethos to pathos or to the "sublime."[85] From Cicero to Quintilian, those supreme rhetorical values were considered equal and balanced against each other,[86] a decision that was realized in the heroic literature of the baroque and in Corneille more in favor of pathos and admiration,[87] and in Lessing and the English Romantics, especially in Wordsworth, more in favor of ethos.[88]

Now we can state more exactly to what extent the elements of Nietzsche's aesthetic epiphany are prefigured in the rhetorical tradition. That is true of the phenomenon of the sudden, the horror that evades reflection. It is also true, however, of the argumentation of Nietzsche's polemics against Euripides and the heroes of his stage, in all their bourgeois mediocrity,[89] against character representation and psychological refinement in tragedy.[90] In theory, this polemic centers in the already mentioned conclusion that the effect of tragedy "never depended on epic suspense"[91] and terminates in the key sentence: "Everything laid the ground for pathos, not for action."[92] Here, the original rhetorical formula of pragma, ethos, and pathos turns most clearly into a pointed argument of pathos against ethos and pragma. The central objection to the epic dissolution of archaic tragedy is prefigured in Longinus' work, especially in the latter's observation that the pathos of great writers dissipates when they "slip off into characterization" (9:15). Longinus' statement that the "dazzling light" of the discourse prevents the audience from becoming suspicious as to the truth expressed by the sophisticated rhetorical figures sheds the strongest light on the rhetorical prefiguration of Nietzsche's theory of appearance: "Now surely sublimity and emotion form a remedy and a wonderful kind of assistance against the suspicion of using figures" (17:2). The orator "veils" the figures of speech by means of the [dazzling] light. This somewhat deceptive process is described as follows: "Now in speeches and writings, since emotion and sublimity lie nearer to our souls—because of a kind of natural kinship and because of their dazzling effect—over and over again they appear to us before the figures, and they cast technique into the shade and keep it hidden." (17:3).

In regard to Nietzsche's complex theory of appearance this argument is particularly interesting because here the "dazzling effect" of the sublime that comes into play in opposition to the merely rhetorical appearance represents an operation that shares elements of structure and content with Nietzsche's model of Apollonian and Dionysian appearance. In terms of structure, Nietzsche employs the idea of a "demotion of appearance to the level of mere appearance" in presenting Apollonian appearance. From "mere appearance" as "the reflection of eternal contradiction, the father of things," "the sole ground of the world" there emerges a "new visionary world of mere appearances."[93] Only that new world makes possible the "serene contemplation beaming from wide-open eyes."[94]

As to the analogy about content: the ecstasy of the Dionysian condition is jeopardized by an opposing force, the lethargy that Hamlet experienced after he looked into the essence of things and became unable to act.[95] The disillusionment that threatens to develop about the recognized horror of existence is removed by the "sublimity" of the aesthetic event. We should mention that Nietzsche's element of "lethargy" is reminiscent of the concept of *memoria* in rhetoric,[96] which, for obvious reasons, played only a small role in the rhetoric of the sublime. The English and German romantics, however, used it as a means of controlling the emotions,[97] in a procedure opposite to the one Nietzsche pursued.

Nietzsche's argument shares with Longinus' the motif of "the dazzling light" that tricks reflection, an "antidote" to the suspicion that these aesthetic joys could be deceptive. And this antidote itself is a deception. Unlike Plato in his *Phaedrus*, Longinus uses unambiguous metaphors of light, with words such as $\phi\omega\varsigma$, $\eta\lambda\iota o\sigma$ (17:10). In *Phaedrus*, Plato uses exclusively words of "brilliance": $\Phi\epsilon\gamma\gamma o\varsigma$ and $\lambda\alpha\mu\pi\rho o\nu$ (250 b). From this distinction alone we cannot yet conclude to what extent the metaphor of appearance in the rhetorical tradition already implies the ambivalence of appearance and illusion. Nietzsche exploited this ambivalence for his aesthetics in his conscious play with the two meanings of the German word *Schein*, "shine" and "appearance."

For our purposes it does not matter whether and how much

Nietzsche the philologist[98] was influenced by the rhetorical tradition of the sublime or by its expression in Burke. Still, Burke was the first to translate Longinus' νψοξ into the sublime "darkness" and "uncertain," where in the place of rhetorical surprise we find the actual "shock,"[99] which could have influenced Nietzsche's aesthetics of the sudden. It follows, however, from the rhetorical character of the central aesthetic concepts that the theory of tragedy is not to be equated with an archaic reconstruction.[100] Directly or indirectly, Nietzsche's idea of aesthetic appearance derives from a stylistic model that has nothing to do with the traditional theory of tragedy, much less with tragedism, the pessimistic reconstruction of the tragic in the nineteenth century, even though Nietzsche contributed to this reconstruction. It is more precise to say that Nietzsche understood the sublime not as Lessing, Schiller, or Wordsworth had, in the sense of ethos, but rather in the sense of pathos. He was guided in this understanding by motifs of preidealist and prerationalist aesthetics, where motifs of classical rhetoric, the delicate tact of the *je ne sais quoi*,[101] and English sensualism unite. This process guarantees the novel irrationalism of a self-consciously revolutionary style and of the senses, not merely the irrationalism of regression into the distant past.

This sensualism is based on an aesthetic conception that includes the beauty of nature. And it seems to me that this fact helps answer to what extent the theory of appearance requires the suspension of history. Unlike Hegel in his *Aesthetics*, Nietzsche included the beauty of nature in his *Birth of Tragedy*. His explanation of the Dionysian event is based on the Dionysian in nature.[102] Although Nietzsche distinguishes this Dionysian aspect in nature from the Dionysian element in art,[103] there is no real difference between the beauty of nature and the beauty of art in Nietzsche's work. The Dionysian in nature furnishes the characteristics that distinguish the Dionysian in art. That does not mean, however, that culture is taken back into nature but that within culture the natural, demonic aspect of physiologically discovered humanity emerges. History does not disappear in prehistory, but in an anthropological structure.

Nietzsche goes beyond classical, rationalistic aesthetics back to the sensualistic eighteenth-century aesthetics of taste that had been handed down in the rhetorical tradition; specifically,

Nietzsche takes up the concept of the sublime as developed by Longinus and adopted by Burke. His recourse to that concept regains for aesthetic theory the knowledge of affect and physicality, knowledge this aesthetic theory then pursued further, to the point of anticipating Freudian motifs. For example, Nietzsche anticipated the Freudian approach in firmly linking the concept of appearance to the dream.[104] Is there possibly a connection between historically obsolete tragedism and the concept of appearance? Our answer is no. The concepts of appearance and appearing are not based on an illegitimate transformation of temporally structured history into a static cultural history[105] but rather on a connection between the aesthetic emotion that was gained in the concept of the sublime and the physiological suspicion of the intellect. The first element of this connection derives from motifs of the English aesthetics of the eighteenth century, which was influenced by the rhetorical tradition. The second element anticipates the modern, physiognomic idea of beauty. Together they form a model of argument in which modernity emerges from cultural regression.

Although history is not blindly banished from the concept of appearance, we still encounter a historical moment isolated within historical time. This isolating procedure was formulated in Nietzsche's 1874 essay, "The Use and Abuse of History," and in its system it is closely related to the concept of appearance. In this essay, the most important expression of Nietzsche's critique of contemporary historicism, one concept is central for our investigation: that of the "present" or of the *closed "horizon."* To summarize Nietzsche's idea briefly, to avoid becoming pure epigones under the weight of the sheer memory of universal history, we must counter this past actively with a strategy: "You can explain the past only by what is most powerful in the present."[106] I will not mention here the significance the emphatic concept of the present has taken on for the historical consciousness sharpened by hermeneutics since Heine's critique of universal history.[107] Nevertheless, we should remember that Nietzsche took this concept, which still had a negative valence in Schiller, and made it hermeneutically more profound by realizing that a foreshortening of the "horizon" would produce such a fruitful "moment."[108] The infinity of the universal historical perspective should be eliminated and only a limited range of vision should be granted. Only with such a restricted "horizon" is it possible to create the fictions and illusions that make action possible.

The problems entailed in such a methodical restriction of temporal perspective to a self-identical moment have been evident since the days of phenomenological research. Ernst Bloch described the most extreme consequence of such a foreshortened moment as emphasis "placed senselessly on one point."[109] Nietzsche, who also characterized the completely unhistorical nature of an animal's temporal horizon as "pointillistic,"[110] hit upon a way out of the dilemma. He replaced the historical argument, which is unable to save the punctualist perspective, with an aesthetic argument and saw in the artist the ideal manifestation of the hermeneutically gifted historian: "For art flies away if you are roofing your deeds with the historical awning. The man who wishes to understand everything in a moment, when he ought to grasp the unintelligible as well as the sublime by a long struggle, can be called intelligent only in the sense of Schiller's epigram on the 'reason of reasonable men.' "[111]

Obviously, we can present a theory of the present, the moment of my now, in contradistinction to a known past that censors it, only through an aesthetic concept. Once again, this concept is the sublime. This proves that Nietzsche's exposition of appearance cannot be transposed into a historical category. Instead, the quasi-historical concept of the moment becomes plausible only with the aid of an aesthetic concept. Does it follow from this that history becomes the history of art? Does the theory of appearance dissolve all historical categories? In the context of his later criticism of Wagner, Nietzsche also criticized the category of the sudden, which is so important for the theory of appearance.[112] Nevertheless, Nietzsche never relinquished the theory of appearance he had developed in the *Birth of Tragedy*. Instead, he reflected on it "under the hammerblow of historical knowledge"[113] and tried to maintain it in the face of this historical knowledge. His criticism was aimed only at a romantic realization of the sudden,[114] not at the phenomenological approach itself. The Dionysian moment as we saw it could not be portrayed as a historical moment; at the same time, it could not be relinquished, because it is imposed on us by nature. The result is a contradiction that could not be glossed over but rather had to be endured as an aporia. This aporia—according to Nietzsche's insight—is hidden within the essence of beautiful appearance, which can no longer be grasped by historical categories. This insight puts Nietzsche in the late 1870s face to face with the problem of redeeming art from history without letting history disappear into art.

Nietzsche's *Birth of Tragedy* and the four sections of *Thoughts Out of Season* were followed by his critical-positivistic revision of the romantic idea of art. In spite of this, he did not at the same time relinquish his phenomenological approach, which was threatened by the factor of history. In fact, he had to put this approach on a new foundation. In 1886, in the preface to the *Gay Science*, he wrote,

> Oh, those Greeks! They knew how to live. What is required for that is to stop courageously at the surface, the fold, the skin, to adore appearance, to believe in forms, tones, words, in the whole Olympus of appearance. Those Greeks were superficial—*out of profundity*. And is not this precisely what we are again coming back to, we daredevils of the spirit who have climbed the highest and most dangerous peak of present thought and looked around from up there—we who have looked *down* from up there? Are we not, precisely in this respect, Greeks? Adorers of forms, of tones, of words? And therefore—*artists?* [115]

In contrast to the justification of the Dionysian and the concept of appearance in *The Birth of Tragedy*, here appearance or surface is linked with human self-reflection and with the historicity of the intellect. And more: the depth of appearance is viewed from the "peak of contemporary thought." If Nietzsche does not portray appearance historically, he does at least introduce the historical consciousness as an element of aesthetic shock. That is, to be sure, a revision of the Dionysian understanding of nature, but it occurs in the service of opposing a concept of history that would make art historically redundant. Nietzsche undertook this attempt in the third section of *Human, All Too Human:*

> Previously, the mind was not obliged to think rigorously; its importance lay in spinning out symbols and forms. That has changed; that importance of symbols has become the sign of lower culture. Just as our very arts are becoming ever more intellectual and our senses more spiritual, and as, for example, that which is sensually

pleasant to the ear is judged quite differently now than a hundred years ago, so the forms of our life become ever more *spiritual*—to the eye of older times *uglier*, perhaps, but only because it is unable to see how the realm of internal, spiritual beauty is continually deepening and expanding, and to what extent a glance full of intelligence can mean more to all of us now than the most beautiful human body and the most sublime edifice.[116]

Nietzsche's insight into the historical aging and intellectualization of art does not lead him—as it did Hegel—to relativize art in relation to the newly found historical point of reference, which for Hegel implies the end of art. What Nietzsche gives up is the "symbolic" character of archaic art, which for Hegel represented the first phase of the development of culture. This renunciation also affects the concept of appearance, which is linked to the "dread" in tragedy. Nietzsche rejects this dread as an aesthetically permissible element. In *Human, All Too Human*, Nietzsche writes that we have "outgrown the symbolism of lines and figures" because we no longer believe in the gods.[117]

This Hegelian argument seems to invalidate the whole terminology of appearance, for, according to Nietzsche, in Greek and in Christian art everything was arranged with a view to an "inexhaustible significance," that is, to mythical interpretation:[118] "Beauty entered the system only secondarily, without impairing the basic feeling of uncanny sublimity, of sanctification by magic or the gods' nearness. At the most, beauty tempered the *dread*— but this dread was the prerequisite everywhere."[119]

For us today, Nietzsche continues, the beauty of a building is "as the beautiful face of a mindless woman: something mask-like."[120] From the position of the skepticism achieved in *Human, All Too Human*, which included a vigorous criticism of romantic art in general, the tragic dread celebrated in the earlier *Birth of Tragedy* as an existing possibility is now definitively declared a thing of the past. Nevertheless, Nietzsche retained the concept of appearance, translating it into that of the mask, which had been prepared in the work on tragedy. We should recall that for Nietzsche the concept of Apollo was primarily relevant for the theory of art and not, as Wilamowitz assumed, as a theorem in the history of religion, whose repudiation would have affected the theory of appearance as well.

This is not true in the same way for the figure of Dionysus. Nietzsche's early theory of art identified itself with that figure as a metaphysical fact. Now it becomes clear, however, that Nietzsche subjugates the Dionysian moment arbitrarily to his primary interest, namely, the aesthetic epiphany. Dionysian ecstasy was the most telling example for this epiphany in cultural history, but it was not a necessary example, and even before Nietzsche wrote his theory of tragedy, the aesthetic epiphany was for him, in a sense, the heuristic principle of a future aesthetics. That is, it was not the "positivistic" result of his studies on Greek tragedy, which he would have had to revise. This epiphany itself served, as we see, merely as a theoretical model for the modern myth that Richard Wagner's operas seemed to promise.

Although Nietzsche continued to use the figure of Dionysus for his metaphysics of art[121] and although he moved the concept of appearance increasingly in the direction of his ethics of cruelty,[122] the importance of the concept of appearance as originally posited must be distinguished from this ideological alteration and its consequences for the history of reception of the concept. In order to maintain the aesthetic relevance of the concept of appearance under the changed condition of historical reflection, Nietzsche actualized his old metaphor of the "mask."[123] Just as the sublime developed from dread of the gods, whatever beauty remains for us develops from the enigmatic: the mask. The metaphor of the mask, we might say, becomes an ironic substitute for the pathos of appearance. "Mere appearance" is the reflection of a first appearance, as the mask reflects something that is a mere semblance: "the beautiful face of a mindless woman." It is clear that the concept of appearance has become even more radical in its aesthetic value than it had been in *The Birth of Tragedy*. Now no being is posited as the final ground of the mirrorings. Beauty and intellect are forever separated, logically and metaphysically. The beautiful appearance is here explicitly accepted as a "deception," and at the same time it is not discredited. The original operation, that of separating beauty from the concept of truth, has become still more aggressive.

Nietzsche rescued appearance, originally experienced and theoretically presented as the archaic-Dionysian epiphany of Greek tragedy, from truth by importing it as a theorem into historical consciousness. He was able to maintain the skepticism he had developed in his early essay, "On Truth and Lie in an Extramoral Sense," as the ultimate foundation of the concept of appearance. As he explained in that essay, there is no "real perception," no "adequate expression of an object in the subject," because "between two absolutely separate spheres, such as subject and object . . . , there is no causality, no correctness, no expression, but at most an *aesthetic* attitude."[124] This sentence can be rearranged to say that every aesthetic attitude can only be judged in itself, not by referring to something else. In other words, the aesthetic attitude is an "absolutely separate sphere." Nietzsche had a metaphor ready for this sphere, the revolutionary concept of appearance, which came to be the leitmotif of European decadence, most obviously in Oscar Wilde's essays "The Decline of Lying" (1889), "The Truth of Masks" (1891), and "The Sphinx" (1887–89).

Still, that does not mean that it is impossible to develop a theory of the model of appearance. Nietzsche's criticism of his early romantic version of the sudden proves how easily the model can be lifted out of its archaic context and placed into a modern one. He measures the chaotic, the revolutionary, the experimental element of late romanticism, the Dionysian, we might add, with the yardstick of the "ideal mask" of the literary age of Goethe.[125] This new concept of the mask or of the "ideal mask" contains the old meaning of appearance. For the "ideal mask" does not aim for "reality" but rather for "allegorical generality."[126] Historical characters and local color are "made mythical and moderated almost to invisibility"[127] in this generality. The "ideal mask," the "allegorical," thus has "mythic" quality. In distinction to the classical period, this "ideal mask" represents no idea, no metaphysical content, no reality; rather, it is the self-referential concept of form juxtaposed to an art of the present that is slipping into naturalistic subjectivity. Nietzsche thus holds on to an "objectivity" that already distinguished the Dionysian artist of *The Birth of Tragedy* from the subjective-romantic artist.[128] The new mythical aspect of the mask is different from the archaic-mythical in that the shudder at the gods is replaced by the shudder at *time* remembered backward. The structural similarity between this allegorical understanding of appearance in Nietzsche's later work and Benjamin's concept of allegory can only be briefly indicated here.[129] Whereas the concept of appearance in *The Birth of Tragedy* is closely linked with that of an emphatic present, the metaphor of the mask stands in no such relation, because the notion of the "twilight of art" implies the objective historical moment.[130]

In summary, we can say that the concept of appearance contains three dimensions with respect to historical time.

1. It is originally presented in a structure one of whose elements is mythical dread. However, this is not a necessary connection; it only provides an image for the necessary, that is, the epiphany of the aesthetic moment. The epiphany, the idea of appearance suddenly manifesting itself, plays a prominent role in the modern theory of art, especially in James Joyce and the surrealists.[131] The most clearly articulated opposing position in modern aesthetics is Brecht's theory of the "epic theater."

2. In the metamorphosis of archaic appearance to the mask, Nietzsche completes his turn to historical consciousness without sacrificing his theory of appearance. The concept of appearance is instead ironically radicalized to oppose literary, psychological, and cultural-critical realism, even to the point of becoming "illusion" or "deception." On the one hand, we can no longer think of a metaphysical referent in connection with appearance; on the other hand, the intensity of the aesthetic effect is heightened. The profundity of art consists in its lack of a ground or, as Nietzsche says, "Everything that is profound loves the mask."[132] The appearance— originally Nietzsche's hermeneutic insight for presenting the concept of aesthetic autonomy—expands in this process to become an aggressive symbol of the movement that has become known under the name aestheticism. This posthistory of the concept of appearance, which deserves its own study, should not be conflated with the question as to the structure of aesthetic surplus value, to which Nietzsche's model provides the most fruitful theoretical answer to date.

3. The concept of appearance is, finally, compatible with history, but its "phenomenal" character resists any temporal determination. That means, however, that Nietzsche decides the tension between nature and intellect in the concept of art in favor of nature.

NOTES

1. Translator's note: The German term is *Schein*, which connotes "mere appearance," "illusion," "semblance." I have usually rendered it as "appearance" except where the context called for distinguishing *Schein* from *Erscheinung*, "appearance," "phenomenon" or another closely related term. In those cases I have usually used "mere appearance."

2. Plato, *The Republic*, trans. Francis Cornford (Oxford: Oxford University Press, 1945), pp. 600d–601 and 604b–605c.

3. Hesiod, *Theogony*, trans. Richmond Lattimore (Ann Arbor: University of Michigan Press, 1959), p. 124. See Herbert Anton, "Minna von Barnhelm und Hochzeiten der Philologie und Philosophie," Sonderdruck aus *Neue Hefte für Philosophie*, 4: *Theorie literarischer Texte*, edited by R. Bubner, Konrad Cramer, Rainer Wiehl (Göttingen: Vandenhoeck und Ruprecht, 1973), pp. 78–79.

4. Wolfgang Franz Haug, *Kritik der Warenästhetik* (Frankfurt/Main: Suhrkamp, 1973), pp. 57–58.

5. Immanuel Kant, *Critique of Judgement*, trans. James Meredith (Oxford: Clarendon Press, 1952), p. 192 (I, § 53).

6. Friedrich Schiller, *On the Aesthetic Education of Man in a Series of Letters*, trans. Wilkinson and Willoughby (Oxford: Clarendon Press, 1967), p. 199.

7. Ibid., p. 197.

8. Schiller began to free himself from Kantian influences in the years 1794–95. The problem of aesthetic autonomy was then subordinated to his concern with the philosophy of history, see Rolf-Peter Janz, *Autonomie und soziale Funktion der Kunst: Studien zur Ästhetik von Schiller und Novalis* (Stuttgart: Metzler, 1973), pp. 61–62. See also Jörn Rüsen, *Ästhetik und Geschichte: Geschichtstheoretische Untersuchungen zum Begründungszusammenhang von Kunst, Gesellschaft und Wissenschaft* (Stuttgart: Metzler, 1976), p. 20. Rüsen suppresses the difficulties that Schiller had in these years with the aesthetic phenomenon in favor of a portrayal of Schiller's philosophy of history. He deals with the aesthetic problem only as part of the question of means in the historical process, that is, as an instance of reconciliation between nature as intelligible and as appearance (*Ästhetik und Geschichte*, p. 20). This approach obscures the problem of autonomy, of which Schiller was well aware, as we have demonstrated. It is as if Rüsen approaches Schiller as a philosopher of history and fails to see Schiller's dilemma as an aesthetician.

9. Schiller, *On the Aesthetic Education of Man*, p. 197.

10. All modern aesthetics of truth can be traced to Schiller's idea of art as a phase in the development from sensuous human being to moral

human being, which derives from his philosophy of history. See Rüsen, *Aesthetik und Geschichte*, p. 20.

11. Walter Benjamin, *Der Ursprung des deutschen Trauerspiels*, in Benjamin, *Gesammelte Schriften*, ed. R. Tiedemann and H. Schweppenhäuser (Frankfurt/Main: Suhrkamp, 1974), 1: 281.

12. Walter Benjamin, *Gesammelte Schriften*, 1: 831.

13. Georg Wilhelm Hegel, *Aesthetics: Lectures on Fine Art*, trans. T. M. Knox (Oxford: Clarendon Press, 1975), pp. 598–99.

14. Schiller, *On the Aesthetic Education of Man*, p. 57.

15. Hegel, *Aesthetics*, p. 599.

16. Plato, *Phaedrus [or On the Beautiful, Ethical]*, in *Plato in 12 Volumes*, trans. Harold North Flower (Cambridge, Mass.: Harvard University Press, 1914), 1: 485 (250b).

17. Ibid. (250b–c).

18. Ibid. (250d).

19. Ibid. (250d–e).

20. Ibid. (250e).

21. Ibid., p. 487 (251a–b).

22. Alfred Bäumler, *Das Irrationalitätsproblem in der Ästhetik und Logik des 18. Jahrhunderts bis zur Kritik der Urteilskraft* (Darmstadt: Wissenschaftliche Buchgesellschaft, 1975), p. 104, emphasizes this point. Bäumler correctly points to Winckelmann's "tact regarding what cannot be comprehended in beauty" (p. 106). In contrast to the classical reception of Winckelmann as an idealizing thinker, Bäumler notes the individualizing and psychologizing aspect of his interpretation of works of antiquity: "For beauty is one of the great secrets of nature, whose effect we all see and experience, but a universal, clear concept of whose essence remains an undiscovered truth." Bäumler's distinction between "effect" and "essence," with a slight favoring of effect for an empirical doctrine of art, is closer to the aesthetic theory of Nietzsche and the aestheticism of the late nineteenth century than to the aesthetics of German classicism (see J. J. Winckelmann, *Geschichte der Kunst des Altertums* [Darmstadt: Wissenschaftliche Buchgesellschaft, 1972], p. 139).

23. Kant, *Critique of Judgment*, p. 192 (I, § 53).

24. Friedrich Nietzsche, *The Birth of Tragedy* and *The Case of Wagner*, trans. Walter Kaufmann (New York: Vintage Books, 1967), p. 36.

25. Arthur Schopenhauer, *Die Welt als Wille und Vorstellung*, ed. Arthur Hübscher (Zürich: Diogenes Taschenbuch, 1977), pp. 439–40.

26. Ibid., p. 438.

27. Ibid., p. 439.

28. Friedrich Nietzsche, *The Will to Power*, trans. Walter Kaufmann and R. J. Hollingdale (New York: Vintage Books, 1967), p. 526.

29. Kant, *Critique of Judgement*, p. 191 (I, section 53).

30. Nietzsche, *The Birth of Tragedy*, p. 40.

31. Ibid., p. 80.

32. Friedrich Schlegel, *Das Gespräch über die Poesie*, in Schlegel, *Kritische Schriften*, ed. Wolfdietrich Rasch (München: Hanser, 1970), p. 502.

33. Gotthold Ephraim Lessing, *Hamburgische Dramaturgie*, in Lessing, *Sämtliche Werke*, ed. Karl Lachmann (Berlin, 1839), 7: 332; seventy-seventh essay.

34. Max Kommerell, *Lessing und Aristoteles: Untersuchungen über eine Theorie der Tragödie* (Frankfurt/Main: Klostermann, 1970).

35. Gotthold Ephraim Lessing, Moses Mendelssohn, Friedrich Nicolai, *Briefwechsel über das Trauerspiel*, ed. J. Schulte-Sasse (München: Winkler, 1972), p. 54.

36. Ibid., p. 55.

37. Ibid., p. 106.

38. Lessing, *Hamburgische Dramaturgie*, p. 332.

39. Nietzsche, *The Will to Power*, p. 449.

40. Ibid.

41. Nietzsche, *The Birth of Tragedy*, p. 84.

42. Hegel, *Aesthetics*, pp. 220 ff.

43. Ibid., p. 8.

44. Ibid.

45. Ibid.

46. Ibid., p. 9..

47. Ibid.

48. Ibid., p. 10.

49. Ibid.

50. Ibid.

51. Nietzsche, *The Birth of Tragedy*, p. 34.

52. Ibid.

53. Ibid., p. 45.

54. Ibid.

55. Ibid., p. 35. Translator's note: The German text calls Apollo *der Scheinende*; the German word *scheinen* can mean both "to shine" and "to appear."

56. Ulrich von Wilamowitz-Moellendorff, *Zukunftsphilologie! Eine Erwiderung auf Friedrich Nietzsches "Geburt der Tragödie"* (Berlin, 1872–73), 1: 11. See Martin Vogel, *Apollinisch und Dionysisch: Geschichte eines genialen Irrtums* (Regensburg: Bosse, 1966), p. 37ff.

57. See Vogel, *Apollinisch und Dionysisch*, p. 98. See also M. L. Bäumler, "Das moderne Phänomen des Dionysischen und seine Ent-

deckung durch Nietzsche," *Nietzsche-Studien*, Internationales Jahrbuch für die Nietzsche-Forschung 6 (1977): 123–53.

58. Nietzsche, *The Birth of Tragedy*, p. 35.

59. Ibid.

60. Ibid., p. 45.

61. Ibid., p. 49.

62. Ibid., p. 45.

63. Ibid.

64. In his book on Nietzsche, Heidegger points out this passage in the preliminary work for *The Birth of Tragedy* (1870–71): "My philosophy *topsy-turvy Platonism*: the farther I move from the truly existent, the purer, more beautiful, better it is. Life as illusion is the goal" (see Martin Heidegger, *Nietzsche* (Pfüllingen: Neske, 1961), p. 180). On the psychology of this passage see also Heinrich Niehaus-Pröbsting, *Der Zynismus des Diogenes und der Begriff des Zynismus* (München: Fink, 1979), p. 258.

65. Nietzsche, *The Birth of Tragedy*, p. 45.

66. Ibid.

67. See Gert Sautermeister, who takes *The Birth of Tragedy* as a kind of failed dialectic cultural theory. Sautermeister, "Zur Grundlegung des Ästhetizismus bei Nietzsche: Dialektik, Metaphysik und Politik in der *Geburt der Tragödie*," in Christa Bürger, Peter Bürger, and J. Schulte-Sasse, eds., *Naturalismus/Ästhetizismus* (Frankfurt/Main: Suhrkamp, 1979), pp. 224–43. Nietzsche later criticized his own work on tragedy as offensively Hegelian. That criticism was aimed not at its substance but at its modish tone (it "smells" of Hegelianism) (*Ecce Homo*, trans. Walter Kaufmann [New York: Vintage Books, 1969], p. 271).

68. Nietzsche, *The Birth of Tragedy*, p. 48.

69. Ibid., p. 49.

70. Ibid.

71. Ibid.

72. Ibid. Translator's note: Kaufmann's phrase is "the depth of his being." The German *Abgrund des Seins* seems to me more universal and less personal; hence the elision.

73. Ibid., p. 52.

74. See Ralf Schnell, "Die Zerstörung der Historie: Versuch über die Ideologiegeschichte faschistischer Ästhetik," in *Literaturwissenschaft und Sozialwissenschaften*. 10. *Kunst und Kultur im deutschen Faschismus* (Stuttgart: Metzler, 1968), pp. 17–55.

75. Nietzsche, *The Birth of Tragedy*, pp. 56–57. See also Sautermeister, "Zur Grundlegung des Ästhetizismus bei Nietzsche," pp. 235ff., and

Gert Mattenklott, "Nietzsches *Geburt der Tragödie* als Konzept einer bürgerlichen Kulturrevolution," in G. Mattenklott and Klaus R. Scherpe, eds., *Positionen der literarischen Intelligenz zwischen bürgerlicher Reaktion und Imperialismus* (Kronberg, Czech.: Scriptor, 1973), p. 110. Mattenklott, who emphasizes Nietzsche's elitist position and his hostility to the masses, also elaborates those aspects of Nietzsche's piece that are revolutionary in a cultural sense and do not look backward.

76. For an exhaustive treatment of the idea of tragedism, see Heinz Schlaffer, "Friedrich Hebbels tragischer Historismus," in Hannelore Schlaffer and Heinz Schlaffer, *Studien zum ästhetischen Historismus* (Frankfurt/Main: Suhrkamp, 1975), p. 130.

77. Burke, "A Philosophical Enquiry into the Origin of our Ideas on the Sublime and the Beautiful," passim. On the significance of the category of the sublime for the history of aesthetics, see Hans Robert Jauß, *Ästhetische Erfahrung und literarische Hermeneutik*, vol. 1 (München: Fink, 1977), pp. 119 ff.

78. Kant, *Critique of Judgement*, pp. 121–22 (I, §29).

79. Ibid.

80. Ibid.

81. Longinus, *On the Sublime*, trans. James Arieti and John Crossett (New York, Toronto: Edwin Mellen Press, 1985). I owe thanks to Heinrich Niehaus-Pröbsting for directing my attention to the rhetorical tradition and especially to the work of Longinus.

82. See R. Brandt, "Einleitung zu Pseudo-Longinos," in Pseudo-Longinos, *Vom Erhabenen*, German and Greek, ed. Reinhard Brandt (Darmstadt: Wissenschaftliche Buchgesellschaft, 1966), p. 11.

83. The passages from Longinus will be identified by chapter and section number in the following.

84. Klaus Dockhorn, *Macht und Wirkung der Rhetorik* (Bad Homburg: Gehlen, 1968), pp. 49ff.

85. Ibid., pp. 16, 64.

86. Ibid., pp. 51–52, 62–63, 64.

87. Ibid., p. 63.

88. Ibid., pp. 84, 80. Nietzsche's deviation from Idealistic aesthetics can be seen in the fact that Schiller's concept of the pathetic-sublime does not take up the rhetorical tradition. See Klaus L. Berghahn, "'Das Pathetischerhabene': Schillers Dramentheorie," in R. Grimm, ed., *Deutsche Dramentheorien* (Frankfurt/Main: Athenaeum, 1971), 1: 221 note 10.

89. Nietzsche, *The Birth of Tragedy*, p. 77.

90. Ibid., p. 108.

91. Ibid., p. 84.

92. Ibid. Nietzsche repeated this thesis later, in *The Case of Wagner*, and made it more precise: the Greek (Doric) word *drama* should be translated as "event." It has been a great misfortune for aesthetics that the term has always been translated as "action." Nietzsche, *The Birth of Tragedy* and *The Case of Wagner*, trans. Walter Kaufmann (New York: Vintage Books, 1967), p. 174.

93. Nietzsche, *The Birth of Tragedy*, p. 45.

94. Ibid.

95. Ibid., p. 60.

96. See Dockhorn, *Macht und Wirkung der Rhetorik*, p. 98.

97. Ibid.

98. Nietzsche's philological preoccupation with ancient rhetoric is well known. Hans Blumenberg sees in rhetoric the essence of Nietzsche's philosophy (Blumenberg, *Arbeit am Mythos* [Frankfurt/Main: Suhrkamp, 1979], p. 272). Niehaus-Pröbsting recently pointed out the rhetorical element (see Niehaus-Pröbsting, "Rhetorische und idealistische Kategorien der Ästhetik," thesis presented to the Paderborn Colloquium on Art and Philosophy, 1980, p. 25 note 21). On Nietzsche's relationship to rhetoric see Joachim Goth, *Nietzsche und die Rhetorik* (Tübingen: Niemeyer, 1970). Goth does not mention Longinus' possible influence. See also G. Rupp, "Der ungeheure Consensus der Menschen über die Dinge," *Literaturmagazin* (1979), 10: 179ff.

99. See also Brandt, "Einleitung zu Pseudo-Longinos," in Pseudo-Longinos, *Vom Erhabenen*, p. 24.

100. See also Blumenberg, *Arbeit am Mythos*, p. 661. Blumenberg emphasizes that Nietzsche does not justify the preeminent position of the Dionysian by claiming that it was the archaic mode.

101. See Bäumler, *Das Irrationalitätsproblem*, p. 29–30.

102. Nietzsche, *The Birth of Tragedy*, p. 36.

103. Ibid. p. 37.

104. In this context see also the section "Dream and Culture," in Friedrich Nietzsche, *Human, All Too Human*, trans. Marion Faber with Stephen Lehmann (Lincoln, Nebraska: University of Nebraska Press, 1984), pp. 19–20.

105. Schlaffer described this process using the example of Jacob Burckhardt. Schlaffer, "Jacob Burckhardt: Oder das Asyl der Geschichte," in Hannelore Schlaffer and Heinz Schlaffer, *Studien zum ästhetischen Historismus*, p. 96.

106. Nietzsche, *The Use and Abuse of History*, trans. Adrian Collins (Indianapolis, New York: Bobbs-Merrill, 1957), p. 40.

107. Heinrich Heine, "Verschiedenartige Geschichtsauffassung," in Heine, *Sämtliche Schriften*, ed. Klaus Briegleb (München: Hanser, 1971),

3: 19–23. Nietzsche's admiration for Heine revolves around his antihistorical "will to life" (see Nietzsche, *Twilight of the Idols,* in Nietzsche, *The Portable Nietzsche,* trans. Walter Kaufmann [New York: Penguin, 1954], p. 527). Nietzsche probably knew Heine's essay, which was first published in 1869 under the title "Letzte Gedichte und Gedanken von Heinrich Heine." The structure of Heine's idea of the present could hardly have escaped Nietzsche's hermeneutic instinct.

108. Nietzsche, *The Use and Abuse of History,* p. 8.

109. Ernst Bloch, "On the Present in Literature," in Bloch, *The Utopian Function of Art and Literature,* trans. Jack Zipes and Frank Mecklenburg (Cambridge, Mass.: MIT Press, 1988), p. 218. See also chapter 4 of this book, "The Fear of the Unknown."

110. Nietzsche, *The Use and Abuse of History,* p. 8. However, Nietzsche also recommends the single point to the person who wants to experience happiness on the threshold of the moment. Ibid., p. 6.

111. Ibid., p. 29.

112. Especially in "From the Soul of Artists and Writers," §§149, 155, 156, in Nietzsche, *Human All Too Human,* pp. 104–107. To be sure, Nietzsche also uses the concept of the sudden to characterize his favored art, like that of Bizet. See *The Case of Wagner,* p. 158. From that we can conclude that Nietzsche is not rejecting the temporal unit that the metaphor suddenly announces, but only its romantic or Wagnerian realization. In *The Will to Power,* Nietzsche defines the history of culture as an process of enlightenment in the sense of a "diminishing of this fear of chance, the uncertain, the sudden"(p. 527). This loss of primitivity arouses a need to enjoy the archaic version of the sudden in an aesthetic form (ibid.).

113. Nietzsche, *Human, All Too Human,* p. 42.

114. This distinction is crucial, because otherwise we are left with the false impression that Nietzsche distanced himself from his aesthetics of appearance and revised it in a positivistic direction when he distanced himself from Wagner and when he wrote his critique of late romantic art in *Human, All Too Human.* We do not agree with Ralph-Rainer Wuthenow, who assumes just such a self-correction, a renunciation of *The Birth of Tragedy* in light of the Hegelian philosophy of history (see Wuthenow, *Muse, Maske, Meduse, Europäischer Ästhetizismus* [Frankfurt/Main: Suhrkamp, 1978], pp. 41, 44).

115. Nietzsche, Preface to *The Gay Science,* trans. Walter Kaufmann (New York: Vintage Books, 1974), p. 38.

116. Nietzsche, *Human, All Too Human,* p. 15.

117. Ibid., p. 131.

118. Ibid.

119. Ibid.

120. Ibid.

121. Nietzsche, *Twilight of the Idols*, p. 560; *Ecce Homo*, trans. Clifton Fadiman, in *The Philosophy of Nietzsche* (New York: The Modern Library, 1954), p. 868.

122. The motif of cruelty is central to the literature of decadence. For further development of this idea, see Bohrer, *Die Ästhetik des Schreckens*, pp. 236, 252ff., 273.

123. On the motif of the mask in aestheticist literature see Bohrer, *Die Ästhetik des Schreckens*, pp. 31–32, 34. See also Wuthenow, *Muse, Maske, Meduse*.

124. Nietzsche, "Über Wahrheit und Lüge im außermoralischen Sinn," in Nietzsche, *Werke* (München: Hanser, 1966), 3: 317.

125. Nietzsche, *Human, All Too Human*, p. 136.

126. Ibid.

127. Ibid.

128. Nietzsche, *The Birth of Tragedy*, pp. 38, 48, 52.

129. Benjamin's theory of the allegory, which he developed in his work on the baroque tragedy, means that in the allegorical image of the baroque period the awareness of historical time and of the historical moment guarantees the place, beyond time, of death and nature in a reflexive sense, but also in a melancholy sense (see Benjamin, *Ursprung des deutschen Trauerspiels*, pp. 336–65). Applied to temporal categories, Benjamin also speaks of the "mystical moment" of the symbol and of the "contemplative" tension of allegories in which the "*facies hippocratica* of history appears to the observer as a frozen, primitive landscape" (ibid., p. 342). For Benjamin, the "allegory" is the sign for history as a "history of suffering" (ibid.). Nietzsche's "tragic" conception of existence is echoed in Benjamin's theory.

130. Nietzsche, *Human, All Too Human*, p. 137.

131. See chapter 9 of this book.

132. Nietzsche, *Beyond Good and Evil*, trans. Helen Zimmern, in *The Philosophy of Nietzsche* (New York: The Modern Library, 1954), p. 425.

7 | Nietzsche's "Madness" in a Cultural System

I. The Objectification of "Pain"

Pain is probably the most potent of all physical sensations, outweighing even pleasure. In section 13 of *The Gay Science*, Nietzsche writes about pain as a means of making others feel our power: "One hurts those whom one wants to feel one's power, for pain is a much more efficient means to that end than pleasure; pain always raises the question about its origin while pleasure is inclined to stop with itself without looking back."[1]

That is why some thinkers have considered pain an initiatory motive for acting and thinking. In other words, our fear of pain is greater than our anticipation of pleasure. Pain is thus from the beginning not merely a pointlike event in the body that our consciousness then registers as pain. Pain is preeminently a fact of consciousness. In the most extreme conditions of pain, the human being loses consciousness; extreme physical mutilations are felt as pain only afterward, not at the time when they occur. Moreover, the scientific physiology of pain was less well developed at the time of the "theology of pain" in the nineteenth century than it is today. More than anything else, pain is a threat that resides in time, which we would prefer to avoid at all costs. The most gruesome imagining of human fantasy is not death but the anticipation of death during torture. The elimination of torture by law has therefore been declared the decisive criterion of Enlightenment,[2] just as the description of torture, of harrowing pain, became a motif in the fantastic, quasi anti-Enlightenment literature, for example, in de Sade and Edgar Allan Poe.[3]

If pain was ever considered purely as a negative category of experience, one—like evil—to be avoided, then it was in the ideological alienation of affect of the Christian martyr, as *imitatio Christi*. In the nineteenth century this figure undoubtedly prefigured a suffering whose description in sensual terms could be integrated into culture only as an event of redemption. This prefiguration in the tortured, the crucified, the martyred individual in baroque tragedy of the modern understanding of pain as a mental event is joined by the precise analysis of the capacity of pain to intensify consciousness. In the context of the reflection of the ego and its narcissistic symbols in romantic literature (mirror, doppelgänger), cruelty turned against the self, the experience of pain, offers the possibility of the most intensive experience of the self. Like the glance into the mirror, which says "I" to itself and yet sees another physical entity, pain provides the peculiar experience of literally objectifying the self. The horrendous effect of the description of actual torture (the assassins of Louis XV) or fictional atrocities arises most often when the reader is told about the play of expressions on the face of the person who is observing his own torment. The final consequence of pain is mutilation, or in the case of being burned at the stake, complete disintegration, the annihilation of our physical identity. Pain is the highest index of our self-awareness in its transition to nonbeing, unless we deny, like Schopenhauer and his Indian mentors, any quality of being to physical existence.

From this horizon of the ideological integration of pain into nineteenth century culture, we can now investigate the genesis and structure of the experience of pain in Nietzsche's work—as an anticipation of his "madness." We know that we cannot equate this madness with his final collapse on January 3, 1889, not only because of Karl Jasper's much-needed corrections of the medical record[4]—in which he understood the "biological factor" in phenomenological terms and not merely as a symptom—but also because of our knowledge about the isolation of the social misfit.

Nietzsche wrote to his long-estranged friend Erwin Rohde, whom he saw as a typical representative of scientific reason, for the last time on November 11, 1887, a year before his collapse in Turin. His words give warning of the dangerous character of this calm as a decisive element of the so-called madman: "Who has ever been concerned for me with even the slightest degree of passion and pain! Has anyone had even an inkling of the real cause of my long sickness, whfor my sickness, which I may have conquered after all? I now have 43 years behind me andich I have perhaps mastered now, in spite of everything? I have forty-three years behind me, and am just as alone as when I was a child."[5] Six years earlier, on July 30, 1881, Nietzsche had written to another of his friends from his youth, who never in any way engaged him in a primary sense, the theologian Franz Overbeck. Nietzsche wrote that he had discovered Spinoza as a precursor and a thinker with whom he felt a spiritual kinship and continued: "*In summa:* my solitariness which, as on very high mountains, has often, often made me gasp for breath and lose blood, is now at least a solitude for two. Strange!"[6]

These words give us material to distinguish between "mad" and "not mad" or "premadness" and "period of madness." We may assume a trace of hubris in the "loneliness" letter of 1881, in which Nietzsche compares himself to Spinoza, but here it purports to be, and indeed is, pure objectivity. Then the exaltations of the so-called madness letters, which he signs as "Dionysus"[7] or "the Crucified"[8] and where he says "every name in history is I,"[9] are mad only according to our conventions. These choice self-stylizations are rather the correct words for a draft of himself that was developed much earlier, through the awareness of pain and the endurance of pain. In his letter of February 11, 1883, to Overbeck it is clear: Nietzsche will doubtless perish unless something happens. And then, finding a kind of comfort in a causal explanation, he writes that Europe is about to experience a terrestrial and climatic disturbance, which he, as a sort of seismograph, detects: "How can I help having an extra sense organ and a new, terrible source of suffering!"[10] He imagines the barrel of a gun and adds: "I have always been exposed to the cruelest coincidences—or, rather, it is I who have always turned all coincidence into cruelty."[11]

His search for a meaning of the pain, for a rewriting of the physiological suffering into a meaningful perception, into a deed, shows itself here in two ways. First, Nietzsche experiences himself as the recorder of a European weather condition. Second, he turns the chaotic, accidental aspect of his suffering into a "cruelty" of his own creation. That points us toward the motif that surfaces a few days later, in a letter of February 22, 1883, in his comments about his "sleepless, terribly tormented nights"[12] when drugs could not bring sleep. At the same time he also intensifies his suffering: "Ah, Nature equipped me fearsomely for self-torture."[13] This objectification of suffering, of raging pain, to a historic-symbolic event or a personal myth finds an almost prophetic expression in a letter to Overbeck dated April 14, 1887: "Given, I could soon die—and I do not deny a deepening desire for death—something would remain of me, a piece of culture that could never be replaced by any other."[14]

We must thus place the so-called hubris, which interpreters have called the index of his state of madness, in a much earlier period of the letters and include the bold, aggressive self-presentation of *Ecce Homo* here as well. On the other hand, we must see that hubris as a conscious stylistic means of ironic precision. We have to ask what value the symptomatology of the normal possesses. The answer would be that it is simply the language of the "kingdom of truth,"[15] which conspires against madness. Nietzsche unveiled that kingdom and Foucault, taking up his argument, accused it of repressive rationality.[16] This is not to trivialize the question of organic brain disease, but to set it aside as a problem that yields nothing for us. Then we can discover the real problem: madness as a sign that integration into the objective cultural system is no longer possible. It is impossible not just because the person who cannot be integrated contradicts the norm—as the classic heretic did who contradicted the system using its language— but because that person is no longer integrated into language itself and so slips away from us. An analysis of the language of *Zarathustra*, of *Ecce Homo*, and of the "madness letters" would let us comprehend this slipping as a state of being constantly ahead, which is aware of its own condition and comments on it emotionally. The various forms of intellectual laughter, which Nietzsche described in precise detail a few days before his collapse, had to be discussed with the ironic, burlesque wildness of the illuminated one—we can read all of that as the language of what is no longer heard and can no longer be heard by the existing culture. It is no surprise that even the youth movement of the 1890s misunderstood Nietzsche on a very naive level of "experience."[17] As a matter of interest, the way the youth movement integrated Nietzsche is a good example of the false integration through heretics. It is a false integration because these heretics after all spoke in the same language that they attacked and thus falsely romanticized Nietzsche; they failed to understand his actual protest.

Despite the distance between Nietzsche and the cultural system around him, he loved the culture, which is why he never lost touch with the educated friends of his youth. Those friends understood this relationship to his culture early on. Rohde probably saw it most clearly. After *Human, All Too Human* was published, Nietzsche's final break with Wagner and late romantic art, Rohde wrote Nietzsche on June 16, 1878, full of reproach: "Can you excise your soul and replace it with another? Instead of Nietzsche, now suddenly become Rée?"[18] A year later, however, on December 22, 1879, Rohde wrote again. He now noticed the distance between himself and Nietzsche and was no longer interested in a scholarly dispute, but was trying to save the "human element" in the relationship, a petit-bourgeois trait without any sign of the "class" that Nietzsche always noted as a criterion: "I can never lose you," Rohde wrote, "even if you climb the most distant intellectual mountain peaks."[19] He still pretends to understand the "torments" and to be suffering "sympathetic pain" and talks of Nietzsche's "shadow conversations" taking place "at such height and distance from everything personal."[20] But at bottom he means the opposite and expresses himself falsely, that is, conventionally. As if he were compelled to prove the truth of Nietzsche's distinction between the contemptible "scholar" who, as scholar, is never "personal," and the "philosopher" for whom "there is absolutely nothing impersonal,"[21] Rohde wrote about himself: "I'm moving along in the same track, as it happens with professors: we groan a great deal under our university burden, hardly ever manage to think of ourselves, and must finally understand that in any case we weren't really made for that. I am in very good health, and it's probably also healthy that my wife and child tie me closer to the earth."[22]

The distance, the isolation, the truth that Nietzsche probably was unable to speak with a single soul "personally" apart from his year with Paul Rée and Lou Salomé, allowed him to interpret his pain and suffering relatively early as a kind of badge of the elect and thereby enabled him to bear it better—or to bear it at all. The corresponding rhetorical figure would be that of self-stylization into the sublime. Before he could undertake such an interpretation and salvation of his isolation by reading it into the history of the spirit as he understood it, his rhetorical figures were mere stylizations. Nevertheless, their compulsion to identification is manifest very early, in a letter to Richard Wagner dated September 27, 1876, where Nietzsche asks about the limits of the pain he can bear.[23] He makes suffering into an "investigation" that proceeds "scientifically,"[24] a "study"[25] that repeats itself. He thus translates something he encounters more or less accidentally and whose precise course he cannot know into the language of law and structure. In a letter to Peter Gast dated September 11, 1879, he accepts the pain and his possible imminent death as a condition of his hidden "strengths."[26] Years later, he knows that a "transformation" is "happening"[27] in him, as he writes to Overbeck on February 14, 1884, and at the same time he does not know how he will endure the next moments. This strength to think while in pain allows Nietzsche always to give the pain names that cancel out its deadly effect as an alien enemy that wants to destroy him. A talent for objectivizing is not to be confused with reification.

Even hubris and loneliness change by this process from injuries to occasions for thinking beyond them: as he says, he has experienced contempt, suspicion, and ironic indifference, "all in the cruelest form."[28] And he adds: "Objectively viewed: it was highly interesting."[29] Just as sickness studied him, he studied sickness and loneliness, that is, he entered into a relationship with them that he could recognize in terms of his own premises, because it was a part of himself, no longer something foreign. That is the purpose of the metaphor of the "sick thinker," who can pass through the sickness. Three years before his great collapse, Nietzsche laid a foundation for the "sick thinker" as a figure in his theory of "pain." We must note the image of the "sick thinker" in the second piece of the preface to The Gay Science.[30] In the third section, Nietzsche introduces the concept of "pain." He speaks of "great pain" as the teacher of a "great suspicion," suspicion about the separation of soul and body, even soul and spirit:

> Only great pain, the long, slow pain that takes its time—one in
> which we are burned, as it were, with green wood—compels us
> philosophers to descend into our ultimate depths and to put aside
> all trust, everything good-natured, everything that would interpose
> a veil, that is mild, that is medium—things in which formerly we
> may have found our humanity. I doubt that such pain makes us
> "better"; but I know that it makes us more *profound*.[31]

We should emphasize that pain here is enjoyed as the brother,
the helper, so we can avoid seeing the complexity of Nietzsche's
enjoyment of pain as simple psychological masochism. His masochism, his tendency to "self-torture," as he puts it, is directed at pain
as an organ of revelation, a means to catch the "spirit *in the act.*"[32]
It is true—in addition to this intellectual justification—that motifs
of what we earlier called stoicism also play a role, a reaction to
positivistic science, socialists, politicians of all parties who—in
order to produce great pleasures—propagate a doctrine of least
possible nonpleasure, that is, painlessness. But suppressing the
human experience of pain also means suppressing the experience
of joy. Although Nietzsche defends this pain in section 12 of *The
Gay Science,* offering the prospect of a hedonistic goal,[33] the goal
is not hedonism but "new galaxies of joy,"[34] attained through pain,
as the suffering thinker may perhaps achieve the "voluptuousness of
a triumphant gratitude."[35] It is hard to say to what extent
Nietzsche consciously accepted the pain that visited him intermit-
tently from 1876 on—sometimes to the point of being unbear-
able—and gave it a new name, how often he saw himself as the
"man of sorrows," as the "dismembered Dionysus," as "the crucified." At any rate, he was ready in a naive, rather conventionally
reformulated way to endure everything for the sake of a soldierly
heroism. To consider suffering pain an achievement could obviously make him euphoric: "My spirit is to this moment not yet
bowed by the constant, painful suffering, sometimes it even seems
to me that I am more merry and benign than in my whole earlier
life."[36] This remark, written to Peter Gast on September 11, 1879,
shows a middle position of happy tolerance.

At the outset we spoke of pain as a motif in the literature of
the nineteenth century. We will not trot out literary history to
substantiate that claim here. A single reference is important, that
to Baudelaire. Nietzsche discovered Baudelaire relatively late and

did not immediately consider him a congenial spirit.[37] In the year
before his collapse, he wrote to Peter Gast (February 26, 1888)
about Baudelaire and his relationship with Wagner. He sees Baudelaire as someone who is sensitive in a Wagnerian sense as a decadent representative of high romanticism, as a "libertine, mystical,
satanic."[38] Nietzsche spoke admiringly of Baudelaire's diary, *Mon
coeur mis à nu,* and then dryly reported that Baudelaire, "that
bizarre three-quarter fool" and "the poet of the *Fleurs du mal,*"[39]
was treated with Wagner's music as medicine "in the last days of
his life, when he was half mad and was slowly declining."[40]
Nietzsche here takes a quasi-boyish tone, establishing a parallel in
German scholarly discourse to the language of a Prussian officer's
club, to distance the striking biographical parallels between Baudelaire's life and his own. We offer a concluding reference to Baudelaire's poetry of pain. Baudelaire, like Nietzsche, offered an ironic
commentary on the painlessness of modern civilization. He even
condemned the clinically irreproachable methods of contemporary
French executions with the argument that pain is the last expression of dignity.[41] The word *doleur* (pain) belongs, like *abîme* or
gouffre (abyss), to the central metaphors of the *Fleurs du mal* cycle.
The constellation of the person watching his own pain and the
person causing himself pain is contained in the poem "Heautonti-
moroumenos" (The Self-Executioner), a title reminding us of
Nietzsche's concept. Its final lines read:

> I am the wound, and yet the blade!
> The slap, and yet the cheek that takes it!
> The limb, and yet the wheel that breaks it,
> The torturer, and he who's flayed![42]

And in "Recueillement" (Meditation) Baudelaire directly addresses
"his" pain: "Be tranquil, O my sorrow (*douleur*), and be wise."[43] It
would be wrong to compare Nietzsche and Baudelaire. One was a
poet and prose writer, the other a philosopher although Thomas
Mann imposed the distorting term "cognitive poet" on him.[44]
Then, too, the experience and individual empirical psychology of
each man was very different. Baudelaire's experience of sexuality
and of the numb despair of everyday life in Paris[45] contrast with
Nietzsche's almost boyish naiveté in erotic matters[46] and with his
capacity and inclination for rapturous conditions in his thought,

as, for instance, while writing *Zarathustra* and while in a landscape he enjoyed as "sublime."[47] The absence of a great metropolis experienced as an alienating horror is as determinative factor for Nietzsche as its experience was constitutive for Baudelaire. Thus the metaphor of pain does not contain a psychological-empirical experience common to both men. Nietzsche sensed this and likely reacted to Baudelaire only through the mediation of Wagner. But certainly the language of both highlights the smile in the pain of consciousness. The contents of consciousness are different, but the isolation of someone no longer thinking in the terms of the cultural system is the same. What the two men share is their unwavering insistence on this consciousness; yet it results in forms of viewing pathos and the sublime, which contain the category of pain, that are different for each of them.

II. The Discourse of "Madness" as Method

Nietzsche mastered pain, as we have seen, by giving it names. He thereby transformed pain from unarticulated suffering or a mood that simply happened to him to an organ of his perceptual and intellectual system that could be described in structural terms. As an analogue to the various forms of distancing pain as a preparation and partial anticipation of madness, it now remains to examine this madness itself as it is objectified linguistically in order to understand it as a Foucaultian reversal of the "merciless language of non-madness." I would like to present this on two levels: first, using the example of the last of the so-called madness letters, the letter to Jacob Burckhardt dated January 5, 1889, in the context of the last phase of the letters in 1888 and its marked stylistic and metaphorical "peculiarities," to use the term for the behavior attributed to extreme or pathological states. We will see that we must relinquish the understanding of madness as a mere psychological or medical deviation and employ instead a phenomenological approach. Second, I will elucidate Nietzsche's use of madness for his critique of culture, using sections 14 and 18 of the first book of *Daybreak*. I will pursue alternative interpretations and will try to justify Nietzsche's identification with madness.

From the outset of our investigation, we are interested in a deeper truth inherent in this kind of delusion, a nondelusion or even an instance of the cunning of reason. Our heuristic point of departure, which takes madness to be a linguistic-imaginative construct, does not need to rely on recent psychiatric and anthropological research on the long since noted connection between madness and genius, between creativity and psychosis—any case, that would be something of a derivative procedure. Instead, we can use the evidence of a linguistic text that directly demonstrates the equivalence between madness and truth, the first text to subject madness to the modern suspicion of reason, a text that is central to our cultural discourse: Shakespeare's *Hamlet*.

Polonius' aside, "Though this be madness, yet there is method in't," (II, 2) provides the justification for our recurrent, and always forgotten, suspicion that madness is merely a mask and may well hide its opposite. Because of this early definition that has become part of our cultural knowledge the problem of feigned or real madness, in *Hamlet* or in Nietzsche, cannot be decided in favor of one of the alternatives, but we must consider them together. The *Hamlet* passage substantiates the dual aspect of feigned and real madness as a heuristically useful decision about how we moderns must now read the word *madness*. But that is not all. The analytical characteristics of Hamlet's language of madness, his "method," can also furnish a raster for reading Nietzsche's texts on perception.

Polonius suspects something, but he cannot verify his suspicion. His failure to understand Hamlet's words is the sign that Hamlet may be mad. This failure to understand is primarily due to two disruptions of normal linguistic communication inherent in Hamlet's way of speaking: (1) Hamlet gives unknown names to familiar people and objects, that is, he seems to create false identifications; and (2) he breaks through the conventional, superficial coincidence of word and meaning and thereby arrives at the formulation of a hidden problem that nonetheless transcends the conceptual horizon of the person he is conversing with. The alleged obscurity is in reality only laconic, highly logical compression. Hamlet calls Polonius a "fishmonger" (II, 2) creating the impression that he no longer recognizes the old man. In fact, Hamlet means to use that name to catch Polonius out as one who is dangling bait before him. Hamlet's term captures Polonius' present function precisely. Polonius fails to recognize this. He utterly misunderstands Hamlet's answer to his question: "What do you read, my lord?" Hamlet answers "Words, words, words." We should not call this threefold repetition of the concept "words" a profound answer; rather, it is the most precise answer. As Hamlet gives the simplest, first answer, which is misunderstood as a banality, he formulates an insight that transcends Polonius' understanding, namely, that we read "words" first of all that only gradually become a "something" for us. Words can be interpreted in a variety of ways; they require interpretation. Hamlet thus declares something written to be something in need of interpretation. Polonius' second question clarifies the nature of his failure to understand: "What is the matter, my lord?" Hamlet counters with a response that once again outstrips the understanding of his questioner: "Between who?" Hamlet's irony here targets not only Polonius' harmless, superficial interest in content and plot. His response indicates that language itself could act, that words could act, that is, that they do not passively transmit meaning.[48] Overlooking this indication of a problem from a manneristic linguistic consciousness, Polonius corrects his question to one that cannot be misunderstood—or so he believes. That is, he reduces it to its most banal version: "I mean the matter that you read, my lord." Hamlet reports on his reading at a level of allusion that Polonius understands to relate to himself. That brings him to the half-right conclusion: "Though this be madness, yet there is method in't." The problematization and correction of a falsifying everyday language are taken as an index of madness; Polonius does not recognize them as method. They are the logical elements of this method of madness. They also have an aesthetic side: the aesthetic value of wit—it is no accident that Hamlet calls himself a "jig-maker" (III, i)—that Freud mentions in his study of jokes, that is, the "similarity between dissimilar things," to the point of "bewilderment" and "illumination."[49]

Not only the "method" Polonius finds in Hamlet but also the madness must be characterized with regard to the emotional situation of Nietzsche's texts. That Hamlet is driven by a deep pain is directly stated in his "To be or not to be" soliloquy, and it is also the underlying tone of the melancholy knowledge that supplies the basis for his self-awareness. Hamlet has a kind of foreknowledge that causes him to speak truths to Rosenkrantz and Guildenstern that they cannot grasp: "You would play upon me; you would seem to know my stops; you would pluck the heart out of my mystery" (III, 2). Keeping his secrets, we might say, is the most intimate gesture of a person aware of his loneliness. Hamlet's aggression, his insults, his cynicism, and his scorn, directed in part against Ophelia, who should get herself to a nunnery, are like a scream.

The question whether Hamlet's madness is feigned or real is as old as the history of interpretation, and it is part of our European discourse on madness. The problem of madness, which finds a first modern structure and symbol in Hamlet, is insoluble. That very insolubility creates the precondition for a heuristic formulation of the problem that contains Nietzsche's case not merely as a derivation of intellectual history but also as a phenomenological fact. First of all, Franz Overbeck once said that he could not resist the idea that Nietzsche was always only acting his sickness.[50] A better approach than the "whether or not," which is unproductive for our interests, is to present the relationship between the later Nietzsche and men like Overbeck and Rohde as comic dialogue: Nietzsche as Hamlet, Overbeck and Rohde as Guildenstern and Rosenkrantz. What I mean is this: in the later years, when Nietzsche became so estranged from the friends of his youth,[51] his friends, on the one hand, make a kind of harmless effort to establish a relationship where there is nothing to which to relate; on the other hand, Nietzsche demonstrates the "objective" condescension toward his friends of someone who cannot share his "secret." If these unequal partners had actually faced each other in a dramatic situation, if they had acted, a comic dialogue would necessarily have resulted.

This situation is recapitulated in the so-called madness letters. Here, we have all the elements that could be called constitutive for Hamlet's "mad" speech: (1) the misleading naming, which then proves to create truth; (2) the logical superiority of compressed speech; (3) a sardonic laugh, the joke that emerges from pain.

1. When Nietzsche signs his late letters with "Astu," "the Crucified," or "Dionysus," he is merely giving a final name to what had long since been prepared as a self-interpretation, as an understanding of pain. The integration or distancing of pain into an organ of illumination or an index of its own role at a particular point in the new era[52] permit us to understand the identification with "God" or "the Crucified" or "Dionysus" merely as appropriate punch line. The assumption that Nietzsche actually, psychophrenically "confused himself" with God says little as soon as we have discovered the method in the madness of his language, which antedates the moment

of his collapse. In the same way, the (in any case acute) insight about his first influence as "the great *feuilletonist* of the *grande monde*"[53] is brought from absurdity into clarity by the remarks about contacts with Paris journalists[54] and the interest of important contemporaries like Taine and Strindberg in him,[55] an interest he registered with pride at the end of 1888. The psychological basis for this identification is prepared in the letter to Strindberg dated December 7, 1888: Nietzsche emphasizes his interest in crime—which at this late stage is comparable to Dostoevsky's interest in that subject—and justifies it with the intellectual and moral superiority of the criminal Prado to his judges.[56]

2. Logical compression is part of this tactic of giving names. The single sentence written to Georg Brandes on January 4, 1889: "Once you discovered me, it was no great feat to find me: the difficulty now is to lose me"[57] is itself a masterly expression of the dialectical process of interpretation. The Danish critic Brandes was one of the few intellectuals of the time who understood Nietzsche's significance; that understanding, however, plunged Nietzsche into new, private conflicts. The play on words that he makes with "discover" and "find" points to the problem of evaluation as anticipation, that is, of his own inner realization of something before it has become conceptually clear.[58]

3. Finally, the sardonic laugh, a tone of heartrending composure and grim humor and the morbid jokes also constitute Hamlet's style. That is also true of his calling attention to his own joking, the self-reflection of the "fool," and of the calculated aggression directed not only at individuals but at the world. Nietzsche's attack on Bismarck's son in the Foreign Office[59] was anticipated in the letter to Strindberg mentioned above, in which he speaks of a "declaration of war" against Bismarck himself and the young Kaiser,[60] in a sense crowning his attacks on the Germans of the Empire. In a letter to Peter Gast dated November 26, 1888, Nietzsche very precisely described the psychological cause that gives rise to the attitude, the compulsion, to laughter (interestingly, Gast did not include the letter in his edition of Nietzsche's letters to him): "I make so many silly jokes with myself and have such private

clownish ideas that I sometimes simply grin for half an hour on the public street; I know no other word for it."[61]

I will pass over the argument that every reference to time and place and every mention of daily habits in the last letter to Jacob Burckhardt has its own sense, and will summarize: The madness of the so-called madness letters does not help us prove anything about Nietzsche's psychopathic state at that time, which, in any event, is not at issue here. The vehement, appellative, sometimes excessive tone, including the structure of jokes at the expense of third persons, as well as the artistic compression and pointedness of long trains of thought—whether through an estranging process of naming or through a literally eccentric interpretation of the state of the world—this language represents the method in madness, which even the simple Polonius could not fail to recognize in Hamlet's case and which seemed "dangerous" to King Claudius.[62] Madness as a method is thus our thesis; we leave open the question of whether this is fiction or reality, feigned or actual madness. In his careful, intuitively certain evaluation, Karl Jaspers still noted critically a "lack of restraint" that "narrowed" Nietzsche's "vision."[63] In view of Nietzsche's early idea of a "narrowing" of the "horizon" in the creative moment,[64] Jaspers' criticism seems more the tut-tut of a cultural pedagogue than an exact description of this kind of language of madness. Such moral-scientific indignation in particular slights the relationship of madness to pain, which is a source of the wild rebellion that brings the rebel to the very boundaries of language. Here, too, we recognize in Hamlet's pain the prefiguration of the modern ultimate refusal and escape, a slipping away. That brings us to the question of Nietzsche's conscious reflection of madness, the question as to a possible theory of madness and its meaning in the "history of morality."

From the outset it should be clear that we cannot draw methodological conclusions from our analysis of actual madness or the language of madness as a method of gaining truth as though Nietzsche, because he suspected the nature of his own sickness, had also formulated an emphatic interpretation of madness in history. We even know that while Nietzsche thought of the possibility of a stroke, and imminent, sudden death, he never expected that he would go mad.[65] In any case, we have no need of such conclusions. In Nietzsche's work the figure of the madman always functions as the breaker of a cultural norms. We find variations of this type in the crazy man, the sick intellectual, the Dionysian ecstatic, and Zarathustra. The actualized core of meaning of the 1881 text of section 14, book 1, of *Daybreak* becomes clear through two perspectives: (1) In Nietzsche's work, unlike in Foucault's, the "madman" is not the "forgotten man." Foucault directly refers to Nietzsche's theory of tragedy in interpreting self-forgetting Western history in his foreword to *Madness and Civilization*.[66] (2) In equating the madman of antiquity with the innovative man in history, Nietzsche, as a thinker about creativity, announced from the beginning his interest in a possible model or cultural symbol.

Nietzsche's text is divided into two parts. In the first half, he describes how the new, deviant thought or idea is always "accompanied" by madness in prevailing over the "morality of custom."[67] He asks why it must be madness that breaks the spell of venerated customs and superstition, the very elements of traditional morality that Nietzsche battled against.[68] His answer: because the new can only be assimilated in the form of the archaic, of ritual, as mask of a divinity both for those who believe in the old and for the pangs of conscience of the reformers.[69] Nietzsche knew quite well that, as far as the knowledge the innovator has assimilated is concerned, even he lives from the old, from "custom," from the cultural norm, which conflicts with his new "evaluations."[70] The distinction between actual madness and merely feigned madness is unproductive for Nietzsche's assessment, a fact that logically follows from the ambivalence that marks the ancient innovator, placed between "custom,"[71] to which he constantly threatens to succumb, and his "drives"[72] to destroy it.

In contrast to Foucault, who tacitly cites this interpretation of madness in history throughout his work, by imitating it in its structural description though not in its application,[73] Nietzsche seems to locate the opposition in prehistory. The "new" fights not against the norms of the "kingdom of truth"[74] after the "zero point," as Foucault calls it;[75] rather, the new battles the terrible pressure of ritual in prehistory.[76] Then, however, Nietzsche takes the position that Foucault will also take: only in the prehistoric world could madness have a chance, as authenticity or as mask— the madman, in the time before history, was assumed to be a genius. Today the tables are turned: all geniuses must be mad.[77] This priority of prehistory over "world history" as regards "madness" is made more precise at the end of section 18 of *Daybreak*. Nietzsche anticipates Foucault's hermeneutic idea as to why it is almost impossible for us to empathize with those "tremendous eras of 'morality of custom' which precede 'world history.' "[78] Nietzsche explains that this time constitutes the "actual and decisive eras of history which determined the character of mankind."[79] And then follows the list of archaic qualities, including madness as divinity, change as immoral, and suffering as virtue, with the concluding point that precisely this archaic character is valid today as well.[80] This "optimistic" assessment of our cultural future that also, however, indicates a regression to our prehistoric fate, helps to illuminate the difficult second half of section 14. The following passage is controversial and problematizes the whole meaning of Nietzsche's representation of madness:

> Who would venture to take a look into the wilderness of bitterest and most superfluous agonies of soul in which probably the most fruitful men of all times have languished! To listen to the sighs of those solitary and agitated minds: "Ah, give me madness, you heavenly powers! Madness, that I may at last believe in myself! Give deliriums and confusions, sudden lights and darkness, terrify me with frost and fire such as no mortal has ever felt, with deafening din and prowling figures, make me howl and whine and crawl like a beast: so that I may only come to believe in myself! I am consumed by doubt, I have killed the law, the law anguishes me as a corpse does a living man: if I am not *more* than the law I am the vilest of all men. The new spirit which is in me, whence is it if it is not from you? Prove to me that I am yours; madness alone can prove it." And only too often this fervour achieved its goal all too well: in that age in which Christianity proved most fruitful in saints and desert solitaries, and thought it was proving itself by this fruitfulness, there were in Jerusalem vast madhouses for abortive saints, for those who had surrendered to it their last grain of salt.[81]

Two mutually exclusive interpretations are equally possible. In summary form, one interpretation believes that this passage distances the historically outdated type who merely feigns madness according to a script and has him speak ironically. The genuine "madman" and truly creative person is the subject of the final sentences mentioning "vast madhouses for abortive saints." Concerning actorlike character of the false "madmen" we could also refer to Schopenhauer's chapter on madness, a passage that, however, finally contradicts such a thesis. The madman as actor,[82] Schopenhauer argues, does not rely on a talent for deception but on a very different argument, which is interesting for the alternative interpretation of the Nietzsche passage. The madman as actor relies on the fact that actors destroy the identity of their memory; this results in incomplete memory, which is Schopenhauer's basic criterion of madness.

The other way of reading Nietzsche's passage takes the voices of the "solitary" and "agitated" minds as authentic descriptions of the "madman" though they are, to be sure, spoken through a mask; still, they are intended as descriptions with which Nietzsche identifies. With words and concepts that are to some extent identical, Nietzsche describes his own states of self-doubt, a description that is repeated in section 18 of *Daybreak*. There, in an unmistakable nod to his own, often bemoaned "tortures"[83] and his belief in himself,[84] he calls the heroic souls of the age of "custom" the predecessors of his own progress.[85] The phrase "belief in oneself" as a condition for surviving loneliness appears in Nietzsche's reflections and letters.[86] The "doubt" that is mentioned in section 14 has its counterpart in section 18: the belief in oneself[87] that is becoming difficult and the "pangs of conscience"[88] of the genuine innovators of prehistory. The argument introduced here, that even the innovators are beset with uncertainty about their "custom"-shattering deed, corresponds to the opposition of "doubt" and "law" in section 14.[89] This reflection provides the basis for the argument that Nietzsche is expressing his own renewed idea of "madness." The destructive self-criticism, the doubt whether he will be able to walk his lonely path, is here clothed in the mask of two pairs of concepts. There is another difficulty with this interpretation: How does the solitary know that he is more than the law and not the vilest of all men? Here is the answer: "The new spirit which is in me, whence is it if it is not from you? Prove to me that I am yours; madness alone can prove it."[90]

This passage is very ambiguous. On the one hand, the last sentence seems to say literally that only the evidence of madness itself points to a power that speaks through the "madman" and makes him more than the law. On the other hand, in view of Nietzsche's enduring, serious, and only gradually abandoned attempt to be understood with his shattered laws and norms, the reference to others cannot so easily be ignored. In his radical renunciation of norms, the reaction of humanity was something for which his growing uncertainties hungered. Therefore, I would like to take Nietzsche's view that "madness itself" is a criterion as a proposition that must constantly be renewed because it is always in jeopardy. That would also take account of Nietzsche's perspectivism, which impels him always to consider the opposite too. The duality between the evidence of madness and the reaction of the others is repeated over and over again.

In this actualization of the "madman" as a leading mythologem within the cultural revolution and as a method of achieving a new intellectual deed, purpose, goal—the sort of draft of a program that Artaud later realized in his idea of the "theater of cruelty," which Foucault mentions along with Nietzsche[91]—we are again reminded of the mode of the moment. The example of such a temporal modality of the sudden, the "lightning flash," can be found in *Zarathustra* as well as in *The Birth of Tragedy*. Because Nietzsche, after developing his theories of tragedy and of the foreshortened "horizon"[92] in *The Use and Abuse of History*, tried to conceive of the pure moment against the temporal structure of past and future—under the aesthetic category of "shock"—he was also able, in contrast to Foucault, to seek out the "madman" once again, in the present, in the now-point, in his "I."

Since that time, suddenness has been the mode of intellectual experience. Schopenhauer equated his "true health of the spirit"[93] with "complete memory."[94] Where this facility of memory fails, madness enters. Unlike Schopenhauer, Nietzsche—and this is the progressive, modern aspect of his thought—saw the creative element in the wholly reduced perspective on the "horizon."[95] In *The Birth of Tragedy* he lists the further attributes of this state, which Foucault later reiterates: dreams and ecstasies.[96] And the loss of memory is what influences our brain function in sleep, as Nietzsche writes in the section of *Human, All Too Human* entitled "Dream and Culture": "The utter clarity of all dream-ideas, which presup-

poses an unconditional belief in their reality, reminds us once
again of the state of earlier mankind . . . in our sleep and dreams,
we go through the work of earlier mankind once more."[97]

As Nietzsche formulates it, this variant of the moment, which
most closely approaches madness in the feature of loss of memory,
is a cultural "as if" situation. Nietzsche sees through its deception,
but takes it seriously and uses it as a symbol of our closeness to
prehistory, that is, to our elemental potential and duty. We will
merely note that Nietzsche, here and in the section called "The
Logic of Dreams," anticipates Freud's idea of "dream work," that
is, of the transportation of latent dream ideas into manifest dream
content. The systematic aspect is what is important for us, namely,
Nietzsche's cultural-revolutionary attempt to rescue the concept of
madness for a new culture as a further variation on the creative
moment. This perspective more clearly reveals the great distance
between Foucault and Nietzsche that is evident in Foucault's attempt to achieve the "zero point" of the history of madness through
a procedure of simulation comparable to Nietzsche's dream symbol.
Foucault merely approaches the "action"[98] of the separation of
madness, but Nietzsche actually repeats it or rather reconstitutes it
in himself. That does not refer to his biological breakdown but to
his language of madness as a language of wit. Nietzsche believes
that he can undo this forgetting, but Foucault makes clear why that
is no longer possible today. From the outset Foucault's melancholy
hermeneutic consciousness concerning what we can know about
madness is aware that long ago we tamed the madness whose
wildness we try to understand.[99] Still, Foucault's point means that
the Enlightenment and rationalism were a high point of regressive
rationality, that is, of the "merciless language of non-madness,"[100]
and that this language continues on and on. Foucault's question
about the "structure of rejection,"[101] as he calls it, also amounts to
the formulation of the conditions under which one could draft a
new theory of culture or live a new culture. Through Foucault's
pointed questions we learn to pose our own question about whether
Nietzsche was the victim of an illusion he could maintain only
because he refused to look for a real historical-theoretical foundation and instead consistently and instinctively insisted on an aesthetics with which the avant-garde of the modern period—or at

least its imaginative wing—consciously or not, long kept its head above water in its epistemology. This avant-garde added nothing new to Nietzsche's undertaking. Its aporia was the same aporia Nietzsche had already confronted.

That aporia is clearest if we compare Nietzsche's conception of the madman and of the archaic period with that of his student Foucault:

1. The "madman" for Nietzsche is not the forgotten one but rather the innovator. He is brought back into history. For Foucault, the madman is the ineffectual heretic in a yet-to-be-written history of heresy. Foucault has something of a "sentimental" relation, in Schiller's sense, to the "madman"—his method is scientific and analytical. Nietzsche has a naive relationship to the "madman"—he identifies with him emotionally.

2. For Foucault and Nietzsche, Western history is a history of the rejection of tragedy. Foucault adopted this central idea from *The Birth of Tragedy*. The "birth of history," according to Foucault, is the "death of tragedy."[102] In contrast, Nietzsche believed that it was possible to revive both tragedy and madness as aesthetic consciousness. Foucault thinks in terms of the hermeneutic situation of the modern scientist: we necessarily belong to a world that has already captured the untamed state it tries to comprehend.[103] It is a repetition of the classic parable of the lost innocence of consciousness, which Schiller and Kleist wrote for the first time.

3. For Nietzsche, the reduction of historical consciousness to a foreshortened "horizon" constitutes a kind of hermeneutic model to reiterate the tragic or mad human being. For Foucault all that remains is the chance of understanding how the hegemony of reason over madness was achieved. He is interested in the "zero point," the caesura between reason and nonreason[104] and expresses that interest in his question of what we can know about madness.[105] It is a Nietzschean element that Foucault is not interested in a history of knowledge or in the process of truth in history but in the "gesture" with which madness was once separated out, that is, in the structure of rejection itself. Our culture can be understood

only in this "gesture" of "rejection."[106] There is no rationality without madness. In contrast to the dialectical reflections of Adorno and Horkheimer on the relationship between Enlightenment and myth— which defuse the problem known since Nietzsche and reduce to its current conceivability— Foucault's presentation is fundamentalistic. In rejecting from the outset the obligatory paradigm of reason and hence also a category of telos-oriented history, Foucault takes the "gesture" itself seriously again. That correlates with his attention to suddenly temporalized time,[107] which Nietzsche already saw in the sublime "moment" of madness or of the person in aesthetic rapture: as appearance and as the "point" to which the "horizon" is foreshortened.

NOTES

1. Friedrich Nietzsche, *The Gay Science*, trans. Walter Kaufmann (New York: Vintage Books, 1974), p. 86.

2. See Karl Heinz Bohrer, *Die Ästhetik des Schreckens: Die pessimistische Romantik und Ernst Jüngers Frühwerk* (München: Hanser, 1978), p. 459.

3. Ibid., pp. 173–74; 235–36; 256–57.

4. Karl Jaspers, *Nietzsche: Einführung in das Verständnis seines Philosophierens*, 3d ed. (Berlin: de Gruyter, 1950), pp. 91–92.

5. *Selected Letters of Friedrich Nietzsche (Letters)*, trans. Christopher Middleton (Chicago: University of Chicago Press, 1969), p. 276.

6. Ibid., p. 176.

7. Ibid., p. 346.

8. Ibid., p. 345.

9. Ibid., p. 347.

10. Ibid., p. 206.

11. Ibid., p. 207.

12. Ibid., p. 209.

13. Ibid.

14. *Nietzsches Briefwechsel mit Franz Overbeck*, ed. R. Oehler and C. A. Bernoulli (Leipzig: Insel, 1916), p. 375.

15. See Michel Foucault, *Madness and Civilization*, trans. Richard Howard (New York: Vintage Books, 1965), p. ix.

16. Ibid., pp. x–xi.

17. Ludwig Klages, *Die Psychologische Errungenschaften Nietzsches* (Leipzig: Barth, 1926), p. 11.

18. *Nietzsches Briefwechsel mit Erwin Rohde*, ed. Elisabeth Förster-Nietzsche and Franz Schöll, in Nietzsche, *Gesammelte Briefe* (Berlin and Leipzig: Insel, 1902), p. 544.

19. Ibid., p. 552.

20. Ibid.

21. Friedrich Nietzsche, *Beyond Good and Evil*, trans. Helen Zimmern (London: Allen & Unwin, 1967), pp. 11–12.

22. *Nietzsches Briefwechsel mit Rohde*, p. 554.

23. Nietzsche, *Letters*, p. 148.

24. Ibid.

25. Ibid.

26. Nietzsche, *Briefe*, in Nietzsche, *Werke in drei Bänden*, ed. Karl Schlechta (München: Hanser, 1966), 3: 1157.

27. *Briefwechsel mit Overbeck*, p. 242.

28. Ibid.

29. Ibid.

30. Nietzsche, *The Gay Science*, p. 34.

31. Ibid., p. 36.

32. Ibid., p. 34.

33. Ibid. pp. 86–87.

34. Ibid., p. 87.

35. Ibid., p. 34.

36. Nietzsche, *Briefe*, 3: 1157.

37. On Nietzsche's acquaintance with Baudelaire, see Karl Pestalozzi, "Nietzsches Baudelaire-Rezeption," *Nietzsche-Studien* 7 (1978): 159ff.

38. Nietzsche, *Briefe*, 3: 1280.

39. Ibid.

40. Ibid., p. 1281.

41. Charles Baudelaire, *Mon Coeur mis à nu*, in Baudelaire, *Oeuvres complètes* (Paris: Pléiade, 1961), p. 1278.

42. Charles Baudelaire, *Flowers of Evil*, ed. Marthiel Mathews and Jackson Matthews (New York: New Directions, 1955), p. 69.

43. Ibid., p. 155.

44. Thomas Mann, "Vorspruch zu einer Musikalischen Nietzsche-Feier," in Mann, *Altes und Neues: Kleine Prosa aus Fünf Jahrzehnten* (Frankfurt/Main: Fischer, 1953), p. 260.

45. See Pascal Pia, *Charles Baudelaire in Selbstzeugnissen und Bilddokumenten* (Hamburg: Rowohlt, 1958), pp. 31, 75–76.

46. See the correspondence between Nietzsche and Lou Salomé and Nietzsche's courtship letter to Mathilde Trampedach dated April 11, 1876. Nietzsche, *Briefe*, in Nietzsche, *Werke*, 3: 1117–18.

47. Descriptions of nature in Nietzsche's work and recurrent indica-

tions in his letters point to the physiological and psychological healing that the mountain and forest landscape effects.

48. Translator's note: This interpretation depends on the German text, in which Polonius asks "*Aber wovon handelt es?*," i.e., literally, "but what is the subject matter," "what is it about?" Hamlet replies, "*Wer handelt?*" "who acts?" The German word play depends on the double meaning of the verb *handeln*, "to act" or (with *von*) "to deal with," "be about," whereas the English depends on two readings of the word "matter."

49. Sigmund Freud, *Jokes and Their Relation to the Unconscious*, in Freud, *The Complete Psychological Works*, trans. James Strachey (London: Hogarth Press, 1960), 17: 11–12.

50. See J. P. Stern, *A Study of Nietzsche* (London: Cambridge University Press, 1979), p. 33. Stern, as far as I know, is the first scholar to relate the figure of Nietzsche to Hamlet in terms of cultural physiognomy. However, he did not address the problem of madness.

51. See Jaspers, *Nietzsche*, pp. 87–88.

52. See the letter to Franz Overbeck written two months before Nietzsche's collapse, on October 18, 1888, in Nietzsche, *Selected Letters*, p. 314. See also the letter to Georg Brandes dated November 20, 1888, ibid., p. 326.

53. In the letter to Jacob Burckhardt dated January 6, 1889, ibid., p. 347.

54. Letter to Meta von Salis dated December 29, 1888, ibid., pp. 342–43.

55. Letters to Franz Overbeck dated November 13 and November 29, 1888, ibid., p. 322 (November 13); *Nietzsches Briefwechsel mit Franz Overbeck*, p. 446 (November 29). Also letters to Peter Gast dated December 9 and 16, 1888. Nietzsche, *Selected Letters*, pp. 331, 333. Also letter to Meta von Salis dated December 29, 1888, ibid., pp. 342–43.

56. Letter to August Strindberg dated December 7, 1888, ibid., pp. 328–30. Translator's note: Prado was a Spanish subject who had been living in France and was tried for theft in Paris in 1888. Under cross-examination, his cohabitant accused him of murdering a prostitute, a charge that proved to be true. Prado was sentenced to death.

57. Ibid., p. 345.

58. See chapter 2 of this volume.

59. Letter to Jacob Burckhardt dated January 6, 1888. Nietzsche, *Selected Letters*, pp. 346–48.

60. Letter to Strindberg dated December 7, 1888, ibid., p. 330.

61. Quoted in Jaspers, *Nietzsche*, p. 84.

62. "The terms of our estate may not endure/ Hazard so dangerous as doth hourly grow/ Out of his lunacies." *Hamlet*, III, 3.

63. Jaspers, *Nietzsche*, p. 106.

64. See the discussion of Nietzsche's idea of the "horizon" in chapter 6 of this volume.

65. See Stern, *A Study of Nietzsche*, p. 33.

66. Foucault, *Madness and Civilization*, p. xi.

67. Nietzsche, *Daybreak*, trans. R. J. Hollingdale (Cambridge: Cambridge University Press, 1982), p. 13.

68. Ibid., p. 14.

69. Ibid.

70. Ibid., p. 13.

71. Ibid.

72. Ibid.

73. Translator's note: Richard Howard translated an abridged version of Foucault's *La folie et la deraison* as *Madness and Civilization*. This phrase seems to belong to the omissions.

74. Ibid., p. ix.

75. Ibid.

76. Nietzsche, *Daybreak*, pp. 14, 17.

77. Ibid., p. 14.

78. Ibid., p. 17.

79. Ibid.

80. Ibid.

81. Ibid., pp. 14–15.

82. Arthur Schopenhauer, *Die Welt als Wille und Vorstellung*, in Schopenhauer, *Werke* (Zürich: Diogenes, 1977), 4: 473.

83. Nietzsche, *Daybreak*, p. 17.

84. Ibid.

85. Ibid.

86. See, in Nietzsche, *Selected Letters*, letter to Overbeck dated summer 1883 (pp. 214–16); letter to Peter Gast dated August 14, 1881 (p. 178–79).

87. Nietzsche, *Daybreak*, p. 17.

88. Ibid.

89. Ibid., p. 15.

90. Ibid.

91. Foucault, *Madness and Civilization*, p. xi.

92. On Nietzsche's idea of the "horizon," see chapter 5 of this volume.

93. Schopenhauer, *Die Welt als Wille und Vorstellung*, p. 472.

94. Ibid.

95. See chapter 5 of this volume.

96. Friedrich Nietzsche, *The Birth of Tragedy out of the Spirit of Music,* trans. Walter Kaufmann (New York: Vintage Books, 1967), p. 38.

97. Friedrich Nietzsche, *Human, All Too Human,* trans. Marion Faber, with Stephen Lehmann (Lincoln: University of Nebraska Press), p. 20.

98. Foucault, *Madness and Civilization,* p. ix.

99. Jacques Derrida criticized this aporia in Foucault's undertaking as not being thought through. Derrida, *Writing and Difference,* trans. Alan Bass (Chicago: University of Chicago Press, 1978), pp. 44 ff.

100. Foucault, *Madness and Civilization,* p. ix.

101. See note 73.

102. See note 101.

103. See note 101.

104. Foucault, *Madness and Civilization,* p. ix.

105. Ibid.

106. See note 101.

107. In the foreword to the English edition of *The Order of Things,* Foucault discusses the suddenness with which "certain sciences were sometimes reorganized" (Michel Foucault, *The Order of Things* [New York: Pantheon Books, 1970], p. 12). He emphasizes that these changes must be examined more closely "without being reduced, in the name of continuity, in either abruptness or scope" (ibid.). He also defends himself against the charge that "this work denies the very possibility of change" (ibid.).

8

The Emphatic Moment and Suicide: On the Motif of Suddenness in Heinrich von Kleist

I. Celebration of Death or Suicide

Early death and romantic literature have been coupled since early European romanticism joined them. In literature we associate the longing for death with the names of the English poets Keats, Shelley, and Byron, and with the names of the German poets Novalis, Hölderlin, and Kleist. The motif of death not only plays a prominent role in their poetry—they all also died young, most of them in their twenties. Byron, the oldest, was thirty-five when he died. With their double affinity for death they created a revolutionary cultural and literary tradition. The unholy, unusual writers of the nineteenth century followed that tradition: Büchner, E. A. Poe, Baudelaire, Rimbaud.

However close and noncoincidental the link between death and literature has become since the early nineteenth century, however much his own anticipated death became a sign and a weapon of the bourgeois artist—Rimbaud described himself as a literary suicide—the only genuine suicide among these many death-driven writers was the Prussian noble, officer's son, and sometime officer himself, Heinrich von Kleist. In November of 1811, Kleist, age thirty-four, carefully planned and almost staged a death scene on the shore of the Wannsee outside Berlin. He shot Henrietta Vogel, the terminally ill woman he had enthusiastically befriended, and then he shot himself. Kleist thus followed in the footsteps of the seventeen-year-old English poet Thomas Chatterton, whose suicide had made him a literary myth for English romanticism and aesthetics.

Chatterton created for the following era the vision of suicide as a sublime act. Germany had an analogous figure in Goethe's Werther, but regardless of his effect on imitators, Werther was, after all, purely fictional. A more telling distinction is that the motif of sensibility draws a clear boundary between suicide because of unrequited love and the kind of suicide we mean here, which we will for now call, in analogy to the "art for art's sake" of European aestheticism, suicide for suicide's sake.

It is undisputed that this is Kleist's case. Kleist staged the deaths of himself and his partner in such a way—including the final positioning of the corpses[1]—that this act has been called, without cynicism, his "last literary work."[2] Twenty years later, Marie von Kleist described a farewell letter from Kleist that has since been lost: "There has never been such poetry as in his letter."[3] That also characterizes the extant farewell letters we do know. We find verification of a general death wish in Kleist's correspondence very early, as early as 1801–1802.[4] The first concrete announcement of suicide follows, in his famous letter to his half-sister Ulrike dated October 26, 1803.[5] This early letter, and the suicide games and pacts that have been handed down to us, all these ways of looking forward to his own death not only as a release from earthly woes but as a fascinating goal, anticipate in language, argument, and rhetorical formulas the final announcements of his suicide in the letters to Ulrike and Marie von Kleist.

We can sum up the matter as follows: Kleist's suicide on November 21, 1811, was not only announced over a period of at least ten days before the suicide and justified in literary prose that alternates between depression and exaltation; it had already been announced ten years earlier. The linguistic-imaginative anticipation that occurred a short time before the day of the suicide actually presents a structural identity across a larger unit of time.

We are not inquiring into Kleist's suicide in the sense of looking for an autobiographical cause for a catastrophe that might have been avoided. If there is an autobiographical explanation where there are so many motives—in his well-known letter to Marie von Kleist dated November 19, 1811, Kleist names the lack of recognition in his own life and the alliance between the Prussian King and the French[6]—then we should not look for it, as so many have, in Kleist's "existential" situation but rather in his hopeless social and economic position after the demise of the periodical *Berliner Abendblätter,* which he had taken on only a few months earlier.[7] It is the same misery that drove the starving Chatterton to his death. In both cases the government censors suppressed and finally destroyed the writer's journalistic existence. But this autobiographical reference, which is most convincing because it immediately illuminates the situation of the alienated author, still does not explain Kleist's suicide. The argument of social hard times plays no role in the early anticipations of suicide; those were characterized by joyous rapture—it occupies the central place in the farewell letters of November 9 or 19, 20, and 21, 1811.[8] We could agree with Erich Heller that "Kleist was in love with death," and that would leave us with just another metaphor located indecisively between psychology and cultural anthropology. The problem also cannot be solved with the aid of psychoanalytical analogies, as A. Alvarez has shown. For whatever psychosomatic anomalies we might name to explain the lifelong longing for death *à deux* as a flight from the problems of sexuality or as a deficit in sexual contact[9]—there remains the actual, irreducible core, namely, the language of suicide itself, which is very difficult to determine.

If we take Kleist's suicide seriously, not as a literary act but as the last link in a chain of imaginative acts, then the best approach is to investigate when and how the suicide is prepared in his work. We are not looking for a mysterious complex of motives that caused Kleist to commit suicide; instead, we are looking for the relevant motif of a prose of suicide. We omit the language of his dramas, because we would like to view the problem as unemphatically and prosaically as possible. We start with the assumption that the language of prose and the language of the drama are fundamentally different even when their terminology concerning the concept of death is similar. We privilege Kleist's prose all the more in our inquiry because literary studies of his work have dealt with the motif of death, primarily in *The Prince of Homburg,* but not with the fact of suicide as a problem of Kleist's artistic existence. To emphasize the rapture of death in *Penthesilea* or in *The Prince of Homburg* implies excessive emphasis on the theme, which we would like to avoid.[10]

Kleist scholarship, which has generally focused on his worldview and metaphysics, has not been able to maintain a consistent position on his suicide, neither in its methodology nor in its content. Suicide was a forbidden topic, something immoral, indecent, even obscene, and could only be accepted categorially in its transcendent form as something "absolute" or "existential." This reformulation of a destructive act into a heroic or existential celebration of death was all the easier because Kleist's farewell letters consciously seek the aesthetic category of the sublime, even through their language. They thus provide a conciliatory, cultural-philosophical context. The example of the motif of wings[11] points to the roots of the idea of a reconciled death in the Enlightenment, an idea Kleist knew both from Kant and from Lessing. The most important work in this context is Lessing's essay "Wie die Alten den Tod gebildet" (How the ancients represented death). Death is not to be imagined as a skeleton, as Lessing's opponent in that art-historical and aesthetic debate maintained, but rather like sleep, as a young spirit with wings and an inverted torch. "Being dead is nothing frightful: and inasmuch as dying is merely the step toward being dead, dying cannot be frightful either."[12] This image of death as the gentle brother of sleep coupled with the idea of a perfection of the human being after death, which Kant and the Enlightenment philosophers developed, play an important role in the ideological preparation of Kleist's idea of suicide. He wrote Marie von Kleist the famous sentence about the "triumphal song that my soul begins to sing in this moment of death,"[13] and had the Prince of Homburg say: "Now, Immortality, you are all mine. . . . Wings sprout from both my shoulders, my spirit floats through quiet spaces of ether."[14] A letter from Kleist to Ulrike on the day of his death speaks of "inexpressible merriment,"[15] similar to his feelings when, ten years earlier, on December 23, 1801, he took his leave not from life but from the friend of his youth, Lohse, writing that he felt "so peaceful, so affectionate, as if I were near the hour of my death."[16] In that earlier letter, however, Kleist relativized his words as those of a "stupidly overstressed spirit,"[17] as if commenting for outsiders on the unmotivated extravagance of his emotions. Alvarez reminds us that Montesquieu had already noted the link between joy and suicide when he complained that suicide was often performed, for reasons that he could not explain, in "the very bosom of happiness."[18]

In search of the relevant motif in Kleist's language, we will have to decide between the contemporary selection of norms, that is, the enlightened, eudaimonistic philosophy of death, and Kleist's own incommensurable, deadly word. In his essay "Mourning and Melancholia," written seven years after the Viennese Psychoanalytic Society's symposium on suicide, Freud first developed the mechanism of the "enjoyable" "self-tormenting" of melancholy to the point of suicide. He also mentioned the tendency of melancholy "to change round into mania—a state which is the opposite of it in its symptoms."[19] Part of the normal manifestation of mania, however, is the state of "triumph,"[20] a key word in Kleist's farewell letters. According to Freud, "mania is nothing other than a triumph of this sort, only that here again what the ego has surmounted and what it is triumphing over remain hidden from it."[21] Kleist's early reference to his being overstressed, quoted above, reveals more knowledge of the psychic mechanism than an interpretation of "death" that is interested merely in intellectual history. Goethe's simplistic, although defensive, judgment that Kleist's language aims at a "confusion of feeling" is certainly more accurate than interpretations using concepts of modern existence. For interpretations that celebrate Kleist as a modern writer unintentionally reduce that "confusion of feeling" too quickly to a metaphysics of the ego—an ego that replaces God, history, and society and is thus conceived of as a substance, which in turn cancels out the "confusion." The attempt to explain Kleist's attitude with reference to his various crises, particularly the so-called Kant crisis, whose role, according to recent studies, has been exaggerated,[22] also errs in tracing the Kleistian element of destruction we are looking for too quickly to an educational experience. Kleist, however, was "without ideas," as Erich Schmidt put it, because he was concentrated in the most intense way.[23]

Our interest in the element of destruction mistrusts an understanding of literature that secretly turns literature into a help with the problems of life, that misuses the author as a producer of meaning, and that creates emotional identifications between the artist understood as a hero and the reader looking for a model. Where better to give the lie to this false meaning and to the rash enlisting of literature as a help in coping with life than here, where literature becomes a preparation for suicide? When we emphasize suicide, we oppose the transfiguring subsumption of literature into the "Absolute": as Camus wrote, "An act like this is prepared within the silence of the heart, as is a great work of art."[24]

For these reasons, we will leave behind the harmonizing system that distorts suicide through intellectual history or existential approaches and instead keep to the original, brutally expressed affect of Achim von Arnim, who wrote to the brothers Grimm after Kleist's death and after reading the second volume of Kleist's stories: "It is a death like Wolfdietrich's, when the skeletons of all those he had slain beat him to death."[25] That is a first hint for our cause, namely, seeing Kleist's suicide prepared in his prose, a prose that is murderous because the most horrible things are narrated calmly, coldly, from a distance, allowing us to suspect a hidden complicity on the author's part.

II. The Rhetoric of Paling

The "enjoyable self-tormenting," as Freud characterized the melancholic's state,[26] was nowhere else in the literature of the nineteenth century anticipated as clearly as in Kleist's prose. Cruelty as pleasure, this suicidal affinity, is the link between two polar emotions characterizing all of Kleist's stories. Kleist was well aware of the unique ambivalence of his feelings when he spoke of the simultaneous "filth and radiance of my soul."[27] The cruel character of his prose is already evident in the plot, especially at the end of each story. Strangely enough, this fact is not at all emphasized in Kleist scholarship—something that can perhaps be explained by the preponderance of the metaphysical questions we have already noted. Throughout Kleist's stories we find murders, executions, massacres. In "Michael Kohlhaas," the sentence of drawing and quartering and being broken on the wheel is transformed into beheading; in "Earthquake in Chile" a burning at the stake becomes a beheading, and in place of the beheading we have a sadistic bloodbath; the "Engagement in Santo Domingo" contains yet another description of an execution and ends with the hero's suicide after he has killed his lover. In "The Duel" the heroine's death by burning is anticipated and the duel is fought in a particularly gruesome way. "The Foundling," finally, ends with the hero's execution by hanging after he has killed someone else.

The author's obsession with execution, murder, and mayhem is not explained by the genre of criminal fiction, as in the case of Edgar Allen Poe, whose work shares some features with Kleist's. Instead, Kleist alters the type of the detective story that poses riddles, which has been taken as the "prototype for all of Kleist's novellas,"[28] in favor of a concentration on psychologically unusual events. That means, however, that the cruelty in Kleist's stories, and the accompanying motif of death are independent of the facts of the crime; both have a high degree of structural autonomy. Death, murder, and, as we will see, suicide are the extremes within a system of diametrically opposed, highly emotional states. We maintain, therefore, that suicide and murder are only especially heightened levels of these states. Without an intellectual superstructure, we cannot see a basic difference between Kleist's use of these states and Poe's pathological fixation on death.

Before we approach these states, especially the motif of suicide, we must become acquainted with the system of emotional excess. If we examine the situations portrayed in all the stories, we notice that descriptions of emotions take up an unusually high percentage of the text. The frequency and intensity of the characters' emotional outbursts structure Kleist's prose by contrasting curiously with the narrator's laconic, smooth style of reporting. We will call the resulting effect the rhetorical figure of the announced but delayed catastrophe. In the world represented here, reduced to an objectified style and whose narrator is apparently emotionally uninvolved, emotional scenes erupt at regular intervals. Because of the narrator's silence,[29] this emotionality takes on not only an air of tacit malevolence but also one of punctual finality. The figures appearing in the various scenes know nothing of the catastrophe but are pregnant with it. The structural immediacy and isolation of these emotional scenes gives them an additional, purely formal, intensity. Emil Staiger pointed out this connection between dramatic form and extreme emotional outburst in his stylistic analysis of "The Beggarwoman of Locarno." He concluded it with the sentence: "And with that we have fallen prey to Kleist to the extent that only a jolt can free us from his embrace and redeem us from a way of being human to whose deadliness the author's end bears witness."[30] The "deadliness" Staiger discovered with a sure instinct in the dramatic form of these stories—a deadliness that, as the omnipresence of death, had always been characteristic of this tragedian par excellence—reveals itself explicitly if we understand (1) the kinds of emotions described; (2) their quick succession; and (3) their frequent transformation into their opposites. These are the recurring, nonverbal expressive gestures whose significance scholars have only recently and with hesitation begun to perceive as a result of the observations by Kommerell, Blöcker, and Kunz.[31]

Although we cannot give a statistical presentation here, we can say with sufficient accuracy that in general all the stories deal with emotional states that change or even transcend the characters' normal physical appearance. Either the characters are overcome by alarm, astonishment, speechlessness, loss of consciousness, and pain, or the opposite happens: excessive jubilation and joy. Instead of ordinary middle-value descriptions of characters or situations that only gradually builds to psychological atmosphere, we confront a succession of transitory states. Presenting a character or psyche always primarily in a state of transition prefigures the most radical transition of all, that from life to death. Thus, a rhetorical system emerges that is based on the stereotypically repeated, nearly unchanging conceptual structure of emotion. For example, a list of the nouns chosen in "Michael Kohlhaas" shows that except for varying nuances of ambivalent emotional expression, only two emotions dominate: terror or pain and astonishment.[32] This finding is confirmed by a study of "The Marquise of O—," where words of unease alternate with emotional descriptions of pleasure.[33] It is important to ascertain the existence of this structural net of only slightly changing emotions in order to avoid false interpretations and conclusions. The latter usually amount to giving the famous "emotion" in Kleist a one-sidedly positive significance based on the assumption that the "emotional" view does not deceive the figure but instead allows him or her to find the hidden truth in an ambivalent situation.[34]

The rhetoric of emotion shows, however, that the emotional situation is not exclusively reserved for the emotional hero but is a net of tension that constitutes all the figures including the liars, traitors, moral weaklings. We can draw a preliminary conclusion:

Kleistian emotion is not, as the theory would have it, always an organ of knowledge; it is in the first analysis a mere psychic event in is own right. Feeling does deceive, as the Marquise of O— suspects when she asks: "Can't these vague internal sensations of yours have deceived you?" [35] And the reader can never know when a mention of such feeling points beyond the pure emotional state of the present. What is communicated above all is the impression of the inner life of a human being as a *terra incognita* that is always in jeopardy. Its transitory modality is the outer signal of that jeopardy. Kleistian emotion is thus not simply to be taken as a "symbol." Instead, it is to be taken literally in its physical contingency and perhaps as a dramaturgical rendering of a psychologically overstrained or even pathological situation.

The rhetorical character emerging from the stereotypical repetition of identical or similar nouns, adjectives, and verbs, while it differs from the usual techniques of representation in the nineteenth century psychological novel, does not contradict this psychological quality. It does, however, give that quality the character of a symptom with clinical overtones. It is important to recognize this rhetoric of psychology to avoid reducing Kleist's stories to "certain basic formulas of a mythic world view," [36] whether that mythic world view is that of original evil, that of justice, or that of hidden happiness.

The above-mentioned concepts of "terror" or "confusion" only provide the framework for the special emotional climate and course of action we find in Kleist. Certain adverbial modifiers are more revealing of the deadly quality of his prose. If we limit ourselves to "Michael Kohlhaas" and "The Marquise of O—," we find two modes of emotional gesture repeating themselves with only slight variations at central high points of the stories. Either the characters rapidly change color—that is, they blush or pale. [37] Or—and this gives the pathology of the scene its particular phenomenal character, which points to the structure of suddenness in scenes of perception in modern literature [38]—they look at someone for a moment. [39] This fully corresponds to the importance of the situation in Kleist's stories; it is not a particular intensification but is rather what enables the characters to be characters in the first place. In other words, the characters do not constitute centers of reflection that could be abstracted from them as an idea; rather, they are defined only through their actions and gestures. If the attitudes of the pathological situation we have described so far serve to create atmosphere, the gestures of blushing or paling and of looking at someone confront the reader with a choice about meaning. However, this is not the meaning of a self-contained person but one determined by the mechanism of the situation. The frequency of abruptly changing situations in which characters reveal themselves through a gesture of blushing or paling does not permit a "holistic," substantial conception of them.

In this repertory of gestures, turning pale always implies an impending catastrophe or death. The gesture of blushing was noticed and discussed very early,[40] but scholars overlooked that of growing pale although any systematic treatment of Kleist's repertory of gestures should have precluded that. The reason for the privileged treatment of blushing is once again the theory of "emotion" favored by literary research. Blushing, so this theory maintains, is a palpable symbolic expression of emotion, of inner truth and existential mood,[41] and that is why a metaphysically oriented approach ignores the opposite of blushing, becoming pale. The mechanism of the course of the action in the stories alone should warn us against assigning false meanings, that is, against substantializing the expression. What we are dealing with here is a psychological or psychopathic system, not a symbolic or epistemological one. This is true especially for the scene of a single moment, for glances lasting the blink of an eye. Overemphasizing Kleist's so-called Kant crisis, scholars have read epistemological problems into Kleist's perceptual situation instead of recognizing the pointillism, the dramatic method of the psychologically ambivalent moment—that is, the feverish instability of psychic identity. The instability renders this identity vulnerable to the extreme, even to the point of extinction. The moment of a Kleistian figure, his or her blushing, paling, or gaze, at first can be grasped only in the specific mode of this instability but not as the secret core of an existential illumination. Even the distinction between the emotional gaze that sees the eternal and the gaze that is subject to mortality[42] amounts to a mystification, which, as we can speculate, derives from the philosophy of eternity of the late eighteenth century. While this mystification is echoed in Kleist's letters, it is not supported by the semantics of his prose. To insist on such a supremacy of ideas is to look for a "whole" that does not exist in Kleist.

The extreme moment of blushing or going pale nevertheless contains the theme of a transition from this world to eternity. The dramatic structure of this theme becomes clearer as we free ourselves from idealistic systems of reference and discover its physical and materialist condition. It is only because of the latter that a sudden change in the external appearance of a character becomes a true threat. Our thesis of an emotionality that has a physical rather than a metaphysical basis is reinforced by Kleist's own theoretical observation. In an essay called "Allerneuester Erziehungsplan" (The very newest plan for education), Kleist developed a psychology of polarity in analogy to electrical phenomena, which had fascinated early romantic natural philosophers since the 1790s. A nonelectric body becomes electric in the presence of an electric one and, indeed, takes on the "opposite charge"; human beings react in the same way. Kleist emphasized the element of instability in his essay: "This highly remarkable law also exists in the moral world, in a manner that, to the best of our knowledge, has been little attended; in that a person whose state is indifferent not only ceases to be indifferent the moment he comes into contact with someone else whose qualities are defined in any way whatsoever."[43] His emotional being then swings to the opposite "pole" from the one occupied by the person he encounters. These basic ideas of a psychology of electric reaction, directed against the pedagogy of imitation that sought to educate by good example, were developed in 1810, a year before Kleist's suicide. But we find their precursors as early as 1805–1806, particularly in Kleist's famous essay "Über die allmähliche Verfertigung der Gedanken beim Reden" (On the gradual completion of thoughts while speaking). There he described the famous moment in the ballroom of Versailles, when Count Mirabeau faced the royal master of ceremonies and declared the états to be the representatives of the nation. Kleist considered this moment as nothing more than an electric reaction. He underlined his clever materialistic insight that "all invention derives from the body"[44] with an occasionalist explanation of the French Revolution: "Perhaps, in just this way, it was ultimately the curl of an upper lip or an ambiguous fingering of a cuff that caused the overthrow of the order of things in France."[45]

To derive the French Revolution from a movement in a single moment, this reduction of an idea to a facial expression, to the accident of a gesture—nothing could better comment on the significance of the Kleistian expression of emotion not as a symbolic sign but as a sign of an energetic, psychically ambivalent process. The background of "electrical" psychology explains not only the instability of emotions described in Kleist's prose but also the fact that they always elicit the opposite emotional response. Most of all, however, it explains the sudden structure of the prose moment with all the attendant consequences, that is, the preclusion of metaphysical interpretation. And one last thing: Kleist's understanding of emotional events as electrical, physical contains an aesthetic will such that the eccentric character of appearance, the dramatic *how* of the physical appearance notoriously obscures the *what* of this appearance, which directly explains the differences in interpretation. To that extent, the extreme moment, the moment of annihilation and death, is also willed. Its "occasionalist" character is the stylistic index for the narcissistic affinity: the final or fatal situation is only a last intensification of emotional moments that have always been understood as "electric."

III. Michael Kohlhaas, the Suicide

Where and how do such moments—gestures of change of complexion, paling—actually function as anticipation of death? We should recall that not only do many stories end with executions and murder; in some, the suicide of the hero is the climax, most obviously in "The Engagement in Santo Domingo." Viewed as pure action, what occurs in that story is precisely what Kleist will do: the hero shoots first his lover and then himself. The murder and suicide in the story, the result of passion and error, deviates from Kleist's own case in its psychological conditions. But as we saw with respect to the idea of "electrical" emotion, Kleist was interested not only in the moral content of emotions but also in their energetical history in general. Furthermore, in the story the murdered lover was secretly prepared for death; she even longed for it. This suicidal longing in the form of self-sacrifice is mirrored in the hero's narration about the fiancée of his youth. She died for him on the revolution's gallows because she kept silent although she could have saved herself by speaking.

This female self-sacrifice appears again, albeit in a somewhat veiled form, at the catastrophic end of "The Earthquake in Chile." Josephe, still undiscovered by the murderous mob, makes a last attempt to put an end to the butchery by plunging into the blood-thirsty pack with a cry of "Here, murder me, you bloodthirsty tigers!" and is immediately beaten to death. This story also begins with a suicide: the greater catastrophe, the earthquake, ironically interrupts the smaller, the attempted suicide, only to result in the annihilation of the potential suicide at the end.

In a disguised form, the suicide motif is also present in "The Duel" and "The Foundling." In all these cases, however, it serves only the rather formal function of accompanying and accentuating as a dramatic act the central catastrophe. However, in Kleist's most famous story, "Michael Kohlhaas," the suicide motif can be discerned as a concealed leitmotif. This has so far not been dis-cussed in the Kleist scholarship, for of all Kleist's figures, Michael Kohlhaas in particular has been interpreted primarily from the standpoint of metaphysics and worldview. Like Goethe's Faust, Kohlhaas has become a figure of German myth. Readers have seen him as a "martyr" to his own "sense of justice" ever since Rudolf Ihering, in his 1870 book *Kampf ums Recht* (Fight for justice), paid tribute to the horse dealer Kohlhaas—a reverence Thomas Mann animatedly, though with political undertones, concurred with in his introduction to the American postwar edition of Kleist's stories, which he delivered as a lecture in Zurich in 1954.[46] The thesis of Kohlhaas as suicide has an alienating effect, or even something of blasphemy, in the face of this tradition of research and interpre-tation.

I do not mean to contest the fact that Kleist uses two central traits to characterize his hero as a proponent of justice, however terrifying.[47] As if the legal arguments alone were not enough, the scholarship that relies on them can make use especially of the "horse" motif. The horses that the Junker had allowed to starve into shadows of their former selves, the actual cause of Kohlhaas' private war, are restored to their earlier magnificence at the end of the story. They are symbolic (as a current interpretation has it) of the reparation of the injustice done to Kohlhaas and form the optimistic conclusion of the story.[48] The following reasons militate against this view: (1) in the course of events Michael Kohlhaas and the narrator forget the original motif, that of seeking justice. After a certain point, Kohlhaas no longer seeks justice, but revenge. (2) The feeling of revenge intensifies into an emotion of anticipating his own death with ecstasy if it will lead to the annihilation of the opponent. (3) The quality of this emotion as a suicidal, narcissistic act is documented in the rhetoric of paling and of the moment.[49]

We will elucidate first the revenge that becomes a suicidal emotion, using the example of two key scenes. Then we will discuss the consequences that result for the discussion of justice and the metaphysical or existential interpretation of "Michael Kohlhaas" immanent to it. The first thing to notice is that even in "Kohlhaas," as in the other stories we have mentioned, suicide emerges early on as a blind motif. Kohlhaas threatens to shoot himself if Luther refuses to listen to him.[50] It becomes clear that he intends something monstrous, something he cannot yet properly name, before the thought of "revenge" has been properly introduced: "his soul," as Kohlhaas enigmatically tells his environment and the reader, is "aimed at great things."[51] We must keep in mind that in Kleist's terminology the concept of "soul" and the anticipated great "things" are closely linked with the motif of suicide.[52] Thus, already before the first great scene in which Kohlhaas rejects the salvation offered to him in order to annihilate the Elector of Saxony, the scenery is already characterized by a moribund rhetoric of "souls" and growing pale: "white in the face,"[53] "suddenly pale as a corpse,"[54] "turned pale"[55] "a deathly glance"[56]—those are the external features of the figures around Kohlhaas, which announce the final "pale" condition of Kohlhaas himself.

The description of an image in the church at Châlons-sur-Marne shows that Kleist came to this rhetoric of paling not only by way of the colloquial or literal meaning but rather through a specific aesthetic of the sublime.[57] This image, he writes, fascinates not because of its meaning but through the arousal of the spirit it elicits in those who perceive it. The description of the image itself is as follows: "They are a pair of winged angels that hover down from the abode of heavenly joy in order to receive a soul. The soul lies, inundated with the pallor of death, on its knees, its dying body reclining into the arms of the angels."[58]

Mentioning the gaze of the dying eyes of the soul, Kleist concludes, " I have never seen anything more touching and elevating."[59] The connection between deathly pallor and the idea of the sublime is a Kleistian topos that runs through all his letters. He described his friend Pfuel's appearance while reading about the death of Penthesilea as follows: "You know his 'ancient' gaze: when he has read the final scene, one sees the death on his countenance. That made him very dear to me."[60]

The "Marquise of O——" is particularly sublime in this sense. Just as in "Michael Kohlhaas," moments of deathly pallor structure the progressive approach to the climax, which in this case is the discovery of the biological father. The scene of discovery reads: " 'Oh no, surely not for him!' she cried, suddenly turning around and shooting the Count a look that crackled like lightning while a deathlike pallor spread across her face."[61] The rhetoric of pallor announces a deadly outcome, namely the possible suicide, which, as in other Kleistian endings, is avoided only with the help of a kind of superimposed epilogue. Blöcker opined: "The most noble poetic creations of this suicide must prove themselves in living, in remaining alive, not in dying."[62] That is the comfort and the wisdom of existential identification. However, it cannot disguise the impression that Kleist often protects his figures from the final consequence of their affinity for death only through a technical narrative decision. The remark of a French critic is apropos here. After the triumphant production of the *Prince of Homburg* with Gérard Philippe in the title role, he wrote: "The German Hamlet will not die and will engender many children."

We do not know how many children the Marquise of O—— still had. What we do know is that the narrator removes her from the deadly moment of the soul and of great things. Not so in the case of Michael Kohlhaas. Here, the first peak scene of consciously anticipated death, the execution of the self, follows the moment when the Elector offers Kohlhaas freedom and life in exchange for a secret note in which the future of the Saxon ruling house can be read. The note, which is sealed and whose contents Kohlhaas at this moment does not know, was given to him by a gypsy woman whose mysterious identity does not concern us here. Kohlhaas refuses to enter into this life-saving deal. When the Junker, the Elector's agent, asks him why, he answers:

> Noble sir, if your sovereign should come to me and say, "I'll destroy myself and the whole pack of those who help me wield the scepter"—destroy himself, mind you, which is the dearest wish of my soul—I would still refuse him the paper, which is worth more to him than his life, and say, "You can send me to the scaffold, but I can make you suffer, and I mean to." And Kohlhaas, with death staring him in the face, called a trooper over and invited him to have the large portion of food left in his dish.[63]

Later, Kohlhaas has an opportunity to retract his decision. Then, however, we read: "Kohlhaas, who exulted in the power given him to wound his enemy mortally in the heel at the very moment that it was treading him in the dust."[64] The complex emphasis, anticipating his own death and transforming it into joy at the enemy's pain—concentrated in the words "with death staring him in the face"—appears long before the execution scene. From this moment on the reader knows that Kohlhaas no longer wants to have his horses, and with them his rights, restored but instead is looking for death. The execution scene at the end does not confirm, as is so often repeated, that the horses, the symbols of justice,[65] are the center of the story. Instead, it reveals the center as a deadly revenge that includes the annihilation of the enemy. This scene, which is unique in the psychological literature of the nineteenth century, makes the act of execution secondary to the final aggression of the hero, who annihilates himself in order to bring down his enemy: "Kohlhaas, striding up in front of the man with a suddenness that took his guard by surprise, drew out the capsule, removed the paper, unsealed it, and read it through; and looking steadily at the man with the blue and white plumes, in whose breast fond hopes were already beginning to spring, he stuck the paper in his mouth and swallowed it."[66]

Without calling upon the aid of the psychoanalytical theory that suicide is murder directed against one's self,[67] we can note here that the peculiar identity between destruction of another and destruction of the self is obvious. Verbs of joyous aggression determine the psychological moment of gazing at the other: "annihilate," "hurt," "swallow." The choice of words is similar to that in Kleist's farewell letters: hurt—pain.[68] His last letter to Marie von Kleist explicitly combines the idea "of the most glorious and voluptuous death"[69] with an intuition of the "bitter pain"[70] that Kleist's death will cause Marie. The end of the story "The Found-ling" provides a variant of "Kohlhaas": Piachi, the condemned murderer of the traitorous Nicolo, has been sentenced to death by hanging and refuses the absolution that could save his soul from damnation: "I don't want to be saved. I want to go down to the lowest pit of hell. I want to find Nicolo again, who won't be in heaven, and take up my revenge again, which I could only satisfy partly here!"[71]

Traditional Kleist scholarship has been accused of "metaphysical obscurantism" by more recent works focused on political argu-ments.[72] This objection would be more convincing if the obscuran-tism had not been replaced by an explanation in terms of the philosophy of law that transforms the murderous end of the story into a kind of political happy ending.[73] But how are we to explain the contradiction between catastrophic facts and Kohlhaas' final high spirits? We assert that it is always grounded in the joy of the subject and not due to some cause outside the subject.

Achim von Arnim once said that Kleist was the most candid, almost cynical person he had met in a long time,[74] an insight that Erich Schmidt valued[75] but that has been lost by the following generation of scholars. "Cynicism" in this case means the bound-less freedom from concern about prevailing norms. Kohlhaas and Piachi also sang the "triumphal song," just as Kleist's "soul" did at the moment of his death. Kohlhaas feels the same "inexpressible cheerfulness"[76] that Kleist mentions shortly before his suicide. We can take this word as a semantic index for the suicidal mania Freud analyzed in his essay "Mourning and Melancholia."

But we have only given a literary description of a symptom. The battle that has raged since Durkheim about whether suicide is more psychologically or more socially determined cannot be resolved by pointing to the suicide of the artist as a third thing, something incommensurable. It would only be "literary" camouflage if we thus refused to consider all verifiable causal data. However we characterize the triumphal suicide song of Kleist and his heroes— "sickness of the ego," pathology, ecstasy, or socially conditioned neurosis—it is certainly the reaction of an extremely lonely person. We can describe this loneliness more exactly in a historical sense than through metaphors of modern existence. Kleist himself described it prophetically in his early letters to Luise von Zenge, written from Paris in 1801. It is the loneliness of someone who has dropped out of any kind of social association, who has become an unbound atom in the urban crowd.[77] The horrifying sight of this urban crowd will become the great theme of E. A. Poe's and Baudelaire's equally deadly literary works. Kleist anticipated this perspective all the way to its logical consequence of suicide.

NOTES

1. See Joachim Maass, *Kleist: Die Geschichte seines Lebens* (München, Bern: Scherz, 1977), p. 377.

2. Günther Blöcker, *Heinrich von Kleist oder das absolute Ich* (Frankfurt/ Main: Suhrkamp, 1977), p. 100.

3. Quoted in Helmut Sembdner, *In Sachen Kleist: Beiträge zur Forschung* (München: Hanser, 1974), p. 177.

4. As in the letter to Heinrich Lohse dated December 23 (29), 1801. Kleist takes leave of his friend with language that indicates that it is not just a matter of giving up their shared accommodations but of something more, and something ominous: "I want to take leave of you for ever, and in so doing I feel so peaceful, so affectionate, as if I were near the hour of my death" (Kleist, *Sämtliche Werke und Briefe* (*Werke*) [München: Hanser, 1977], 2: 709). Similarly, in a letter dated May 1, 1802, to Ulrike von Kleist: "—in short, I have no other wish than to die, once I have succeeded in three things: a child, a beautiful poem, and a great deed. For life has nothing more sublime than this, that we can sublimely throw it away" (ibid., p. 725). And also in the letter dated May 20, 1802, to Wilhelmine von Zenge: "I have no other wish than to die soon" (ibid., p. 726).

5. Kleist announces his intention to join Napoleon's army on its expedition to England. Consciously or unconsciously returning to the death motif of his letter of May 1, 1802, Kleist now says that he has rejected his "work"—he means the fragmentary drama, *Robert Guiskard*— that fame is denied him. "I cannot show myself worthy of your friendship, I cannot love without this friendship: I plunge myself into death. Be calm, you sublime one, I will die the lovely death of battle" (ibid., p. 737).

6. Ibid., pp. 883–84.

7. On this subject see Kleist's correspondence with Friedrich von Raumer, who was then government counsel, and with Chancellor Karl

August von Hardenberg. See also his letter of May 20, 1811, to Prince Wilhelm (ibid., pp. 862ff.) and the letter of June 6, 1811, to Friedrich Wilhelm III (ibid., pp. 869–70).

8. This argument is valid regardless of the dating problem noted by Sembdner, the editor of Kleist's *Werke*, especially the problem surrounding the letter of November 9 or 19, 1811 (see Sembdner, "Zu Heinrich und Marie von Kleist," in Sembdner, *In Sachen Kleist*, p. 178). Sembdner argues that it is unlikely that Kleist would have announced his suicide so emphatically twelve days before the deed. That psychological argument is less convincing if we consider the very early "suicide" letters mentioned above. They contain in part not only the same motifs as later ones (lack of social and private recognition), but they also seek, as a kind of substitute for the fame that Kleist has failed to win, the sphere of the sublime (letter to Ulrike dated October 26, 1803, in Kleist, *Werke* 2: 737), which characterizes his last letters. Very early on, Kleist's anticipation of death is to be understood as a literary gesture. As a mere psychological expression of a "stupidly overstressed spirit" (see letter to Lohse, December 23, 1801, in ibid., pp. 708–711), it would border on involuntary comedy: to announce the magnificent deed without ever doing it.

9. Gerhard Schmidt, "Der Todestrieb bei Heinrich von Kleist," *Münchner medizinische Wochenschrift* 10 (1970): 762.

10. We can name as examples of the metaphysical overemphasis on the motif of death as a tendency in scholarship: Josef Kunz, "Die Thematik der Daseinsstufen in Kleists dichterischem Werk," in Walter Müller-Seidel, ed., *Heinrich von Kleist: Aufsätze und Essays* (Darmstadt: Wissenschaftliche Buchgesellschaft, 1973), pp. 672–706. For the interpretation of the *Prince of Homburg* in this sense, see especially Eleonore Frey-Staiger, "Das Problem des Todes bei Kleist," *Modern Language Notes* 83 (1968): 821ff. See also Walter Silz, "On Homburg and the Death of Kleist," *Monatshefte für deutschen Unterricht* 32 (1940): 325ff. The style of the dramas, in contrast to Kleist's prose style, has contributed to the metaphysical overemphasis on the death motif, see Müller-Seidel, "Die Struktur des Widerspruchs in Kleists Marquise von O . . . ," in Müller-Seidel, ed. *Heinrich von Kleist*, p. 245 note 2. Arthur Henkel, on the other hand, warned about the danger of this overemphasis very early on: "Respect for the secrets of a person also forbids mythologizing this death or taking it as a kind of art work, as Kleist's last unwritten tragedy" (Arthur Henkel, "Traum und Gegensatz im Prinzen von Homburg," in Müller-Seidel, ed., *Heinrich von Kleist*, p. 577).

11. In the death monologue of the Prince of Homburg and in his farewell letter to Sophie Müller dated November 20, 1811, Kleist mentions the wings that sprout on the shoulders of those who are ready for

death. On the Enlightenment roots of the idea of reconciled death, see Gerhardt Schmidt, "Der Todestrieb bei Heinrich von Kleist."

12. Gotthold Ephraim Lessing, "Wie die Alten den Tod gebildet," in Lessing, *Sämtliche Werke*, ed. Karl Lachmann (Berlin, 1839), 8: 247.

13. Kleist, *Werke* 2: 884.

14. Ibid., 1: 707.

15. Ibid., 2: 887.

16. Ibid., 2: 709.

17. Ibid.

18. Alfred Alvarez, *The Savage God: A Study of Suicide* (New York: Random House, 1972), p. 101.

19. Sigmund Freud, "Mourning and Melancholia," trans. James Strachey, in Freud, *The Complete Psychological Works* (London: Hogarth Press, 1957), 14: 253.

20. Ibid., p. 254.

21. Ibid.

22. See Manfred Lefèvre, "Kleistforschung 1961–1967," *Colloquia Germanica* 3 (1969): 4, 17, 52. See also Ernst Cassirer, *Heinrich von Kleist und die Kantische Philosophie* (Berlin: Reuther & Reichard, 1919).

23. Erich Schmidt, "Heinrich von Kleist als Dramatiker," in Müller-Seidel, ed., *Heinrich von Kleist*, p. 4.

24. Quoted in Alvarez, *The Savage God*, p. 99.

25. Quoted in Gerhard Schmidt, "Der Todestrieb bei Heinrich von Kleist," p. 761.

26. Freud, "Mourning and Melancholia," p. 251. Compare Nietzsche's and Baudelaire's concepts of self-torment or self-execution (see chapter 7 in this volume).

27. Kleist, letter to Marie von Kleist of late autumn 1807. *Werke*, 2: 797. On the discussion about the reading of *Schmutz* (filth) instead of *Schmerz* (pain), see Sembdner, "Schmerz oder Schmutz?" in Sembdner, *In Sachen Kleist*, pp. 76–87. Kleist's modern joining of the cruel with sexuality was emphasized by Ernst Fischer, "Heinrich von Kleist," *Sinn und Form* 13 (1961): 810. See also R. S. Lucas, "Studies in Kleist: Michael Kohlhaas," *DVJS* 44 (1970): 163. Bernhard Blume also emphasized the cruel element in Kleist but believed that Kleist suffered the chaotic but did not glorify it (Blume, "Kleist und Goethe," in Müller-Seidel, ed., *Heinrich von Kleist*, pp. 160–61, 169).

28. Helmut Koopmann, "Das 'Rätselhafte Faktum' und seine Vorgeschichte: Zum analytischen Character der Novellen Heinrich von Kleists," *Zeitschrift für deutsche Philologie* 84 (1965). Compare with: Claus Reinert, *Detektivliteratur bei Sophokles, Schiller und Kleist* (Kronberg, Czech.: Scriptor, 1975), p. 76.

29. On this point, see Wolfgang Kayser, "Kleist als Erzähler," in Müller-Seidel, ed., *Heinrich von Kleist*, p. 237.

30. Emil Staiger, "Heinrich von Kleist, 'Das Bettelweib von Locarno': Zum Problem des dramatischen Stils," in Müller-Seidel, ed., *Heinrich von Kleist*, p. 129.

31. Max Kommerell, "Die Sprache und das Unaussprechliche: Eine Betrachtung über Heinrich von Kleist," in Kommerell, *Geist und Buchstabe der Dichtung*, 3d ed. (Frankfurt/Main: Klostermann, 1944), pp. 243–318; Blöcker, *Heinrich von Kleist oder das absolute Ich*, pp. 188–89; Josef Kunz, "Die Thematik der Daseinsformen," p. 680 note 2.

32. See Heinrich von Kleist, "Michael Kohlhaas," in Kleist, *The Marquise von O— and Other Stories*, trans. Martin Greenberg (New York: Ungar, 1973), pp. 108, 113, 115, 116, 119, 124, 129, 138, 170, 172, 173, 178, 179, 180.

33. Kleist, "The Marquise of O—," in Kleist, *The Marquise von O— and Other Stories*, trans. Martin Greenberg (New York: Ungar, 1973), pp. 45, 47, 50, 56, 59, 60, 62, 63, 64, 65, 72, 75, 79, 80, 82.

34. A fundamental revision of this point of view was introduced by Walter Müller-Seidel in his book *Versehen und Erkennen: Eine Studie über Heinrich von Kleist* (Köln: Böhlau, 1961), see particularly pp. 129–30. His work did not, however, prevent the repetition of the thesis that emotions cannot be deceived. See Eleonore Frey-Staiger, "Das Problem des Todes bei Heinrich von Kleist," pp. 826–27.

35. Kleist, "The Marquise of O—," p. 61. Translator's note: It is actually the Marquise's mother who poses the question to the Marquise.

36. This objection to a prominent view in German scholarship was formulated by Erna Moore, "Heinrich von Kleists 'Findling': Psychologie des Verhängnisses," *Colloquia Germanica* (1974): 275. She writes: "Instead of a metaphysical fate, psychological problems lie behind the event" (ibid., p. 276). For all her necessary criticism of fundamentalism, Erna Moore does not escape the danger of a psychologism that oversimplifies the ego problem of the portrayal of characters determined by the situation, as Hans Peter Herrmann has clearly shown (see Herrmann, "Zufall und Ich: Zum Problem der Situation in den Novellen Heinrich von Kleists," in Müller-Seidel, ed., *Heinrich von Kleist*, p. 397).

37. Scenes of blushing or paling in the "Marquise" are to be found in Kleist, *The Marquise of O—*, pp. 43, 45, 47, 49, 51, 54, 60, 64, 66, 67, 69, 76, 80, 81. The scenes in "Michael Kohlhaas" are ibid., pp. 94, 96, 99, 104, 108, 109, 110, 112, 124, 128, 131, 140, 141, 142, 151, 153, 160, 167.

38. On this point, see Karl Heinz Bohrer, *Die Ästhetik des Schreckens:*

Die pessimistische Romantik und Ernst Jüngers Frühwerk (München: Hanser, 1978), pp. 186–87, 367ff.

39. The scenes of looking or of the specific gaze in the "Marquise" are in Kleist, *The Marquise of O—*, pp. 48, 50, 58, 60, 67, 81, 82, 83. In "Kohlhaas," the scenes are ibid., pp. 89, 110, 124, 128, 130, 131, 132, 134, 135, 138, 140, 142, 153, 155, 166, 167, 170, 171, 177, 180, 182.

40. See Kunz, "Die Thematik der Daseinsstufen in Kleists dichterischem Werk," p. 680 note 20. See also Ditmar Skrotzki, *Die Gebärde des Errötens im Werk Heinrich von Kleists* (Marburg: Elwert, 1971).

41. Even Skrotzki emphasizes the appropriateness of concepts from existentialist philosophy, see *Die Gebärde des Errötens*, p. 6 note 15. Thus the author assumes that the gesture of blushing constitutes meaning (ibid., pp. 17–18). He links blushing with states of shame, in which their truth reveals itself. Müller-Seidel, who early on recognized the way in which the pure moment can change abruptly in Kleist, concluded that this was due to a "fate" and excluded anything "coincidental" (Müller-Seidel, "Die Struktur des Widerspruchs," in Müller-Seidel, ed., *Heinrich von Kleist*, p. 249). Klaus Müller-Salget, on the other hand, developed the idea of "coincidence" as a constitutive element ("Das Prinzip der Doppeldeutigkeit in Kleists Erzählungen," *ZfDPh* 92 (1973): 194). Ernst Fischer accepted the concept of coincidence but separated it from any irrationalist interpretation (Fischer, "Heinrich von Kleist," p. 780).

42. Eleonore Frey-Staiger makes this distinction in "Das Problem des Todes bei Heinrich von Kleist," pp. 826–27.

43. Kleist, "Allerneuester Erziehungsplan, "in Kleist, *Werke* 2: 330.

44. Kleist, Letter to Ulrike von Kleist, January 12, 1802, in Kleist, *Werke* 2: 713.

45. Kleist, "Über die allmähliche Verfertigung der Gedanken beim Reden," in *Werke* 2: 321.

46. Thomas Mann, "Introduction to Kleist," *The Marquise of O— and Other Stories*, pp. 30–31. The one-sidedly positive evaluation of Kohlhaas' feeling for justice has been corrected in the Anglo-Saxon scholarship, especially by Lucas, "Studies in Kleist: 'Michael Kohlhaas,'" pp. 125ff. See also Walter Silz, "Three Themes in 'Michael Kohlhaas,'" in Silz, ed., *Heinrich von Kleist: Studies in His Works and Literary Character* (Philadelphia: University of Pennsylvania Press, 1961), p. 180.

47. Early in the Kohlhaas story, we read: "His sense of justice turned him into a brigand and a murderer" (Kleist, "Michael Kohlhaas," p. 87). A little later, we read: "But his sense of justice, which was as delicate as a gold balance, still wavered" (ibid., p. 93).

48. On the discussion about Kohlhaas, see Müller-Salget, "Das Prinzip

der Doppeldeutigkeit in Kleists Erzählungen," pp. 185–91. See also Le-fèvre, "Kleistforschung," pp. 26, 36.

49. Müller-Seidel, who emphasizes the change from a feeling for jus-tice to revenge, does not admit that revenge is the final attitude, because in that case the novella would end "in a nihilism beyond compare" (Müller-Seidel, *Versehen und Erkennen*, p. 150).

50. Kleist, "Michael Kohlhaas," p. 124.

51. Ibid., p. 105.

52. The soul is one of Kleist's central concepts of emotion, which early on appears to be assigned to the sphere of eternity, death, an eccentric state altogether. From the letters to Pfuel dated December 23, 1801, and August 31, 1806, and the description of the image of a church in 1807, to the suicide letters of November 10, 19, 20, and 21, 1811, this concept is repeated again and again in the same context.

53. Kleist, "Michael Kohlhaas," p. 99.

54. Ibid., p. 112.

55. Ibid., p. 104.

56. Ibid.

57. Kleist, letter to Marie von Kleist dated June, 1807, in Kleist, *Werke* 2: 781–82.

58. Ibid., p. 783.

59. Ibid.

60. Letter to Marie von Kleist, June 1807, ibid., pp. 781–82.

61. Kleist, "The Marquise of O—," p. 81.

62. Blöcker, *Heinrich von Kleist oder das absolute Ich*, p. 228.

63. Kleist, "Michael Kohlhaas," p. 166.

64. Ibid., p. 177.

65. On the objections against the view that the symbolism of justice is central, see Lucas, "Studies in Kleist: Michael Kohlhaas," pp. 132ff.

66. Kleist, "Michael Kohlhaas," p. 182.

67. See Freud, "Mourning and Melancholia," p. 252.

68. Kleist's farewell letters reflect, not without some satisfaction, the pain of others after he has put an end to his own pain or transformed it into joy. See the letters of November 10 and November 19 to Marie von Kleist, in Kleist, *Werke* 2: 883–85.

69. Letter dated November 21, 1811, in ibid., p. 887.

70. Ibid.

71. Kleist, "The Foundling," in Kleist, *The Marquise of O— and Other Stories*, p. 247.

72. As by Peter Horn, "Was geht uns eigentlich der Gerechtigkeitsbe-griff in Kleists Erzählung 'Michael Kohlhaas' noch an?" *Acta Germanica* 8 (1973): 91.

73. Ibid., pp. 61, 91–92. To Horn's acute analysis of competing concepts of justice and right we must object that it treats Kleist's text as a random type of political or historical text. The decision about the meaning of the conclusion must, however, be made as a decision about its aesthetic value, and that perspective disposes of the metaphysical-symbolic interpretation that Horn attacks.

74. In a letter to Wilhelm Grimm dated April, 1810, quoted in Curt Hohoff, *Heinrich von Kleist in Selbstzeugnissen und Bilddokumenten* (Hamburg: Rowohlt, 1958), p. 129.

75. See Erich Schmidt, "Heinrich von Kleist als Dramatiker," in Müller-Seidel, ed., *Heinrich von Kleist*, pp. 3–4.

76. See the letter to Ulrike von Kleist dated "on the day of my death," Kleist, *Werke* 2: 887. Before we come to the actual satisfaction of the revenge scene, Kohlhaas is said to speak "cheerfully" (Kleist, "Michael Kohlhaas," p. 181).

77. See the letter to Luise von Zenge dated August 16, 1801, in Kleist, *Werke* 2: 686.

9

Utopia of the Moment and Fictionality: The Subjectivization of Time in Modern Literature

I

The debate about the utopian content of Walter Benjamin's "Theses on the Philosophy of History"[1] is not over, but one fact is not disputed: Benjamin's dissolution of historical continuity and its replacement by the concept of discontinuous time. There is controversy about whether his attempt "to blast open the continuum of history"[2] for the sake of revolution can be connected with a meaningful concept of historical materialism or whether the messianic motif of Judeo-Christian redemptive theology cuts through the Marxist assumption of a history that is already determined, even in its progression. Since Gershom Scholem's mystical exegesis of the "angel" motif,[3] which occupies a central position in the "Theses on the Philosophy of History," and since Jürgen Habermas' thesis that Benjamin's view of art and the past is not only not a critique of ideology (like Marcuse's view) but is "in the most eminent sense conservative,"[4] or even "conservatively revolutionary,"[5] the problem of the concept of time has presented itself as the alternative that Rolf Tiedemann formulated: "Historical materialism or political messianism?"[6]

The discovery of conservative elements in Benjamin's work,[7] his sustained relationship to Carl Schmitt's category of the "state of exception,"[8] and the messianic, mystical metaphors[9] of the "The-ses on the Philosophy of History" that contradict the Marxist, dialectic conception of history, all merely point to an inventory of ideas from intellectual history but do not tell us anything about the specific strategy of their application as conceptual figures, which is our only source of information about Benjamin's utopian horizon in view of the fascist threat in 1940. The proof that messianic and Marxist concepts can be united, as Tiedemann shows,[10] also fails to cancel out the aporetic structure of Benjamin's idea of temporal discontinuity, that is, the distinction between the concept of the moment and the theory of a continuous, progressive, and theoreti-cally interpreted historical time. The concept of the moment ap-pears in the fifth, the sixth, and the fifteenth of the "Theses"; though perhaps not always compatible with the concept of the present (in the second and sixteenth thesis and in section A), it is at least functionally coordinated with the latter.

The term *present,* which is central for the philosophy of history and which was covered by Heinrich Heine's critique of universal-ism,[11] organizes Benjamin's hermeneutic objection to bourgeois historicism and to social democracy's "empty" concept of progress. However, the actual aporia of Benjamin's utopian draft, that is, the quasi-surrealist methodology[12] of reducing historically prog-ressing time to a moment of "illumination," is concentrated in the concept of the moment. According to Benjamin's sixteenth thesis, in the concept of the present, the "historical materialist" under-stands his "experience" with history. Whereas historicism posits the " 'eternal' image of the past," the "historical materialist" has an "experience" with it that is "unique." He blows open "the continuum of history." "The present" then does not mean "transi-tion" but rather a moment "in which time stands still and has come to a stop."[13] In these moments when time comes to a "stop" the "historical materialist" revises bourgeois historiography, which, as the seventh thesis tell us, was always only empathy for the victor,[14] and retroactively compensates a "redeemed mankind" for its suffering, as the third thesis maintains.[15] The goal of history is firmly bound up with the utopian promise of a redemption (second, third, sixth theses) of "mankind," which has up to now been defeated. This goal, however, is not necessarily immanent to his-tory; it is a subject-centered event: "History is the subject of a structure whose site is not homogeneous, empty time, but time filled by the presence of the now [*Jetztzeit*]."[16]

Such a concept of the "now" implies the category of "decision," that is, a value derived from the moment of the subject. The category of the moment, characterized in the three above-mentioned passages applies the model of the present from the history of philosophy to that of intuitionist evidence. The "true picture of the past flits by," it "flashes up," it can be seized "at the instant when it can be recognized" (fifth thesis). In contrast to the interest of bourgeois historicism, the issue is not to determine "the way it really was" but to "seize hold of a memory as it flashes up at a moment of danger" (sixth thesis). As opposed to historical materialism, the historical subject exists only in the act of his "citable" moments (third thesis). This is the reason why Benjamin can say that the revolutionary classes "blast open the continuum of history" (fifteenth thesis). Revolution is not vouched for by the continuum of time but only in the unrepeatable image of a past that becomes visible only for a moment. What was promised disappears behind the act of promising itself. This temporal modality of the "now" that transforms "empty" time, the metaphor of the "second" that dissolves traditional categories of time and space (section B), of flashing, flitting, of the "flair" for the "topical" (fourteenth thesis), of the transitory, the "tiger's leap into the past" (fourteenth thesis), are opposed to the Marxist construct of a course of history that naturally progresses toward revolution.[17] We might say that even though Benjamin has not renounced the utopia of world revolution, he has at least retracted its ordered process or temporal course into a utopia of the moment, the moment in the remembering subject of a regained past that has become just. Standard criticism explains the incoherence of Benjamin's thought by referring to his "surrealist"[18] inconsistency or declaring it an "eccentric"[19] deviation, and the plausibility of the conceptual image of the moment itself has been called into question as a kind of methodological decisionism that cannot be resolved.[20]

Ernst Bloch delivered an early, suspicious commentary on the critical point about Benjamin's category of the "now"—characteristically, Bloch does not use the still more ambivalent word *moment*—and just managed to save it from the interpretation that offers itself here: that "the emphasis as well as the messianic content of the 'now-time' will be placed senselessly on one point if it is not defined within an objective 'anticipation,' "[21] if the "tendency" of history does not make itself felt.[22] Benjamin's blasting open of history, according to Bloch, does not mean "to focus on one point, not even to turn something into a monad." Instead, "to explode is a liberating act that frees all essentially related, utopian moments from before and after within the respective dawning of now-time and relays their directions."[23] To be sure, that is a reading that does not systematically explore the problem of time implicit in the category of the moment.[24]

This greater or lesser concern with the aporia of Benjamin's conceptual image rests on a none-too-high estimation of its theoretical capability on the part of ideological-critical analysis. Such an analysis examines Benjamin's reduced moment in detail only when its explicit messianic or eschatological message (second, sixth, ninth, seventeenth, eighteenth theses, sections A, B) is in danger of being coopted by an interpretation that is not utopian but theological. Scholem's reference to the precursor of the later theory of the moment in the Kabbala's "now" and the "moment" of the angels before God[25] has not been disputed because of the mystical context of Benjamin's motifs, which no one calls into question. Lack of dispute is made easier since what is "new" in this tradition is placed in a quasi-dialectical relationship with the "already there" and thus avoids being subject to sheer immediacy through a conservative turn backward.

Gerhard Kaiser's attempt is more questionable. He tries to link Benjamin's "Theses on the Philosophy of History," especially the "appellative character" of the "momentary,"[26] which he developed in detail, with the thesis of a secularized eschatology that is supposedly in irreconcilable conflict with the "Hegelian-Marxist idea of process."[27] Tiedemann and Osterkamp[28] refuted this thesis by focusing on the dialectical interpretation of the meaning of the "angel of history" (ninth thesis) who, his face turned toward the past, strides backward into an undecided future—an enigmatic image that Kaiser exploited for his theological interpretation in discussing Benjamin's critique of the socialist idea of progress.[29]

The competing claims to messianic terminology by quasi theology and philosophy of history both overlook one fact. Benjamin's metaphor of the moment of memory or of "commemoration" can be understood in its newly coined, not merely traditional, utopian content only by recognizing its systematic and historical connection with the phenomenological modification of the concept of time, which was formulated in certain representative works of literary modernism of Benjamin's time that were part of European aestheticism. It is well established that these works had a profound influence on Benjamin's thought. If we look at Benjamin's metaphor of the moment in light of this literary temporalization of time, then our task is to emphasize its nature as moment without resorting to the concept of an actual Messiah. Put in the terms of these literary models, the topos of the suddenly appearing moment does not point to a Messiah but rather is the moment of a politicized aesthetics of perception.

That Benjamin's theory of the moment was directly influenced by the problem of time in Proust and to a lesser extent by Baudelaire is substantiated by works on the two French authors that precede the "Theses on the Philosophy of History." Bergson's 1896 work, *Matière et mémoire*, is the key to understanding the modern thinkers who emphasize time. Benjamin deals with that work in detail and emphasizes the "structure of memory" as "decisive for the philosophical pattern of experience."[30] At the same time, Benjamin points out how uninterested Bergson himself was in attaching a "specific historical label" to memory.

In this context, Benjamin mentions Bergson's most significant literary student, Proust, and his work *Remembrance of Things Past*. Benjamin, Proust's translator, was always aware of the elective affinity between his own ideas and Proust's and discussed Proust's concept of time, apart from the Baudelaire studies, in the essay "The Image of Proust."[31] We see there the central concept of "recollection" for the "Theses on the Philosophy of History "; that is, the presentification of the *durée* or of "completing time"[32] in a "passing moment."[33] The momentariness of Proust's *mémoire involontaire*, as Benjamin says in both his study of Baudelaire and in that of Proust, does not indicate something lived through but rather something experienced,[34] because an "experienced event" is "finite," confined within one "sphere of experience," whereas "remembrance"—Benjamin also calls this "recollection" and "experience"—is "infinite."[35] And from these two central concepts of

his own philosophy of time Benjamin arrives by way of a psychological detour at the concept of the "quest for happiness" that he
believes runs through Proust's work.[36] Benjamin here anticipates
his own aporia: he does not view the subject-centered concept of
time as theoretically annihilated in the subjectivity of "something
lived through," but yet he maintains the utopia of a mystical "happiness."

Here, we can only present a brief sketch of Benjamin's interpretation of Proust. Benjamin's crucial use of a concept of time whose
subject-object dialectic, in the form of a metapsychology of time
that is "experienced," not merely "lived through," is an indication
that this theory of the moment was not a special case of Benjamin's
esotericism, derived only, as we have seen, from relatively apocry-
phal sources or ideas from the philosophy of history. Instead, this
seems to be a normal case of the newly emerging literature of
consciousness. Along with Proust, representative authors of the
literature of consciousness are James Joyce, Virginia Woolf, André
Breton, and Robert Musil. All of them tried to translate the
category of consciousness of the subjective moment into the objectivity of a utopia. Benjamin's intellectually formulated aporia is
even less resolvable in the case of aesthetic constructs; on the
other hand, however, it is reconciled in the aesthetic realm.

The fact that it is always a matter of subjectifying the "empty"
concept of time and thus reducing utopian contents and goals to
the interiority of a subject with a utopian mood points to the crisis
of the utopian motif as anticipation, whether it is the enlightened-
scientific type of utopia, the political type characterized by progressive thinking, or the imaginative type like Mercier's. The crisis can
be dated to about 1870.[37] A hundred years after Mercier, the
political background was the overthrow of the Paris Commune,
the creation of German unity in the national—not the liberal—
sense, the beginning of European imperialistic politics. In place of
the optimistic constructions of classical utopia and the continuations of the socialistic and technological utopianism of the early
nineteenth century, we now see a new genre: the pessimistic utopia, or anti-utopia.[38] William Morris' *News from Nowhere* (1871),
H. G. Wells' *The Time Machine* (1895), Aldous Huxley's *Brave
New World* (1932), and George Orwell's *1984* (1948) are the most
notable examples; one could also name Kubin's *Die andere Seite*
(1909), Kafka's "The Penal Colony" (1919), and Ernst Jünger's

Auf den Marmorklippen (1939). It is hard to say why the English predominate among these authors. Perhaps it is due to the existence of a traditional English genre (Swift). Or perhaps, unlike the German authors with their more pronounced morally and socially apocalyptic view, the liberal English elite, trusting in stable constitutional institutions and imbued with the idea of progress, is here expressing its sudden doubts or even horror. The aesthetics of the contents of individual works and the aesthetics of production complement each other here. The pessimistic utopias in the critical works by Wells, Huxley, and Orwell invert the utopian contents of the traditional time-place utopia.

The alternative to this genre, the prose of the utopian moment, does not invert the utopian content but rather dissolves it. If the anticipation of collective happiness and normative exempla has become questionable, then happiness may perhaps be redeemed in individual moments. The authors of the intensified moment, Proust, James Joyce, and Musil, replace the description of a state of social harmony or its inverse with the "I" in a state of emphatic perception, an "ecstasy" of "happiness" that transcends both social and purely private reality. Objective reality is no longer conceived as transformable into a utopia, futuristic anticipation disappears altogether, and utopian fantasy moves to the interior of the subject.[39]

II

This intensifies the problem that has always been part of the question of literary utopias because now we can clearly see the dual aspect of the utopian impulse. On the one hand, we are dealing with a moment of the fictional subject that is described or reflected by the author. We will call this possibility hypothetically an *aesthetic* utopia. On the other hand, we are dealing with an appeal to the reader that emerges from the fictionality of this portrayal of the moment. We will call this hypothetically the utopia of the *aesthetic*.[40] This utopia of the aesthetic is not identical with Adorno's or Bloch's conception of the utopian aspect of art.[41] For them, art promises another reality, a promise that negates the poor empirical reality without ever being fulfilled, whereas the above-mentioned model refers to the affective appeal to the reader's boundless fantasy. The "brilliance" of utopia, captured for Bloch and Adorno in the reflection of the "not yet,"[42] lies in the utopia of the aesthetic in the brilliance itself.[43] The question whether fictionality itself always contains a utopian element[44] can be answered at the outset by specifying the fictional: the opening up of the reader's fantasy potential, which is the condition of a utopia of the *aesthetic*, is less likely with a descriptive style in the sense of mimesis than with the various forms of modern literature characterized as "surrealistic" or "magical." The description of a society characterized as utopian does not necessarily constitue a utopia of the *aesthetic*, and the description of a nonutopian, real society is quite capable of triggering the above-mentioned effect. If classical utopias trigger the aesthetic-utopian effect, it is not simply because of their unambiguous utopian content; a mere additive inventory of utopian elements, for instance, would not be utopian. Instead, the effect depends on the work's "as if" structure,[45] that is, on its suggestive contribution to the sense of possibility that invites the reader to perform complementary fantasy work.[46]

In Proust, Joyce, and Musil, the "I" in the ecstasy of the moment unites elements of a utopia of the aesthetic with elements of an aesthetic utopia. The latter is announced by the names of Musil's and Joyce's heroes: the "man without qualities" and the winged man "Daedalus" announce an objective utopia. Neither, however, is a doer; they do not belong to the *Übermenschen* of modern literature.[47] They do as little as Proust's narrator, that is, they are not beings of action oriented toward goals or norms, but media of the momentary state of consciousness. Nevertheless, motifs and symbols of traditional utopian genres—the idyll and its opposite, satire—appear in these works, and this contradicts their distance from the paradigm and must be explained. Just as the ideal of the traditional utopia always implies the opposite of the impoverished present,[48] the utopian moment of the "I" that is alienated from society always presupposes a conscious, decisive, and radical critique of that society. This interdependence between idyll and satire, happiness and aggression, is necessary for the concept of the moment, and this refutes the suspicion that the utopian reduction will turn out to be a purely solipsistic maneuver of the great heirs of decadence. In the case of Walter Benjamin, it was not his political position but rather his recourse to the concept of the moment that gave rise to this suspicion. In the case of the cultural pessimists Proust, Joyce, and especially Musil,[49] the assumption of a resigned, if not reactionary, reduction of an objective social utopia to a subjective utopia of the pure "state of being" is justified. A comparative analysis of the emphasis on the moment in Proust, Joyce, and Musil will reveal its quality as a utopian topos with critical contents despite the fact that it is motivated by cultural pessimism. After that, we will be able to determine the revolutionary meaning of Benjamin's theory of the moment.

Proust's mémoire involontaire

Adorno, who, in contrast to the violent Benjamin, was incomparably receptive to Proust's work, writes, among many other precise comments: "Proust is concerned with an intellectual splitting of the atom, trying to lay open the most minute elements of the real and show them as force fields."[50] These words characterize the method of Proust's style, which can redeem the ideal connection among things that is created by our traditional categories of time and space only by shattering it and holding up the universal to the touchstone of the particular. The world Proust describes is a priori one in which the continuity of time is guaranteed only in the sum of moments of the visible. The rigidity with which true reality is sought only in the most intimate fragment of the "here and now" prevents us from mistaking this method for impressionism.

In order to correctly evaluate the concentrated, reflexive power of this momentariness, which prepares us for the utopian moment but does not yet complete it, we must recall the epistemological works of the Viennese psychologist Ernst Mach. From the analysis of our incoherent sensory impressions, Mach concluded that the ego is a fiction. This conclusion had a far-reaching effect on the literary generation of the turn of the century[51] and gave considerable impetus to the phenomenological question of the smallest unit of time[52] as a fact of consciousness, a question that was being debated at the time.[53] Hugo von Hofmannsthal's "Chandos" crisis can be seen as the most important datum of loss of the object before Proust's *Remembrance*. Its formal-aesthetic index: Hofmannsthal's prose is characterized by intuitive moments.[54]

Thus, to the extent that the transient, profane element of the Proustian moment of perception concerns a fragment of a particle of reality, must not be confused with a merely atmospheric or mood-setting element. Walter Pater, who, with Nietzsche, was the most important representative of the theory of aestheticism and influenced the epiphany of the moment in Joyce's early work,[55] juxtaposed the concept of the "situation" to that of "continuity" and looked for the "extraordinary" in the "situation."[56] But just as the special, mysterious hour in Verlaine, "L'heure exquise" in the cycle "La bonne chanson" as well as the discovery of the aesthetically celebrated moment in the decadent artists' experience of time finally limit the moment in subjective experience, Pater the theorist also ultimately did not cross this boundary in a utopian sense, even though he elevated "experience" to an aesthetic one. In comparison with Proust, Joyce, and Musil, Pater's concept of the "moment" lacks the dialectic reflection of a dual opposition, which alone makes the perception of the moment in the continuity of time into a utopian moment: the opposition of reflecting the moment and the opposition of being aware of the external world. Pater's particular moment was the final intensification of late romantic, neo-Platonic sensualism. It was not yet a focusing on the problem of personal "identity of experience instantaneously present to itself"[57] as formulated in Husserl's phenomenological essay, which was written at about the same time as Proust began his *Remembrance*. Husserl determined the concept of punctualism in such a way that "a punctual phase can never be for itself alone,"[58] but at the same time he determined the "actual now-point" as the "source-point"[59] of temporal-reflective modes of the course of events. The "actual *now*" is, to be sure, the focal point of "retentions,"[60] but it remains something "point-like."[61] Husserl insists on a priority of every "now" of our perception, so that Jacques Derrida was able to speak of the "punctuality of the instant" as a "myth" in his study of Husserl.[62]

Although Proust could not have been familiar with the phenomenological system that was developing in Germany, the reference to this system is necessary not merely because of a general analogy between the philosophical and literary discovery of the "punctual now" but also because of the particular similarity between Husserl's assumption of an interdependence between the "point" and "retentions" on the one hand and Proust's "scanned moment" and the *mémoire involontaire* on the other. These conceptual pairs correspond to Musil's distinction between manic and contemplative ecstasy. This analogy shows the qualitative leap from the aesthetic sensation of decadence to the profound stop of time in Proust. Only the opposition of "now" and "earlier" contained in the model of consciousness that Husserl developed and that Proust intuitively discovered creates the precondition for the moment to become not only emphatic but also utopian.

Several looming moments of this structure are found in the thirteen books of *Remembrance*.[63] For a grasp of the utopian moment, we will limit ourselves to the scene from the first part of *Swann's Way*, which has become known as the "madeleine scene." The first-person narrator describes a scene from his childhood when he hesitantly obeys his mother's exhortation to drink a cup of tea, dissolving the pastry known as a madeleine in a spoonful of the tea. The textual passage that is important in our context reads: "No sooner had the warm liquid, and the crumbs with it, touched my palate than a shudder ran through my whole body, and I stopped, intent upon the extraordinary changes that were taking place. An exquisite pleasure had invaded my senses, but individual, detached, with no suggestion of its origin."[64]

This passage contains the first element of the utopian "moment": the pure self-presence of the "now" in the temporal setting of the instant. Its metaphorical equipment as a specific fact of consciousness contains the reference to a "shudder," a feeling of being "intent upon the extraordinary changes," something "unusual" whose cause is unknown. What is known is an "exquisite pleasure." The purely punctual quality of this uniquely self-referential "now" achieves systematic precision through the indication that the feeling of happiness is "individual, detached" [*isolé*], its "origin" remains unknown [*sans cause*]. Up to this point the moment portrayed by Proust means the procedure that Bloch criticized and called placing emphasis "senselessly on one point," "monadizing," where the "now" point no longer corresponds with other "now" points.[65] Proust, however, allowed the momentum of the pure "now" to be followed by the momentum of reflex, if not of reflection. That forms the second element of the utopian moment: The first-person narrator describes how the instant of happiness is immediately followed by the need for "truth," for clarifying the cause of this experience. As if in an experiment, he reproduces in memory the "unremembered state" (*état inconnu*) [66] of the moment that has just passed, at first without finding an explanation, until the phase of reconstruction reaches a moment of intensity that is still stamped by unknown causes but rouses something "palpitating" in him,[67] introducing the second element, that of remembering: "Will it ultimately reach the clear surface of my consciousness, this memory, this old, dead moment which the magnetism of an identical moment has traveled so far to importune, to disturb, to raise up out of the very depths of my being?"[68]

As the experience thus progresses, the original "punctualizing" is dropped. The narrator intuits the same structure for the utopian moment that Bloch characterized with an eye to Benjamin's "blasting open" of time, a phrase embodying political intentions.[69] Proust carried the process of cognition—that is, remembering under the category of the "moment-like"—to the point of enlightenment: "And suddenly the memory returns"[70]—that is, the conscious memory of the taste of the madeleine in the long-ago days at Combray. This conscious memory makes clear that the unknown cause of the feeling of happiness lay in the memory that remained *unknown*, the *mémoire involontaire* that was elicited by tasting the madeleine. This coupling of the present, sudden moment with a temporally distant moment, which enables the present moment to exist without robbing it of its dignity, completes the second element of the utopian "now."

Husserl would call this "retention."[71] The phenomenon of the "unusual" state of consciousness called up by the *mémoire involontaire* is no mere repetition of the first phenomenon.[72] The temporal distance between original and remembered experience does not constitute a mere mechanical, causal connection of justification but rather the foundation of the feeling of "happiness" in the secondary moment.

Here, with quasi-phenomenological precision, we have the myth of charm and grace lost through reflection and never again to be achieved, which Kleist told for German classical aesthetics in his parable about the young man recognizing himself in the mirror in the essay "Über das Marionettentheater" (On the puppet theater). But the myth is altered to serve a different purpose: happiness (charm, grace) is now retained or achieved precisely through an act of the unconscious consciousness. Kleist's parable concluded with a cultural utopia: eating from the tree of knowledge again in order to fall back into the state of innocence, "that is the final chapter in the history of the world."[73] The coincidence of two similar but not simultaneous "now" points creates in the second moment that unconscious happiness in which scholars early on recognized a suspension of time.[74] And this extinction of past and future in a moment of objective ecstasy of the "moment" can be seen as the temporal structure of utopian happiness in Proust, Joyce, and Musil.

It is essential to see that for Proust the moment grounded in memory loses nothing of its contingency.[75] Jauß, as Adorno also indicated, excluded the Platonic misunderstanding of the moment and pointed out the pure "immanence" of an "experience."[76] The rediscovered time does not point back to a "transcendental home," but to an "earthly beyond."[77]

We can indicate here only briefly how Proust's complex temporal structure is continued in the fact that the remembered time is doubly remembered: remembered in the consciousness of the boy and re-remembered in the consciousness of the writing author.[78] To that extent, as Jauß demonstrated, the *promesse de bonheur* is not contained in the utopianism of the narrated memory but is extended into the future of the work to be written, in this real identification that remains for the author.[79] This argument implies, to be sure, the suspicion that the "negativity of coincidence"[80] places too great a burden on the utopian quality of the *souvenir involontaire*. As a result, Jauß adds a flanking support to the utopia of the moment in the form of a subject-oriented, not phenomenon-oriented, concept of a quasi entelechy of the artist. The utopia of the moment guaranteed by phenomenology is thus transformed into a utopia of contents, of the idea. We will disregard this alternative result.

The boy's "unheard-of feeling of happiness" is based, as it turns out, on the not-yet-comprehended memory of the moment of an earlier time in childhood. The remembered childhood is the only consistently graspable sign of personal identification: "Proust's fidelity to childhood is a fidelity to the idea of happiness, which he would not let himself be talked out of for anything in the world."[81] It is a traumatic holding fast to the points of narrative concentration, as if each temporal step past them would mean loss of identity. This productive regression recalls Freud's explanatory model of artistic creativity: the fantasy of the poet is stimulated by the memory of an early childhood experience whose wish repeats itself and manages to find sublimated fulfillment in the aesthetic act.[82] Novalis anticipated this Freudian model of the return to childhood in his aesthetic myths.

In a formal aesthetic sense and in terms of genre history, recourse to childhood means evocation of the idyll and all its utopian implications. This recourse to the topos of childhood or utopian idyll is enhanced by the accompanying images of peaceful, charming nature: garden, river landscape, clouds, sea. The moments of "Balbec"—they all form a symbolic inventory that, since the Arcadian Renaissance, has utopian features.[83] Ernst Bloch warned that the time-and-place utopia of the paradise of childhood and nature could congeal into a resigned pattern of flight from reality.[84] However, the sequence or dialectic we have described of now-point and memory guarantees that no representation of place occurs; rather, a metaphor is established for the temporal consciousness that the idyll in this remembered sense is indeed past.

In Proust, the occasional flaring up of childhood and nature is a sign of undistorted ideology, of social criticism: the poetic locations are untouched by the satiric qualities that characterize the society Proust describes. The participation of the grand bourgeois and millionaire Proust in this society, the attitude of the dandy and his savoring, even reverent connoisseurship of a code and a civilizing system of order[85] cannot obscure his thoroughgoing distance from the emptiness of this society. The precision of accumulated moments of social situations, which characteristically do not "light up," presents a specific form of objective satire. Laughter comes not from the partisanship of the satiric gaze but from the authenticity of the material itself. Benjamin calls it a "physiology of chatter,"[86] and Adorno points out the radical nature of this satiric gaze by tracing Proust's ability to listen "to reality with such precision" to a refusal of the compulsion to adapt.[87] Proust did not go through the "false maturity of resignation" and "kept faith with the childhood potential for unimpaired experience."[88] The utopian "moment" in the form of the "happiness" of remembered childhood, we may conclude, here serves the function of social criticism. Idyll and satire are necessary opposites in the structure of this utopian "moment" in this life.

James Joyce's Epiphany

Proust did not present his utopian moment in a theoretical sense. Joyce, however, from his early period at the beginning of the century on called the related phenomenon in his work epiphany, and Joyce scholarship has focused on the origin and theoretical meaning of the term.[89] The term appears for the first time at several points in Joyce's early novel *Stephen Hero*. Its varying meaning has led to divergent intellectual-historical derivations. Umberto Eco[90] has convincingly refuted the once dominant view that Joyce's Thomist studies not merely influenced the concept but actually shaped it.[91] Not only the Thomist interpretation but also every variant of it implying a concept of substance would be of crucial importance for the utopian "momentary" structure of the "here and now." Therefore, we will gather and compare the defining characteristics of the epiphany in *Stephen Hero* before we consider the epiphany in its literary form. In that form, it appears explicitly in *A Portrait of the Artist as a Young Man* (1916) and less prominently in *Ulysses* (1922 in Paris; first legal English edition, 1936).

The first definition: during an evening walk, Stephen witnesses a trivial, ambiguous exchange between a young woman and a young man. Stephen hears only fragments of their conversation. The reflection on this scene reads:

> This triviality made him think of collecting many such moments together in a book of epiphanies. By an epiphany he meant a sudden spiritual manifestation, whether in the vulgarity of speech or of gesture or in a memorable phase of the mind itself. He believed that it was for the man of letters to record these epiphanies with extreme care, seeing that they themselves are the most delicate and evanescent of moments.[92]

This reflection and definition of epiphany is followed by the experience of such an epiphany. In observing a clock in a public place, he describes its impression along with other street impressions by means of the temporal characteristics of the epiphany: he notices suddenly, he knows "all at once," that he is experiencing an "epiphany" and characterizes the "glimpses" of the clock as the "gropings of a spiritual eye" that becomes a "vision" when concentrated on an "exact focus."[93] Finally, we have the concluding characteristic that leads the previous attributes of the particular, accidental, and temporal back to the concept of substance that supported the Thomist interpretation: "It is just in this epiphany that I find the third, the supreme quality of beauty."[94]

The allusion to a "supreme quality" of beauty is doubtless an unambiguous reference to Joyce's reading of Thomas' definition of beauty in its three aspects: *integritas* or *perfectio, proportio* or *consonantia,* and *claritas.*[95] Joyce, who simplified this schema in his translation as wholeness, harmony, and radiance,[96] apparently identified the aesthetic quality of the epiphany in *Stephen Hero* with Thomas' *claritas,* which he translates as radiance. This translation contains a clear displacement of the Latin meaning. Whereas the Thomist concept of *claritas* implies a metaphysical ontic quality[97] as well as the theological meaning of "light and reason," as represented by the "word" and the "son,"[98] Joyce emphasizes an accidental property or effect, the immanence of "radiating," as we have seen in the analysis of the conversation he witnessed. This difference between "radiance" as a substantive concept and "radiance" as an aesthetic effect has become significant for the history of aesthetics. It can be traced from Plato's definition of the beautiful in *Phaedrus* to the rhetoric of the late classical period, especially Longinus' *On the Sublime,* to Burke's and Kant's aesthetics of the sublime,[99] and finally to its dramatization in Nietzsche's *The Birth of Tragedy.* As if the concept of *claritas* still obscured Joyce's specific idea of the way in which phenomena surprise the percipient, Joyce equated it with the Latin word *quidditas,* which he again connects to the temporal modality of the epiphany he describes: "This is the moment which I call epiphany."[100]

In *Portrait of the Artist,* which contains the actual description of illuminated moments but no longer the concept of epiphany, Joyce repeats the concept of *quidditas.* The explanation[101] of the term completes the rejection of the Scholastic idea of beauty that was obvious even in *Stephen Hero.* Joyce again calls the "radiance" of beauty *quidditas.* He no longer derives the radiance of the object that triggers an epiphany from the "structure" of a "soul" that appears in it, as he had in *Stephen Hero*. Instead, he derives it from the isolated moment of radiance itself: "The instant wherein that supreme quality of beauty, the clear radiance of the esthetic image, is apprehended luminously by the mind which has been arrested by its wholeness and fascinated by its harmony is the luminous silent stasis of esthetic pleasure."[102] Joyce no longer refers to an ideal content of beauty but lets the phenomenal effect and the recipient's situation shine through the Thomist conceptual structure. Thus he also speaks of a "mysterious instant," which Shelley compared to a "fading coal."[103] The temporal isolation in the moment of effect is joined by a spatial isolation that distinguishes the act of aesthetic perception from others: "The first phase of apprehension is a bounding line, drawn about the object to be apprehended. An esthetic image is presented to us either in space or in time. But, temporal or spatial, the esthetic image is first luminously apprehended as self-bounded and self-contained upon the immeasurable background of space or time which is not it."[104]

Looking back on the analogy between Proust's and Husserl's ideas of the interdependence between the "now-point" and "earlier," we see clearly how Joyce, taking the traditional aesthetics of Aristotle and Thomas as his point of departure, also arrives at a phenomenological definition of the aesthetic as a boundary phenomenon. The accompanying isolation of aesthetic concentration on a single point in space and time is the method that Bloch has criticized as monadizing.[105] We must now ask how the demonstrated change in the theory of epiphany affected the actual literary presentation of the moment and to what extent it is still useful to speak of an epiphany in the case of the ecstatic moments described in *Portrait*. We should recall that in one of the above-mentioned early definitions of the epiphany Joyce spoke of two variants: the "vulgarity of speech or of gesture" or "a memorable phase of the mind itself." He called both types a "sudden spiritual manifestation." Jacques Aubert suggested doing away with the concept of epiphany altogether, at least as far as the works after *Stephen Hero* are concerned, because its original meaning of "accidental revelation" changed to the "*mode* of appearing of the meaning."[106] Umberto Eco, on the other hand, retained the concept of epiphany because he did not believe it was necessary to rely on the Scholastic tradition but instead found the concept anticipated in D'Annunzio,[107] whose work, as Eco showed, manifests striking parallels to *Portrait*.[108] Whatever we may think of this concept, it is clear that Aubert and Eco agree in their rejection of the Scholastic interpretation established by Noon and focus on the fact that Joyce's epiphany concept belongs to the realm of the aesthetics of reception.

If Eco on the one hand concludes that Joyce's word *epiphany* comes directly from D'Annunzio's title *Epifania del fuoco*,[109] and on the other hand—and with good reason—finds essential elements of the epiphany prefigured in Walter Pater's afterword to his work on the Renaissance,[110] then it makes sense to retain the concept as a technical term for the phenomenal moment without limiting it to an exclusionary thesis of derivation.

In *Portrait*, the ecstatic moment is announced relatively early on, namely in the second chapter. There it shows the same connections that struck us in Proust's happiness of memory, which recaptured nature and childhood. Stephen feels the calming effect of the "peace of the gardens" but does not want to play with the other children. He searches in the real world for the "unsubstantial image" that his soul so constantly beheld. He knew that he and the image would encounter each other. Then they would be alone, surrounded by "darkness and silence." In that "moment of supreme tenderness he would be transformed."[111] He would "fade into something impalpable." His transfiguration would take place in a "magic moment."[112] In that magic moment, weakness, timidity, and inexperience would fall away from him. It is not memory but anticipation that is here described as an event of consciousness. But it is the consciousness of a young boy, triggered in the idyll of a garden. The "magic," which is contained within a single "moment," dissolves the categories of time and space, as does Proust's *mémoire involontaire*. It is transfigured into the invisible, where physical time no longer exists.

Finally, a conceptual image for the entelechy of the artist appears, which in Proust, as we indicated, represented the remembering process of writing itself. In a happy intuition the boy, who knows "that he was different from the others,"[113] anticipates the Daedalus motif, which is later made explicit. This introduction of the motif of the "moment" is followed in the fourth chapter by two interconnected scenes that Eco compared with D'Annunzio's text as examples of the epiphany. The first scene takes up the transformation motif of the "magic moment" and begins by identifying "Stephen" with "Daedalus" in the image of a "hawklike man flying sunward above the sea."[114] The sensory association, first established by a voice that seems to come from "beyond the world," occurs in a "timeless" time that admits only the characteristic of "mood."

The image of this moment is the realized prophecy of the first magic moment. The second, which now follows, is characterized as follows: "His heart trembled; his breath came faster and a wild spirit passed over his limbs as though he were soaring sunward. His heart trembled in an ecstasy of fear and his soul was in flight."[115] This "soul" approaches the "ecstasy of flight" that made his eyes "radiant," his breath "wild," and his limbs "tremulous and wild and radiant." It is the "soul" that had "arisen from the grave of boyhood."[116] To understand the subjective character of this epiphany it is essential to see how the objective myth of the artist-artificer is once more bent back into the motif of remembered childhood. The ecstasy, characterized as one of "fear" and of "flight," is not grounded in any other thing but is a self-referential state. It is the state of highest experience of the self,[117] whereby the "new" is experienced as the old, the prophecy of childhood.

This scene of epiphany is followed by a second one composed of two phases: the appearance itself and its effect on the observing subject. The appearance is the girl on the beach, to whom momentary magic has given the look of a strange and beautiful seabird, hinting at a secret affinity between male and female bird-humans.[118] After the silent girl has become aware of the observer's gaze, she looks at him for a long time,[119] turns toward the ocean again, and "a faint flame trembled on her cheek."[120] The effect on Stephen, sunk in contemplation of her, is introduced by the phrase "profane joy."[121] That recalls the earthly horizon of the utopian moment. The girl is to him an "angel of mortal youth and beauty,"[122] a pairing of concepts that recurs twice. What is said of the first impression of the appearance, that a blush "trembled on her cheek," is repeated in the description of the state of the reflecting observer: after the "moment of ecstasy" has disappeared, the observer closes his eyes and once more experiences the sensation of sensual "swooning."[123] It is not like the first experience, but rather a state in which the first experience is reflectively remembered and its transitoriness made conceptually definite without imbuing it with transcendence.

The temporal structure of three successive psychic sensations is not identical with the past and present "now-points." Still, that structure shows a phenomenological perception at work here that dismantles classical categories of time and space.[124] These sensations, to be sure, point to a cause of the utopian effect. The effect is not grounded in an ideal set of symbols or archetypal metaphors but in the discovered happiness of the perceiving, reflecting moments. "Nature," which Proust had already recognized as part of the utopian moment, is integrated into these moments. The metaphor of the ocean is central to the image of the bird-girl. Descriptions of a paradiselike nature,[125] which sometimes even take on the characteristics of the heroic idyll, form the beginning and end[126] of the bird-girl episode. These images of nature do not become rigid archetypical symbols, just as they do not in Proust; they remain particles of aesthetic perception. The importance of Eco's claim that Joyce was influenced by D'Annunzio's *Epifania* is primarily that it proves the pure immanence of the moment, much as our relating Benjamin back to Proust did. Aubert saw this clearly when he said that after *Stephen Hero* the epiphany was no longer the "revelation" of a "soul" but must be understood as the "*mode of appearance of meaning.*"[127] Whether the relationship between Joyce and D'Annunzio is as compelling as Eco believes is not the point. Eco bases his thesis primarily on the fact that Joyce and D'Annunzio both use metaphors of "lightning," of "shimmering radiance," of the "shudder," of "flame," of the "sun."[128] We used Nietzsche's aesthetics earlier in this volume to show that these metaphors all belong to the rhetorical arsenal of the sublime,[129] a fact that has been underestimated because of the traditional favoring of mystical and neo-Platonic traditions in the study of premodern irrationalism.[130] The analogies between Joyce and D'Annunzio can thus be traced to the rhetoric of the sublime that Nietzsche and Walter Pater rediscovered and that the Decadents took up and transformed regardless of any real influence of D'Annunzio on Joyce.

On this secure basis of a purely aesthetic immanence, we can now name the difference between Joyce's utopian moment, the aestheticist moment of D'Annunzio, and the Decadents. Eco believed that Joyce's epiphanies were the "sensory-concrete precipitate of intellectual potentialities."[131] The utopian quality, we might add, lies in the specific graduation of experiences grasped as isolated points in time, where the pure "now" forms a circle with the "afterward" that has become a part of it. That is the structure of the pure "state." In *Ulysses*, the reflection of this relationship of times as the intensive "moment" of imagination is expressed more clearly and definitively than anywhere else. "In the intense instant of imagination, when the mind, Shelley says, is a fading coal, then that which I was is that which I am and that which in possibility I may come to be."[132]

For Proust's time complex it was characteristic that the vanishing point of remembered time presupposed the precision of real time. The minor utopian forms of the idyll and satire complement each other. Childhood, retained and never relinquished, guarantees the acuity of Proust's vision of society. This correspondence of idyll and satire, timelessness and time, childhood and grown-up world, nature and society is only hinted at in *Portrait*. It will unfold fully in *Ulysses*. The epiphanies, which appear there and in the prose pieces with the same title, correspond to some extent to the concept of the "vulgarity of speech" mentioned in the first variant of the epiphany quoted above from *Stephen Hero*. On the one hand this guarantees the "sudden spiritual manifestation," the connection between past and present "moments" in the lightning flash of a "by the way," which the surrealists also sought. On the other hand, the attack on the world becomes more radical. Idyll and satire, nature not mythicized but mythologically remembered and culture regarded blasphemously, complement each other to the point of synaesthesia, in which the sea is "snotgreen" and yet the evocation of "Thalatta."[133] Richard Ellman has emphasized that Joyce grants the past no hegemony over the present.[134] Joyce's reaction to C. G. Jung's interpretation of *Ulysses* is revealing for this rejection of myth. In a letter to his German translator, Georg Goyert, dated October 22, 1932, Joyce said of Jung: "Did you see Jung's article and his letter to me. He seems to have read *Ulysses* from first to last without one smile. The only thing to do in such a case is to change one's drink!"[135]

Through this rejection of mythology, Joyce's moment has become what Benjamin called "profane illumination" and sought but did not find in the surrealists, especially Breton.[136] A comparison between the topos of the utopian moment in Breton's *Nadja* and a Joycean epiphany would show the social-critical potential in Joyce's case still more clearly. The history of oppression by British civilization is recalled as a "profane illumination," in the sense of Benjamin's "Theses on the Philosophy of History," and the history of the "victor" is ridiculed.[137]

Musil's "Other State"

Like Joyce, Robert Musil was not only a portrayer but also a theorist of the moment. Unlike Joyce and Proust, he explicitly named this moment "utopia." In his *Man Without Qualities*,[138] Musil most comprehensively gave voice to and analyzed the phenomenon and concept of the utopia reduced to a moment. That is true for both the intellectual foundation of this utopia, the phenomenological aspect of the "now-point" between past and future, and its metaphorical expression: the images of timeless happiness, especially those having to do with Eros and nature. The historically advanced character of Musil's analysis and evocation of the moment is evident in the fact that he—unlike any of the writers before him who emphasized the moment—constantly asked about the objective relevance of the "sudden" experience, which, as we have seen, remains the only datum after the collapse of all objective referentiality. In a more exacting way than Proust's, Musil's work presupposes a critical acquaintance with Ernst Mach's psychological investigations[139] as well as with the problem of the "now" that Husserl discusses in phenomenological terms, but especially the empirical psychologism of Carl Stumpf and Franz von Brentano.[140] The young Max Scheler, in his early work *Die Transzendentale und die Psychologische Methode* (Transcendental and psychological method), had answered in the negative the question that Musil, more strongly in the grips of doubt, dramatized in the *Man Without Qualities*: whether the here and now of our state of consciousness is an original datum or not.[141] The opposition between idyll and satire implied by the utopia of the "moment" is repeated in Musil as the intellectually dramatic contradiction between phenomenological mysticism and positivist, Enlightenment

skepticism. The reduction of utopia to the pure fact of consciousness of the "moment" and the conflict between the esoteric "I"
and real society are here developed most rigorously and represent a
pure realization of the formula Karl Mannheim coined for utopian
consciousness: "Utopian is a consciousness that finds itself out of
joint with the 'being' that surrounds it."[142]

The "empty" quality of this formula announces the problem of
utopia in Musil's moment so precisely because its lack of traditional
utopian content is accentuated. The utopian moment in Musil
most explicitly liberates the thesis that all dominant and past
ideas, convictions, myths, that is, the cultural objectifications
that function as utopias in terms of their contents, have been
ideologically destroyed and are thus untrue. Musil's emphatic motifs complement a structure of the utopian moment in which the
elements found in Proust and Joyce are repeated in their particular
stylistic context, but are more sharply juxtaposed in Musil's heroic
experiment. That is why Musil's work offers the most favorable
conditions for putting the concept of the reduced utopia to the
test. For now we can more clearly answer whether the model of a
utopia reduced to the "emptiness" of the emphatic consciousness
remains an unresolvable intellectual paradox. The internal contradiction arises because the experienced "now-point" cannot do
without the traditional metaphors of happiness, whereby, however,
an ecstasy that completes itself in time becomes a utopia of place,
or even admits a perspective on the historical future.

Before we answer this question using Musil's reduced utopia, the
so-called "other state," we must clear up two methodological difficulties:

> 1. Musil, independent of his theory of the "other
> state," set up alternative utopian models.[143] These mental
> attitudes, characterized as the "utopia of precise living," the
> "utopia of essayism," the "utopia of the motivated life," and
> the "utopia of the inductive inclination,"[144] all stand, to be
> sure, in a specific, either dialectic or merely additive relation-
> ship to the utopia of the "other state" while definitely and
> explicitly differing from the latter's character of reduction.
> The utopia of the "other state" is thus only the mystical and,
> ultimately, thematically the most significant variation of the

utopian "sense of possibilities" whose "subjunctive passion" and rationalist-enlightenment presuppositions Albrecht Schöne has demonstrated.[145] We will discuss these theorems of the "hypothetical" life that circle around utopia as a sense of possibilities only to the extent that they are necessary for an understanding of the "other state" as a utopia of the moment.

2. Apart from the preliminary states and prefigurations that function like leitmotifs ("The forgotten, exceedingly important affair with the major's wife"), the "other state" is presented in the two sections published by Musil himself— especially in the second book, entitled "Into the Millennium"—as one of contemplation ("Holy Conversations"; "A great event is on the way. But no one has noticed it"), whereas the immediacy of mystical states ("Beginning of a Series of Wondrous Events," "Moonbeams in Daylight") is authorized only in the form of galley proofs corrected by the author.[146] Finally, the completion of the incest, which up to then had been restrained in the potentiality of the subjunctive ("The Journey to Paradise"), is part of the literary estate, whose significance in Musil's unfinished work is still disputed by scholars.[147] Because we are not concerned with evaluating the *Man Without Qualities* as a whole work, we will set aside these editorial and conceptual problems.[148]

We choose the model of the "other state" independently of its time of origin and authorization by Musil. From the labyrinth of the finally unresolvable questions about the composition of the work, we can still derive a preliminary conclusion about the utopia of the moment in Musil. This form of ecstasy of the ego is from the beginning a matter of two conflicting possibilities: the state that is esoteric, behaves hypothetically, vacillating indecisively between theory and contemplation, and the state of absolute erotic exaltation from the I to a Thou, which violates the taboo of incest. In anticipation, we can also conclude that this alternative corresponds to the dual attributes that make the moment model of utopia generally so complex: the dialectic of the intuitions of time and space and the dual aspect of aesthetic utopia and utopia of the aesthetic developed above. We must ask, therefore, to what extent the "other state" represents a happy emphasis on consciousness, that is, to what extent it remains reflective and in opposition to the "surrounding being" (Mannheim) and whether the incest of the siblings entails a loss of this reflective moment, thus completely eliminating time and engendering a mythology of paradigmatic space—and here that would represent the heroic idyll—in which there is no longer any relationship to real society. Finally, we must ask to what extent the fictionality of the "other state," either as discussed in theory or portrayed vividly in the work, vouchsafes a utopia of the aesthetic that no longer requires the particular sensation of the violation of sexual boundaries.

In Proust's *Remembrance of Things Past,* the linguistic gesture "in those moments" and the linguistic gesture "in this moment" freeze time either reflectively or by suggestively presentifying it. In a similar way, an unending chain of formulas for the moment of "now" runs through Musil's *Man Without Qualities,* such as "only for a fleeting moment,"[149] "in that fraction of a second,"[150] "all at once."[151] The pure point between "past and future"[152] is here the metaphorical indication of a fact of consciousness with whose analysis Musil was familiar, primarily through his study of Franz von Brentano's *Psychologie vom empirischen Standpunkt aus* (Psychology from an empirical standpoint, 1874),[153] although we should not assume a conscious imitation of the epistemological-psychological aspect of the phenomenon of the moment.[154] For Musil, Brentano's crucial insight was that temporality always only meant what was "currently present."[155] H. W. Schaffnit has explored the effect of empirical psychology on Musil's idea of the "here and now." Here, we can consider this effect only in its literary translation, that is, in the dramatization of the "now-point." From the analysis of time by Mach, Stumm, and Brentano, Musil drew the conclusion that there was no reality beyond or outside the here and now, that the physical sensation in this moment was the only psychic certainty we ever have. Musil as writer, that is, as creator of an "unheard-of event," of necessity had to work on a fundamental deepening of such a "now-point." Positivistic psychology, which Husserl had already attacked in the *Logical Investigations,*[156] never lost its imperceptible influence on Musil. The metamorphosis of the "now-point" to a mystical event understood as a phenomenon could thus not occur without the most severe epistemological scruple.

This scruple contains the question: what is an experience? How does a moment in time become an experience if I do not simultaneously encounter it as an "idea" that is soon exhausted and loses the dignity of its sudden appearance? As Ulrich explains it to Clarisse:

> For you are an idea yourself, one in a particular state. You are touched by a breath of something, and it's like when the quivering of strings suddenly produces a note. And then there's something there in front of you like a mirage, and the tangle of your soul takes on shape, becoming an unending cavalcade, and all the beauties of the world seem to stand along its road. Such things are often brought about by one single idea. But after a while it comes to resemble all the other ideas that you have had before, subordinating itself to them and becoming part of your outlook and your character, your principles and your moods. By then it has lost its wings and taken on an unmysterious solidity.[157]

Musil at first grasps the "idea" as a sudden, previously unknown phenomenon, much as Kleist analyzed and, so to speak, discovered it in his "Über die allmähliche Verfertigung der Gedanken beim Reden" in the passage on Count Mirabeau's political insight.[158] The same idea then appears not only in the state of exhaustion, of having lost its temporal modality of suddenness, but also in its necessary transition to ideology within a personal life history. The "idea" loses the metaphors of "wings" and "mystery." The concept of idea implies the temporal "always," which, applied to consciousness, means: what came before. But Musil's argument, and his emotional truth, is that "lived experience" can then never be kept pure. The harmony of intellectual certainty and mysterious immediacy is the ideal "now," which Musil seeks but never finds. This "now" already contains the déjà vu of old ideas that have become ideologies. Ulrich's problem is that he does not want to admit the possibility of "events without 'meaning' "; he searches for an "unending state" in contrast to "eternal, vain momentariness."[159]

The model of the utopian moment that contains the "other state" thus has a structure that remains paradoxical: it contains psychic events, spiritual momentariness, which at the same time should not be "in vain" but "should be as meaningful as possible."[160] It is this model that complements in a utopian sense the novel's negative opening question about the extent to which the human being can be a center. The dissolution of the anthropocentric principle makes itself felt because the "private" self is taken to be superannuated: "for the belief that the most important thing about experience is the experiencing of it, and about deeds the doing of them, is beginning to strike most people as naive."[161] But Ulrich's drama centers precisely on the ability to "experience." He attributes to others a loss of naiveté that is actually true only of himself. The resultant tension gives rise to the model of the "other state." Musil's debt to empirical psychology, which we noted above, permits him neither Proust's leap into narrated memory nor Joyce's attempt at epiphany. Even Proust's memory is characteristically not a reproduction of what was once experienced. The experiential character of this memory was based on the "unheard-of" sensation of an unconscious remembering. The epistemological aporia of Proust's moment is dissolved in the relation between "now-point" and "retention." It is well known that Musil displaced into the erotic moment his sought-for utopia of an experience that was not discharged in the idea but that nevertheless "signified," his search for the deprivatization of the deeply private and its transportation into "greatness." Only such a moment could transcend the traditional topos of erotic passion—hence the motif of incest or the hermaphroditic self-encounter.[162]

We should recall that the motif of sibling incest here does not derive from the sensation of decadence of late romanticism, as Thomas Mann, taking the theme from Wagner, once again staged it in his story "The Blood of the Volsungs." Instead, it is an allegory of cultural prehistory, as Benjamin notes in relation to Goethe's symbolism in *Faust II*.[163] The erotically charged encounter between Stephen Daedalus and the bird-girl belongs in this context as well, where motifs from cultural anthropology (regression) and psychoanalysis (superego) intersect. As long as the series of Musil's attempts— or rather self-experiments—presents itself as erotic reflection or perceptual-motor conversations of the siblings, their ecstasies or mystical moments[164]—Musil uses the phrase "daylight mysticism"—have the quality of *contemplatio*. Brosthaus pointed out Musil's own distinction between two forms of the "other state," motor ecstasy and sensory ecstasy. He calls sensory ecstasy contemplation.[165] Its opposite, motor ecstasy, is partially represented in the manic states of Clarisse and Moosbrugger, and in the "other state" of incest in "The Journey to Paradise." In this variation, the reflective suddenness that is anchored in contemplation gives way to an irrationalism whose ideological implications extend from Musil to the analysis of para-fascist motifs to a parallel between incest and the outbreak of World War I.[166] Musil thus withdraws to a moral criticism of the violation of the cultural norm and does not pursue the utopian potential of breaking the taboo itself, a goal the novel aims for in its "Moosbrugger" and "Clarisse" episodes.

Like Proust's *mémoire involontaire* and Joyce's epiphany, Musil's "other state" is furnished with mysterious-wondrous images of nature.[167] The prefiguration of the "garden" as idyll gives the siblings the same dignity, removed from all reality, as in Proust's remembrances of childhood and in the moments at the seashore of Joyce's young man. Here as there we find that time is suspended; the pure present of the "trembling" joy of contemplation rules. But this "stop" of time in the garden scenes is always prevented from hardening into a mythology by the passages sublimating their pointillistic precision and by their reflective difference in perception.[168] While the siblings carry on their theoretically endless dialogue, in which the mystical moments of the "garden" and the "summer day" remain integrated, those moments are still open to eschatological metaphors: the "millennium," the "kingdom of love," this utopia that Novalis brought into modern literature, could "break out at any moment."[169] Such an eschatological moment has always been in opposition to the normal state. From Musil's theoretical compulsion to wrest a "dual aspect" from every state,[170] we can conclude concerning the reduction to the utopian moment that the reality of the "whole" never disappears.

This reflective intellectual attitude does not lead to an inference of a "new" eschatology, that is, a myth. The eschatological concepts remain self-conscious quotations of an infinite conversation, that is, much like Benjamin's "Theses on the Philosophy of History," they can only be understood as allegories that "make use of" a set of theological concepts.[171] We can conclude this from the utopian topos itself and not from Musil's private disposition. As soon as Musil no longer discussed the mental process of utopian longing in the precise and original terms of epistemological and psychologistic analysis but had to present it in images, he had to rely on eschatological metaphors, because of all the available images they most closely approached the boundary where one transgresses the cultural norm.

In contrast to the idyll of the garden of contemplation, the presentation of the ocean in "The Journey to Paradise" exhibits all the symptoms of an image that has congealed into a myth.[172] The idyll of the garden of endless conversation has become a heroic idyll in which European cultural myths are cited. The heavily symbolic scene of the "rocky coves of the Aegean Sea" in *Faust II* and Nietzsche's panic fear[173] are probable corresponding elements to which the symbolic moment of the ocean between cliffs and midday stillness refers. The change in the metaphors of nature is thus guaranteed by a paradoxical shift in the meaning of the garden motif. The garden idyll of conversation contains all the characteristics of "paradise" whereas the "Journey to Paradise" introduces the fall into sin. The subject-oriented utopia of the moment and the indeterminate fact then disappears, however, and transforms itself into a utopia of place. Accordingly, the dialectical relationship of idyll and satire, which was characteristic of Proust's and Joyce's moment and also of Musil's contemplative moment, disappears here. The contemplative variant of the "other state" necessarily presupposes the ironizing of contemporary myths: Walter's[174] and Diotima's[175] culturally conservative idealism, Leinsdorf's "great idea,"[176] Clarisse's cult of genius centered on Nietzsche,[177] Arnheim's world view of the soul and economy,[178] the presentation of all the prefascist private myths in Meingast,[179] Hans,[180] and not least the comic leitmotif of "parallel action"—all of these represent interwoven scenes of a great satire[181] on bourgeois society at the end of the epoch of its certainties. Its life-ensuring myths are unmasked as false, that is, as ideological, because the novel's hero is at work on a "contentless" utopia, one no longer determined by "ideas" that cannot keep pace with his "sense of facts." "Schmeisser's"[182] socialist utopia is drawn into this satire, and that precludes any political solution to the hero's utopian longing and points up the interiority of the utopia of the "other state," which relativizes all objective utopias as "ideas." Two polar perspectives open up: the perspective on a movement of progressive

moments even though such a movement is experienced only sub-
jectively, and the perspective on the symbolism of place, which is
distanced from the subject and in which categories of utopian
immanence, such as happiness and freedom, lose all meaning because the experience merely takes place but without being understood save through recourse to archetypal images.

III

Is the utopia of the moment a negative utopia? Does this negativity
have anything to do with fictionality? In examining how Proust,
Joyce, and Musil vary in structuring their emphasis on the moment, we saw that the "monadizing" that Bloch so distrusted, that
is, the isolation of a temporal point within the forward progress of
time, occurs only in Musil's second variant of the "other state,"
which is represented primarily in the chapter "The Journey to
Paradise." The reduction of time to a psychologically presentified
"now" is not blind in the works of Proust, Joyce, and Musil but
instead implies an "earlier" and even a "later," that is, it still
retains the normal time of history as an alternative.

To be sure, for these three authors normal time contains no
datum of happiness—and this is where the question about negativity arises. Even in Benjamin, the political concept of progress is
distanced, and in Musil it is relinquished explicitly, whereas in
Proust and Joyce it is implicitly renounced. The fact that Benjamin
and Musil hold up to ridicule or ironize only an unreflective variant
of the socialist idea of progress should not lead us to conclude that
the idea of progress of scientific Marxism would be more acceptable
to them. Benjamin and Musil both engage instead in eschatology.
Musil speaks of a "millennium" that could begin at any "moment,"[183] Benjamin cites Hegel's reference to the "Kingdom of
God"[184] and refers to the Jewish tradition that the Messiah could
arrive "every second."[185] However, for both of them this messi-
anic-eschatological set of metaphors does not have a theological
character but is a symbolic semantics for a utopian horizon that
evades any reduction to a concept and that uses eschatological
concepts merely as an allegorical reference. A theological interpretation would represent a conventional misunderstanding of these
two profane mystics. In both cases, the metaphors are instruments

for a hope for another reality that argues in a certain "decisionistic" way.

These metaphors are instruments not merely in the sense of a technique for forming methodological analogies. Instead, they reverently evoke the allegorical power of a past cultural-religious image for a "now" that, logically and psychologically, cannot exist as a total presence but that still must be dramatized as existing if we are to avoid falling prey to the compulsion of cultural norms, the history that has already been written, and outworn ideas. For Joyce the eschatological moment is indicated in the leitmotif of the "Daedalus"-self climbing to the sun, where the subject-reflective tension prevents the mythologizing absorption given by the image itself. Ascending in space here implies also the category of a future time or a personal entelechy. Even if the examples cited here do not yield a content-specific goal for the utopian movement, they are still intentional acts, not resigned movements of flight.

That is true also of the concentration of Proustian voluntary-involuntary memory, which resembles a self-experiment. Thus from the topos of the moment itself we cannot necessarily conclude that we are dealing with a resigned, conservative, or negative reduction of the classical utopia. The application of this type of moment does not preclude the revolutionary sense we asked about concerning Benjamin's work. By the same token, it does not necessarily include it.

And here we encounter a decisive difference between Benjamin's political decisionism[186] and the apolitical emphases of Musil and Joyce and, to a lesser extent, of Proust. The last three authors' ecstasies of the moment contain no explicit political or social motif, but Benjamin refers to the name of Blanqui, whose "hatred" social democracy had "erased" as a motive for revolution.[187] This reverence for Blanqui, the utopian communist and leader of the Paris Commune revolt on October 31, 1870, who was then condemned to death and served thirty-six years in prison and in a penal colony, shows exactly what kind of messiah Benjamin had in mind in 1940: the conqueror of the "Antichrist."[188] After the German-Soviet pact at the zenith of Nazi hegemony in Europe, it was difficult to grasp the political idea that one might still think about a naturally completed "salvation" of humanity or of the proletariat.[189] For that reason, Benjamin refers to the "sudden" revolutionary deed, reduced to the smallest unit of time. Rolf Tiedemann developed in detail the anarchistic origin of this idea as well as its theoretical consequence in the "Theses on the Philosophy of History"[190] and criticizes it in connection with Engels' critique of Blanqui and his followers as "activistic naiveté."[191] In any case, the criticism of remoteness from practical life, with which Benjamin's Marxist interpreters reproached him, has nothing to do with our question about the revolutionary potential of the utopian moment. Part of the concept of utopia is that it stands in opposition to reality. It follows that Benjamin's moment fulfills the condition of the utopian and the revolutionary consciousness and necessarily precludes the concept of political praxis. Benjamin's example shows that any possible political content of the utopian moment is to be found only in its anarchistic quality. Any qualities having to do with realpolitik or the social system are to be excluded.

Do the moments of Proust, Joyce, and Musil contain anarchistic elements? In the context of Benjamin's example this question must be answered in the negative. Musil as a theorist characterized the "anarchic experience"—he does not use the term "anarchistic"— as one pole of an "either-or" characterized by a peculiar "naiveté," "appropriate to a judging person but not an intellectual, for whom oppositions are resolved in a series of transitions."[192] The "experiences" Musil as a writer presents are characterized by the fact that they cannot be reduced to any graspable concept, and the attempt to do so constitutes Ulrich's utopian adventure.

To resolve the "oppositions" into a series of transitions is also the method of all three authors for making the presentified "now" conceptually plausible. In dramatizing this making plausible and its failure, one could recognize in Musil the "anarchic" quality of his moments. However, they are not identifiable in the political sense of Benjamin, but rather states of extreme intensity with the hidden tendency to shatter cultural taboos. Brosthaus reminds us of Ulrich's question, with which the last fair copy of *The Man Without Qualities* ends, as well as Musil's answer. The question: "Why are we not realists?" The answer: "Neither of them was a realist, neither he nor she, their thoughts and actions left no doubt of that; but they were nihilists and activists, and sometimes one thing and sometimes the other, according to how things went."[193]

The "decisionism" of Ulrich and Agathe that Musil here characterizes is an anarchy of the "soul" in its critical phase, but it also reveals parallels to the political irrationalism of other figures in the novel who are connected with them (Clarisse, Moosbrugger, Meingast). At this point the transition of the utopian moment to the negative utopia begins to announce itself. It is a proven fact that Musil not only relativized the positive utopias of Enlightenment provenience and mistrusted democracy but still considered fascism a viable alternative as late as 1938.[194] Without a social perspective, a satiric view of society must always reveal a "nihilistic" consequence or at least elements of it. This possibility is present even in Joyce's satiric presentation of English civilization. It is excluded only because Joyce includes the authors of the Irish renaissance, even his much-admired Yeats, in the satire.[195] The mythological elements of *Ulysses,* its specific forms of "idyll" and the aesthetic evocation, never turn into a national utopia.

But with respect to the question of the aesthetics of production and the history of function, one revealing answer is possible for Joyce, Proust, and Musil, and, with reservations, also for Benjamin's "conservatism." The reduction to the utopian moment corresponds to the educational history of products, if not of the *grande bourgeoisie* as in the case of Proust and Musil, then of an elite secondary and university education that early on shaped an estericism of thought and a defense against the "profane." This "aristocratic" isolation within a society that was becoming progressively more democratic, which characterizes Musil's Ulrich, Joyce's Stephen, and even Proust's first-person narrator, is the socio-psychological condition for the formation of the utopian moment, which we have discussed here primarily in its structure and not in its social implications. We must point out the most important implication of the utopian quality: obviously it is no longer the political philosopher who is drafting this utopia, nor the dreamer or prophet of Mercier. Rather, it is the imaginative bourgeois artist whose negativity created a deep chasm between himself and the scientific concept of "truth." One can no longer speak of the utopian as the prototype of the intellectual.[196] This unity has been broken. In the future, the objective utopia will be formulated only by scientists,[197] while the artist distrusts it as an ideology. The concept of utopia makes clear that in modern intellectual history it is no longer possible to link intellectual and artistic attitudes as they had been linked prior to this period.

Nevertheless, these conditions do not allow us to fix the historical time of the emphasis on the moment at the crisis of the bourgeois elite at the turn of the century. As Elias has shown, motifs of a radical quasi-bourgeois "romanticism"[198]—and, structurally, that is where the utopian moment belongs—begin to manifest earlier than has traditionally been assumed. Walter Pater developed his theory of the aestheticist moment in the conclusion of his work on the Renaissance. It is instructive in our context that there he refers to Rousseau and his description of how the drive to write was aroused in him through "intellectual excitement" and suspense.[199] The experience of illumination in Vincennes that Rousseau describes in his *Confessions* appears, in the context we have developed, as a prefiguration of the utopia of the moment. An analysis of the "Letter to M. de Malesherbes" and of the *Rêveries du promeneur solitaire* would show the structures of the moment that warn us not to fix the date of the emphasis on the moment at too late a point in history. On the other hand, such an analysis would also show how Rousseau manages without the later development of metaphorical or symbolic intensification and becomes aware of the discovery of his presentified subjective self while remaining in a sense innocent. After a hundred years, this simple sensation is worn out, and not only in literature. It has passed through the phenomenological analysis of consciousness, or else it needs the support of mythological figures or of myths themselves. That is true of Musil, Joyce, Proust, and Benjamin. The moment they portray can be traced to new intellectual and political conditions, not to conditions of a simple postfiguration derived from genre aesthetics. But Rousseau's moment and the reflection of the Age of Sensibility[200] (Kleist's essay "Über die allmähliche Verfertigung der Gedanken beim Reden" [On the gradual completion of thoughts while speaking], 1805–06, and Schleiermacher's *Reden Über die Religion* [Talks on religion], 1799) offer themselves as temporal boundaries. To assume an earlier date seems problematic. The elements of suddenness in the early bourgeois novel, especially in Defoe's *Robinson Crusoe,* are certainly ruptures in the temporal flow,[201] which no longer functions as a continuum. But the author does not yet reflect on their temporal quality. The moment here is still a metaphor and linguistic gesture of the "event" involving the endangered, dynamic person. It is synonymous with a philosophy of "danger," of "necessity," which Defoe knew from Locke and from Hobbes.[202] Only the modification of "danger" into a temporal element would allow us to speak of a conscious utopia of the moment in the eighteenth-century novel. Structurally, however, such a utopia is prefigured there.[203]

The moment always coincides with the experience of happiness: in Proust, Joyce, and Musil, remembered, contemplative, or erotic moments are, as we have seen, occasions of an extreme feeling of happiness. With this, these texts evoke a central category of eudaemonistic Enlightenment, which received a strictly political meaning in the humanitarian rhetoric of the American and French revolutions and in later English utilitarianism.[204] The right to happiness is vouchsafed in the American Constitution[205] and has shaped reformist and leftist social policy in Anglo-Saxon societies, particularly in England, up to the present. Walter Benjamin's moment leaves no doubt that he implied the anticipation of this political idea of happiness: he writes that "the order of the profane world has to accommodate itself to the idea of happiness."[206] This political identification of happiness is definitively renounced in the moments of Proust, Joyce, and Musil in favor of the purely subjective feeling of happiness. The metaphor of the garden and of paradise (in Proust, Joyce, and Musil) as well as the "Kingdom of God" (in Musil) correspond to the sites of happiness that Kant used.[207] But we saw that such metaphorical objectifications never transcend the fact of feeling itself, if we disregard the "negative" utopia of incest in Musil, which in any event is no longer compatible with what Kant and the Enlightenment meant by happiness. The moments thus remain subjective, earthly, one-sided. We must, however, differentiate between Proust's emphatically non-metaphysical interest in happiness, Joyce's "pathology," and Musil's scientific mysticism. Günther Bien pointed out this modern separation between subjective and objective happiness in his discussion of Freud's designation of the feeling of pleasure and happiness as a "pathological" principle.[208]

If the link between the utopian moment and the category of happiness could be imagined only as mediated by a psychic event in the hero of the novel, then we would have the model of an aesthetic utopia, a utopia we perceive in a sense from outside, intellectually, and in which we ourselves would not participate. We see, in that case, the utopian moment as the highest "self-realization"[209] of the hero. However, as readers we are indeed emotionally involved in all these moments. Our involvement is not merely due to our identification with the hero;[210] after all, that would mean that we merely participated indirectly in the act of "self-realization," which is emotional but not necessarily aesthetic or utopian. We would treat the happiness of the novel's hero as the happiness of a friend, that is, not the fiction but its real aspect and its content would guide our emotion. The subjective feeling of happiness on the hero's part, in which we participate, is changed in our consciousness into a higher-ordered, objective fact of consciousness: The utopian moment itself, which has become language, and not the narrated psychological relation between the hero and his "experience" evokes the "utopian" effect in the reader. The narrated relation has the semantic value of "information."

The portrayal of the moment, on the other hand, is not thinkable as "information," but has fictional character. This fictionality introduces the utopian phase of aesthetic reception. The subjective happiness of the hero becomes the objective happiness of the reader through the fantasy work the fictionality ensures. This explanation can be made more convincing by a counterexample. The utopian moment reaches its greatest intensity in the novel's hero when the latter enters into a reflective relationship to the moment. The classical case of this situation is the *mémoire involontaire* of Proust, and it is an extension of this argument that in Proust the moments of reading have become identical with the moments of memory in utopian happiness. In the work of Musil and Joyce, too, we see the retardant effect in the happiness of the moment: either as "contemplation" or as "profanity." When the utopia of the moment is not only an aesthetic utopia but also implies a utopia of the aesthetic, then we can conclude that it has avoided becoming a "negative" utopia. The reduction to a moment is a symptom of doubt, but this doubt, consistent with its nature as doubt, does not posit itself as absolute and keeps the utopian horizon, as Musil the mathematician would say, "indeterminately" open.

We can draw the following conclusion concerning the utopia of the moment as a variant of the "negative" utopia: it no longer recognizes the paradigm. We are no longer dealing with a paradigm shift. This means that we can no longer speak of "secularization." The value of the utopia of the moment, which has become aesthetic, can no longer be qualified in terms of the philosophy of history, but must be viewed instead in terms of anthropology and psychology. Telos, ethos, and regulative idea, which are categories applicable to the conceptual comprehension of the traditional forms of utopia, are of no use here. The utopia of the moment shares the criterion of incommensurability with the phenomenon of the aesthetic itself. For that reason, the reduction of the exhausted content of a utopia also contains a radicalization: it is the last conceivable replacement of eschatological history by language, that is, a strategy of discharge for the no longer anticipated but not excluded real case. The total incongruence between fiction and history, in a sense, recharges the utopia that has run down: with a hypothetical anticipation. To be sure, the rejection of the paradigm also entails a nihilistic consequence, which can be avoided only if the aesthetic mythologem replaces the paradigm.

NOTES

1. The title authorized by Benjamin was "On the Concept of History," see Rolf Tiedemann, "Historischer Materialismus oder politischer Messianismus?" in Peter Bulthaupt, ed., *Materialien zu Benjamins Thesen Über den Begriff der Geschichte* (Frankfurt/Main: Suhrkamp, 1975), p. 115 note 9.

2. Walter Benjamin, "Theses on the Philosophy of History," in Benjamin, *Illuminations*, trans. Harry Zohn (New York: Schocken, 1968), p. 262.

3. Gershom Scholem, "Walter Benjamin und sein Engel," in Siegfried Unseld, ed., *Zur Aktualität Walter Benjamins: Aus Anlaß des 80. Geburtstages von Walter Benjamin* (Frankfurt/Main: Suhrkamp, 1972), pp. 87–138.

4. Jürgen Habermas, "Bewußtmachende oder rettende Kritik: Die Aktualität Walter Benjamins," in *Zur Aktualität Walter Benjamins*, p. 186.

5. Ibid., p. 211.

6. Tiedemann, "Historischer Materialismus," p. 77.

7. See, in addition to Habermas, Burkhardt Lindner, " 'Natur-Gesch-

ichte': Geschichtsphilosophie und Welterfahrung in Benjamins Schriften," *Text + Kritik* 31/32 (1971): 43, 47, 53, 57. See also Michael
Rumpf, "Radikale Theologie: Benjamins Beziehung zu Carl Schmitt,"
in *Walter Benjamin: Zeitgenosse der Moderne* (Kronberg/Czech.: Scriptor,
1976), pp. 37–50. Gerhard Kaiser presented the most radical view of
Benjamin's conservatism in "Walter Benjamins Geschichtsphilosophische
Thesen," in Bulthaupt, *Materialien zu Benjamins Thesen,* pp. 43–76.

8. See Rumpf, "Radikale Theologie," pp. 46–47.

9. See especially Gerhard Kaiser, "Walter Benjamins Geschichtsphilosophische Thesen."

10. Tiedemann, "Historischer Materialismus," p. 95, pp. 113–14.

11. Heinrich Heine, "Verschiedene Geschichtsauffassungen," in
Heine, *Sämtliche Schriften,* ed. Klaus Briegleb (München: Hanser, 1971),
3: 19–23. Heine worked on the text, which was published in 1869 from
his literary remains, in September 1833. It anticipates in metaphor and
concept something of Nietzsche's critique of historicism from the second
"Untimely Meditation," "On the Use and Abuse of History."

12. On Benjamin's surrealist method, see K. H. Bohrer, *Die Ästhetik
des Schreckens: Die pessimistische Romantik und Ernst Jüngers Frühwerk*
(München: Hanser, 1978), pp. 359–60, p. 389.

13. Benjamin, "Theses on the Philosophy of History," p. 262.

14. Ibid., p. 258.

15. Ibid., p. 254.

16. Ibid., p. 261.

17. See Tiedemann, "Historischer Materialismus," p. 106.

18. See Habermas, "Bewußtmachende oder rettende Kritik," p. 176.

19. See Tiedemann, "Historischer Materialismus," p. 91.

20. See Harro Müller, "Literaturwissenschaft zwischen Hermeneutik
und Materialismus," unpublished thesis, Bielefeld, 1979, p. 6.

21. Ernst Bloch, "On the Present in Literature," in Bloch, *The Utopian Function of Art and Literature: Selected Essays,* trans. Jack Zipes and
Frank Mecklenburg (Cambridge, Mass.: MIT Press, 1988), p. 218.

22. Ibid.

23. Ibid.

24. On the difference between Benjamin's and Bloch's historical
thinking, see Ernst Osterkamp, "Utopie und Prophetie: Überlegungen zu
den späten Schriften Walter Benjamins," in Gert Ueding, ed., *Literatur
ist Utopie* (Frankfurt/Main: Suhrkamp, 1978), p. 116.

25. Scholem, "Walter Benjamin und sein Engel," p. 99.

26. Gerhard Kaiser, "Walter Benjamins Geschichtsphilosophische
Thesen," pp. 49–50.

27. Ibid., p. 51.

28. Tiedemann, "Historischer Materialismus," p. 80 and pp. 84–85; Osterkamp, "Utopie und Prophetie," pp. 113–14.

29. Gerhard Kaiser, "Walter Benjamins Geschichtsphilosophische Thesen," pp. 53–54.

30. Walter Benjamin, "On Some Motifs in Baudelaire," in Benjamin, *Illuminations*, p. 157.

31. Walter Benjamin, "The Image of Proust," in Benjamin, *Illuminations*, pp. 201–16.

32. Benjamin, "On Some Motifs in Baudelaire," p. 181.

33. Ibid., p. 185.

34. Ibid., and Benjamin, "The Image of Proust," p. 202.

35. Benjamin, "The Image of Proust," p. 202.

36. Ibid., p. 203.

37. See Ferdinand Seibt, *Utopica: Modelle totaler Sozialplanung* (Düsseldorf: Schwann, 1972), pp. 284–85.

38. Ibid.

39. On the intellectual and historical genesis of this modern tendency, see Gerhard vom Hofe and Peter Pfaff, *Das Elend des Polyphem: Zum Thema der Subjektivität bei Thomas Bernhard, Peter Handke, Wolfgang Koeppen, und Botho Strauß* (Königstein, Czech.: Athenäum, 1980), pp. 1–27.

40. Gert Ueding also uses this concept in characterizing Schiller's *On the Aesthetic Education of Man*. See Ueding, *Literatur ist Utopie*, p. 12. Although he uses the example of Schiller to establish a distinction between the utopia of "content" and "aesthetic experience," the latter does not stand for the specific fantasy work that fictionality demands. Instead, it finally amounts to an anthropological general denominator (the idea of play), which makes this concept of utopia seem much too broad.

41. On Adorno's and Bloch's ideas of utopia, see Osterkamp, "Utopie und Prophetie," pp. 103–4.

42. On the concept of "not yet," see Ernst Bloch, "Phantasie, künstlerische Produktivität und Werkprozess," in Bloch, *Ästhetik des Vor-Scheins* (Frankfurt/Main: Suhrkamp, 1974), 2: 80. Adorno spoke in dialectical terms of the relationship between art and utopia: "Being a negative of the old, the new is subservient to the old while considering itself to be Utopian. One of the crucial antinomies of art today is that it wants to be and must be squarely Utopian, as social reality increasingly impedes Utopia." Theodor Adorno, *Aesthetic Theory*, trans. C. Lenhardt (London: Routledge & Kegan Paul, 1984), p. 47.

43. See my discussion of Nietzsche's concept of appearance in chapter 6 of this book.

44. Early on, Lars Gustafsson pointed out the relationship between

aesthetic fiction and utopia. See Gustafsson, "Richtofens Problem," in Gustafsson, *Utopien: Essays* (München: Hanser, 1969), pp. 64–65.

45. The extent to which an "as-if" structure is given when the fiction is treated as reality and is revealed as fiction only through certain ironic hints—as is the case with the work that founded the genre, Thomas More's *Utopia* of 1516—can be determined only by gaining insight, through the aesthetics of reception, into the horizon of expectations of the reader in the Renaissance. See Michael Winter, *Compendium Utopiarum: Typologie und Bibliographie literarischer Utopien. 1. Teilband, Von der Antike bis zur deutschen Frühaufklärung* (Stuttgart: Metzler, 1978), p. xix.

46. On the reader's fantasy work, see primarily Wolfgang Iser, *Der Akt des Lesens: Theorie ästhetischer Wirkung* (München: Fink, 1976), pp. 153, 185–86. Iser analyzes the progressive "moments of reading" (p. 186) each of which opens up a new "horizon." Each is situated by changing points of view that are established by information in the text. This pure immanence of the reader's perspective within the fictional material does not yet create a utopian attitude. Only the "places of indeterminacy" (p. 284) are the precondition, in terms of the aesthetics of reception, for the formation of a utopian concept of fictionality, as can be demonstrated in the "dismissal" of *Ulysses* that Iser mentions (p. 325). The reader is forced to constantly change the direction of his or her activity of structuring. That becomes a utopian attitude when the self-steering mechanism—and Iser does not proceed beyond the analysis of this mechanism—is no longer guaranteed and the decisions of the reader are therefore no longer contained within concepts that belong to the aesthetics of reception or to textual linguistics. H. R. Jauß's reference to the "energy of the fascinated glance" points more precisely at the unending process of a thing in the act of aesthetic perception. See Jauß, *Ästhetische Erfahrung und literarische Hermeneutik* (München: Fink, 1977), 1: 101.

47. See Gotthart Wunberg, "Utopie und fin-de-siècle: Zur deutschen Literaturkritik vor der Jahrhundertwende," in Ueding, ed., *Literatur ist Utopie*, p. 273.

48. See Winter, *Compendium*, p. xviii.

49. On Musil's political mentality, see Ingo Seidler, "Das Nietzschebild Robert Musils," in *DVJS* 39 (1965): 335. See also Irma Hande-Tjaden, "Der freie Geist und die Politik: Zum Problem des Politischen bei Robert Musil," Ph.D. dissertation, Freiburg, 1962.

50. Theodor Adorno, "On Proust," in *Notes to Literature*, trans. Shierry Nicholson (New York: Columbia University Press, 1992), 2: 313.

51. See chapter 3 of this book. On Mach's influence, see Adorno, "Short Commentaries on Proust," in Adorno, *Notes to Literature*, 1: 177.

See also Gotthart Wunberg, *Der frühe Hofmannsthal: Schizophrenie als dichterische Struktur* (Stuttgart: Kohlhammer, 1965), p. 31.

52. On the epistemological background, see Hans-Wolfgang Schaffnit, *Mimesis als Problem: Studien zu einem ästhetischen Begriff der Dichtung aus Anlaß Robert Musils* (Berlin: de Gruyter, 1971).

53. See chapter 3 of this book.

54. See chapter 3 of this book.

55. See Umberto Eco, *Das offene Kunstwerk* (Frankfurt/Main: Suhrkamp, 1973), pp. 329–30. See also Eco, "Joyce und D'Annunzio: Die Quellen des Begriffs der Epiphanie," in K. Reichert and F. Senn, eds., *Materialien zu James Joyces "Ein Porträt des Künstlers als Junger Mann"* (Frankfurt/Main: Suhrkamp, 1975), p. 279.

56. See Wolfgang Iser, *Walter Pater: Die Autonomie des Ästhetischen* (Tübingen: Niemeyer, 1960), pp. 205, 47.

57. See Jacques Derrida, *Speech and Phenomena, and Other Essays on Husserl's Theory of Signs*, trans. David Allison (Evanston: Northwestern University Press, 1973), p. 60.

58. Edmund Husserl, *Zur Phänomenologie des inneren Zeitbewußtseins*, ed. R. Boehm, *Husserliana*, vol. 10 (Den Haag: Nijhoff, 1966), pp. 47–48.

59. Ibid., pp. 28–29.

60. Ibid., p. 30.

61. Husserl, *Ideen zu einer reinen Phänomenologie und phänomenologischen Philosophie*, vol. 1, *Husserliana*, vol. 4 (Den Haag: Nijhoff, 1952), § 81.

62. Derrida, *Speech und Phenomena*, p. 61.

63. Maurice Blanchot, *The Sirens' Song*, trans. Sacha Rabinovitch (Bloomington: Indiana University Press, 1982), p. 66ff., and Ernst Robert Curtius, "Marcel Proust," in *Französischer Geist im zwanzigsten Jahrhundert* (Bonn: Bouvier, 1984), pp. 285ff., interpreted this masterfully. For the basis of the problem of time in Proust, see H. R. Jauß, *Zeit und Erinnerung in Marcel Prousts "A la Recherche du temps perdu": Ein Beitrag zur Theorie des Romans* (Heidelberg: Winter, 1955). See also Jauß, *Ästhetische Erfahrung und literarische Hermeneutik*, vol. 1, pp. 132ff.

64. Marcel Proust, *Swann's Way*, trans. C. K. Scott Moncrieff (New York: Vintage, 1970), p. 34. The French reads: "Mais à l'instant même où la gorgé mêlée des miettes du gâteau toucha mon palais, je tressaillis, attentif à ce qui se passait d'extraordinaire en moi. Un plaisir délicieux m'avait envahi, isolé, sans la notion de sa cause" (Proust, *A la Recherche du temps perdu*, ed. Pierre Clarac and André Ferré [Paris: Gallimard, 1954], p. 45).

65. Ernst Bloch, "On the Present in Literature," p. 218.

66. Marcel Proust, *Swann's Way*, p. 35.

67. Ibid.

68. Ibid. The French reads: "Arrivera-t-il jusqu à la surface de ma claire conscience ce souvenir, l'instant ancien que l'attraction d'un instant identique est venue de si loin solliciter, émouvoir, soulever tout en fond de moi" (Proust, *A la Recherche*, p. 46)?

69. Bloch, "On the Present in Literature," p. 218.

70. Proust, *Swann's Way*, p. 36.

71. Husserl, *Ideen 1*, p. 81; and *Phänomenologie des inneren Zeitbewußtseins*, p. 33.

72. On this point see Blanchot, *The Sirens' Song*, p. 67.

73. Heinrich von Kleist, "Über das Marionettentheater," in Kleist, *Sämtliche Werke und Briefe*, ed. Helmut Sembdner (München: Hanser, 1977), 2: 345.

74. Examples are Curtius, "Marcel Proust," p. 291, and Blanchot, *The Sirens' Song*, p. 67.

75. See Proust, *Swann's Way*, pp. 34–35.

76. Adorno, "Short Commentaries on Proust," p. 184. Jauß, *Ästhetische Erfahrung und literarische Hermeneutik*, 1: 133.

77. Jauß, ibid.

78. Blanchot distinguished the four different times in Proust, *The Sirens' Song*, p. 67.

79. Jauß, *Ästhetische Erfahrung und literarische Hermeneutik*, 1: 135.

80. Ibid.

81. Theodor Adorno, "On Proust," in Adorno, *Notes to Literature*, 2: 316.

82. Sigmund Freud, "Creative Writers and Day-Dreaming," trans. James Strachey, in Freud, *The Complete Psychological Works* (London: Hogarth Press, 1953), 9: 151.

83. On this point see Klaus Garber, *Der Locus amoenus und der Locus terribilis: Bild und Funktion der Natur in der deutschen Schäfer- und Landlebendichtung des 17. Jahrhunderts* (Köln: Böhlau, 1974).

84. Ernst Bloch, *Vom Hasard zur Katastrophe: Politische Aufsätze aus den Jahren 1934–1939* (Frankfurt/Main: Suhrkamp, 1972), p. 315. See also Karl Heinz Bohrer, *Der Lauf des Freitag: Die lädierte Utopie und die Dichter* (München: Hanser, 1973), pp. 110–11.

85. On this point see Curtius, "Marcel Proust," pp. 326–27.

86. Benjamin, "The Image of Proust," p. 206. This unmasking speaks against the thesis, formulated by Peter Bürger, of an "aesthetic experience of reality" that, in evading the "purposive, rational world," threatens to fall victim to its "inhumanity" (Peter Bürger, *Aktualität und Geschichtlich-*

keit: Studien zum gesellschaftlichen Funktionswandel der Literatur [Frankfurt/ Main: Suhrkamp, 1977], pp. 172–73).

87. Adorno, "On Proust," p. 315.

88. Ibid.

89. See especially the works by Umberto Eco already cited and the bibliographies they contain. See also Jacques Aubert, "Joyce und Thomas von Aquin: Zur Ästhetik des Polaer Notizbuches," in Reichert and Senn, eds., *Materialien zu James Joyce,* pp. 290–304.

90. Especially William T. Noon, *Joyce and Aquinas* (New Haven: Yale University Press, 1957).

91. Eco, "Joyce und D'Annunzio," pp. 279ff.

92. James Joyce, *Stephen Hero* (New York: New Directions, 1963), p. 211.

93. Ibid.

94. Ibid.

95. See, among others, Maurice Beebe, "Joyce and Thomas von Aquin: Die ästhetische Theorie," in Reichert and Senn, eds., *Materialien zu James Joyce,* pp. 270–71.

96. Ibid.

97. Jacques Maritain, *Art and Scholasticism, With Other Essays* (New York: Scribner, 1962), pp. 24–25.

98. See Beebe, "Joyce und Thomas von Aquin," p. 272.

99. See chapter 6 in this volume.

100. Joyce, *Stephen Hero,* p. 213.

101. See Beebe, "Joyce und Thomas von Aquin," pp. 273ff., and Aubert, "Joyce und Thomas von Aquin," pp. 300–1.

102. James Joyce, *Portrait of the Artist as a Young Man* (New York: Penguin Books, 1964), p. 213.

103. Ibid.

104. Ibid., p. 212.

105. Bloch, "On the Present in Literature," p. 218.

106. Aubert, "Joyce und Thomas von Aquin," p. 301.

107. Eco, *Das offene Kunstwerk* (Frankfurt/Main: Suhrkamp, 1973), p. 334 note 48.

108. Eco, "Joyce und D'Annunzio," pp. 278–89.

109. Eco, *Das offene Kunstwerk,* p. 334 note 48.

110. Ibid., p. 329. Pater's influence did not prevent Joyce from parodying him, as he parodied the Irish aesthetes as well. See Richard Ellman *Ulysses on the Liffey* (Oxford: Oxford University Press, 1972), pp. 77, 140.

111. Joyce, *Portrait,* p. 65.

112. Ibid.

113. Ibid.

114. Ibid., p. 169.

115. Ibid.

116. Ibid.

117. On the discovery of the self in aesthetic literature, see Peter Bürger, "Naturalismus-Ästhetizismus und das Problem der Subjektivität," in Christa Bürger, Peter Bürger, and Jochen Schulte-Sasse, eds., *Naturalismus/Ästhetizismus: Hefte für kritische Literaturwissenschaft*, vol. 1 (Frankfurt/Main: Suhrkamp, 1979), pp. 39ff.

118. Joyce, *Portrait*, p. 171.

119. Ibid.

120. Ibid.

121. Ibid.

122. Ibid., p. 172.

123. Ibid.

124. Eco emphasizes this without wishing to establish a direct connection between Joyce and phenomenological philosophy. *Das offene Kunstwerk*, pp. 347–48 note 64.

125. Joyce, *Portrait*, pp. 170, 172.

126. Ibid.

127. See note 108 above.

128. Eco, "Joyce und D'Annunzio," pp. 284–85.

129. See chapter 6 of this book.

130. See Klaus Dockhorn, *Macht und Wirkung der Rhetorik* (Bad Homburg: Gehlen, 1968), pp. 47–48.

131. Eco, "Joyce und D'Annunzio," p. 286.

132. James Joyce, *Ulysses* (New York: Modern Library, 1946), p. 192.

133. Ibid., p. 7.

134. Ellmann, *Ulysses on the Liffey*, p. 21.

135. James Joyce, *Letters*, ed. R. Ellman (New York: Viking, 1966), 3: 262.

136. Benjamin, "Der Surrealismus," in Benjamin, *Angelus Novus: Ausgewählte Schriften* (Frankfurt/Main: Suhrkamp, 1966), 2: 202.

137. See Ellmann, *Ulysses on the Liffey*, p. 21.

138. The first parts of this work appeared during Musil's lifetime, in 1930 and 1933. The first volume issued from the literary estate was published by Martha Musil in 1943, and in 1952 Adolf Frisé published the complete edition, based on Musil's literary estate.

139. See H. W. Schaffnit, *Mimesis als Problem*, pp. 551ff. See also Wilfried Berghahn, *Robert Musil in Selbstzeugnissen und Bilddokumenten* (Reinbek: Rowohlt, 1963), p. 55.

140. See Schaffnit, *Mimesis als Problem*, pp. 48–49; pp. 55ff.

141. Max Scheler, *Die Transzendentale und die Psychologische Methode: Eine grundsätzliche Erörterung zur philosophischen Methodik* (Leipzig: Meiner, 1900), p. 165.

142. Karl Mannheim, "Ideologie und Utopie," 5th ed. (Frankfurt/ Main: Schulte-Bulmke, 1969), p. 169.

143. See Hermann Wiegmann, "Musils Utopiebegriff und seine literaturtheoretischen Konsequenzen," in Ueding, *Literatur ist Utopie*, pp. 309ff.

144. Ibid., p. 310.

145. Albrecht Schöne, "Zum Gebrauch des Konjunktivs bei Robert Musil," in Jost Schillemeit, ed., *Deutsche Romane von Grimmelshausen bis Musil* (Frankfurt/Main: Fischer, 1976), pp. 290–318.

146. On the problems accompanying editions of *The Man Without Qualities* see, in addition to Adolf Frisé's afterword to the 1966 edition, the notes to the literary estate in Frisé's expanded and revised edition of 1978. See also Wilhelm Bausinger, "Studien zu einer historisch-kritischen Ausgabe von Robert Musils Roman, *Der Mann ohne Eigenschaften*," Ph.D. dissertation, Tübingen, 1962. Also see Heribert Brosthaus, "Zur Struktur und Entwicklung des 'anderen Zustands' in Robert Musils Roman, *Der Mann ohne Eigenschaften*," DVJS 39 (1965): 461–62 note 29. And see Ulrich Karthaus, "Musilforschung und Musildeutung," DVJS 39 (1965): 426 note 33; and Renate von Heydebrand, *Die Reflexion Ulrichs in Robert Musils Roman "Der Mann ohne Eigenschaften"* (Münster: Aschendorff, 1969).

147. See Brosthaus, "Zur Struktur und Entwicklung des 'anderen Zustandes,' " pp. 461–62 note 29.

148. In the following, I will cite from the fifth edition as well as from Frisé's 1978 edition. Translator's note: The author is not consistent in this undertaking.

149. Robert Musil, *Der Mann ohne Eigenschaften*, ed. Adolf Frisé (Hamburg: Rowohlt, 1965), p. 618. (1978 edition: p. 618). Translator's note: The English edition presently consists of three volumes. A fourth was planned but has not appeared. Where possible, I have quoted from the English as well as the German editions. Where no English translation exists, the translations are mine. Here: Musil, *The Man Without Qualities*, trans. Eithne Wilkins and Ernst Kaiser (London: Pan, 1979), 2: 395.

150. Musil, German edition, p. 878 (p. 878). English edition, 3: 250.

151. Musil, German edition, p. 622 (p. 622). English edition, 2: 399.

152. Musil, German edition, p. 1423 (p. 1669). No published English translation.

153. See Schaffnit, *Mimesis als Problem,* p. 55.

154. Ibid., p. 59.

155. Ibid., p. 57.

156. Edmund Husserl, *Logische Untersuchungen,* Husserliana XVII (Den Haag: Nijhoff, 1975), 1: 130–31.

157. Musil, German edition, p. 354 (p. 354), English edition, 2: 61.

158. Heinrich von Kleist, "Über die allmähliche Verfertigung der Gedanken beim Reden," in Kleist, *Sämtliche Werke und Briefe,* ed. Helmut Sembdner (München: Hanser, 1977), 2: 320–21. For more on this passage, see chapter 4 of this volume.

159. Musil, German edition, p. 1216 (p. 1427); no English translation.

160. Ibid.

161. Ibid., German edition, p. 150 (p. 150); English edition, p. 175.

162. From the siblings' first encounter, this motif is accompanied by the symbolism of a "pierrot" costume (Musil, German edition, pp. 675ff.; English edition, 3: 8ff. It is continued in the motif of the "Siamese Twins" (Musil, German edition, pp. 899ff.; English edition, 3: 275ff.). The idea is treated explicitly in the early draft "Hermaphrodit" (German edition, pp. 1379ff.; no English).

163. Walter Benjamin, "On Some Motifs in Baudelaire," in Benjamin, *Illuminations,* p. 187.

164. Musil, German edition, p. 1091; no English. On the meaning of the mystical components as opposed to the psychologistic, see Schaffnit, *Mimesis als Problem,* p. 61.

165. Brosthaus, "Zur Struktur und Entwicklung des 'anderen Zustands' in Robert Musils Roman, *Der Mann ohne Eigenschaften,*" p. 389.

166. Schöne emphasizes this parallel (see "Zum Gebrauch des Konjunktivs bei Robert Musil," p. 299). Brosthaus also relativizes the position of the incest motif in Musil's final conception of the novel (Brosthaus, "Zur Struktur und Entwicklung des 'anderen Zustands' in Robert Musils Roman, *Der Mann ohne Eigenschaften,*" p. 427 note 35). He does not, however, overlook its aesthetic suggestiveness (ibid., p. 426).

167. On the use of natural scenery, see especially Brosthaus, "Zur Struktur und Entwicklung des 'anderen Zustands' in Robert Musils Roman, *Der Mann ohne Eigenschaften,* pp. 423ff.

168. See K. M. Michel, "Die Utopie der Sprache," *Akzente* 1 (1954): 31.

169. Musil, German edition, p. 1144; no English.

170. Schaffnit worked out the terminological antitheses for Musil's "state" theory (*Mimesis als Problem,* pp. 70–71).

171. On the meaning of Benjamin's concept of *in Dienst nehmen*

(make use of), see Tiedemann, *Historischer Materialismus oder politischer Messianismus*, p. 113.

172. Brosthaus especially pointed out the symbolistic character of a nature that has become demonic ("Zur Struktur und Entwicklung des 'anderen Zustands' in Robert Musils Roman, *Der Mann ohne Eigenschaften*," p. 428). Benjamin's analysis of demonic, lifeless nature in Goethe's *Elective Affinities* corresponds to Musil's treatment of nature in "The Journey to Paradise."

173. On Musil's relationship to Nietzsche, see Ingo Seidler, "Das Nietzschebild Robert Musils," a work that does not succeed in showing the epistemological and ideological-critical influence of Nietzsche on Musil.

174. Musil, German edition, pp. 60ff. (pp. 60ff.); English edition, 1: 65ff.

175. Ibid., German edition, pp. 103ff. (pp. 103ff.); English edition, 1: 118ff.

176. Ibid., German edition, pp. 89–90 (pp. 89–90); English edition, 1: 101–2.

177. Ibid., German edition, pp. 146–47 (pp. 146–47); English edition, 1: 169–70.

178. Ibid., German edition, pp. 108, 281 (pp. 108–9, 281); English edition, 1: 124–25, 1: 333–34.

179. Ibid., German edition, p. 282 (pp. 282–83); English edition, 1: 335–36.

180. Ibid., German edition, pp. 549–50 (pp. 549–50); English edition, 2: 305–6.

181. On Musil as satirist, see Helmut Arntzen, *Satirischer Stil: Zur Satire Robert Musils im "Mann ohne Eigenschaften"* (Bonn: Bouvier, 1960). See also Schöne, "Zum Gebrauch des Konjunktivs bei Robert Musil," p. 312.

182. Musil, German edition, pp. 1322ff (1454ff.); no English.

183. Ibid., German edition, p. 1144 (1241); no English.

184. Benjamin, Theses on the Philosophy of History, p. 254.

185. Ibid., p. 264.

186. Harro Müller uses the concept decision as a formal method in order to keep it free of an already imported political meaning, which offers itself through Benjamin's relationship to Carl Schmitt's category of the "state of exception." The concept should be understood here also systematically and not historically or politically.

187. Benjamin, "Theses on the Philosophy of History," p. 260.

188. See Tiedemann, *Historischer Materialismus oder politischer Messianismus*, pp. 93–94.

189. See ibid., p. 102. See also Osterkamp, "Utopie und Prophetie: Überlegungen zu den späten Schriften Walter Benjamins," pp. 114; 116.

190. Tiedemann, *Historischer Materialismus oder politischer Messianismus*, pp. 107, 110ff. See also Osterkamp, "Utopie und Prophetie: Überlegungen zu den späten Schriften Walter Benjamins," p. 117.

191. Tiedemann, *Historischer Materialismus oder politischer Messianismus*, p. 107.

192. Musil, "Ansätze zu neuer Ästhetik," quoted in Schaffnit, *Mimesis als Problem*, p. 81 note 217.

193. Musil, German edition, p. 1150; no English. See Brosthaus, "Zur Struktur und Entwicklung des 'anderen Zustands' in Robert Musils Roman, *Der Mann ohne Eigenschaften*," p. 438.

194. Seidler verified this fact ("Das Nietzschebild Robert Musils," p. 335).

195. See Ellman, *Ulysses on the Liffey*.

196. On this point see Seibt, *Utopica*, pp. 236–70.

197. The optimistic approach of Jürgen Habermas' social philosophy and Noam Chomsky's critique of the objectivism of American liberal scholars furnish examples for this contention.

198. Norbert Elias, *Die höfische Gesellschaft: Untersuchungen zur Soziologie des Königtums und der höfischen Aristokratie mit einer Einleitung—Soziologie und Geschichtswissenschaft* (Neuwied: Luchterhand, 1969), p. 336.

199. Walter Pater, *The Renaissance: Studies in Art and Poetry* (Berkeley: University of California Press, 1980), p. 295.

200. We should recall the structure of the moment in Goethe. See Peter Pfaff, *Das Glücksmotiv im Jugendwerk Goethes* (Heidelberg: Winter 1965), pp. 21, 27ff.

201. See Bohrer, *Der Lauf des Freitag*, pp. 88, 94–95.

202. Ibid., pp. 123ff.

203. Ibid., p. 120. See also Michael Winter, *Compendium Utopiarum*, pp. 148ff.

204. See Günther Bien, "Die Philosophie und die Frage nach dem Glück," in Bien, ed., *Die Frage nach dem Glück* (Stuttgart, 1968), p. xiii.

205. See Dolf Sternberger, "Das Menschenrecht nach Glück zu streben," in Sternberger, *Ich wünschte ein Bürger zu sein: Neun Versuche über den Staat*, 2d ed. (Frankfurt/Main: Suhrkamp, 1970).

206. Walter Benjamin, "Theologisch-politisches Fragment," *Angelus Novus: Ausgewählte Schriften* (Frankfurt/Main: Suhrkamp, 1966), p. 280.

207. See Manfred Sommer, "Kant und die Frage nach dem Glück," in Bien, *Die Frage nach dem Glück*, p. 132.

208. Bien, "Die Philosophie und die Frage nach dem Glück," p. xvi.

209. On self-realization as a concept in the philosophy of happiness (which is not identical with the emphasis on the decadent "I" mentioned above), see Hans Krämer, "Selbstverwirklichung," in Bien, *Die Frage nach dem Glück*, pp. 21ff.

210. Freud gave simple identification with the hero as the cause of our pleasure in literature. The hero's invulnerability pleases the reader's ego. See Sigmund Freud, "Creative Writers and Day-Dreaming," p. 153.

Index

Designer: Linda Secondari
Text: 11/13 Goudy Oldstyle
Compositor: Maple-Vail
Printer: Maple-Vail
Binder: Maple-Vail